THEMES IN
FUNDAMENTAL MORAL THEOLOGY

Other Books by Charles E. Curran

Christian Morality Today

A New Look at Christian Morality

Contemporary Problems in Moral Theology

Catholic Moral Theology in Dialogue

The Crisis in Priestly Ministry

*Politics, Medicine and Christian Ethics: A Dialogue with
    Paul Ramsey*

New Perspectives in Moral Theology

Ongoing Revision: Studies in Moral Theology

Dissent in and for the Church (Charles E. Curran, Robert
    E. Hunt, et al.)

*The Responsibility of Dissent: The Church and Academic
    Freedom* (John F. Hunt and Terrence R. Connelly
    with Charles E. Curran, et al.)

Absolutes in Moral Theology? (editor)

Contraception: Authority and Dissent (editor)

Themes in Fundamental Moral Theology

CHARLES E. CURRAN

UNIVERSITY OF NOTRE DAME PRESS
NOTRE DAME LONDON

Library of Congress Cataloging in Publication Data

Curran, Charles E
    Themes in fundamental moral theology.

    1. Christian ethics—Catholic authors—Addresses,
essays, lectures. I. Title.
BJ1249.C84   241'.04'2   76-51614
ISBN 0-268-01833-2
ISBN 0-268-01834-0 pbk.

Manufactured in the United States of America

DECANO SOCIISQUE FACULTATIS THEOLOGICAE
COLLEGIS DISCIPULISQUE HUIUS UNIVERSITATIS
QUI DECEM ABHINC ANNOS
AD LIBERTATEM ACADEMICAM DEFENDENDAM
CAUSAM MEAM UT PROPRIAM ADOPTARUNT
APRILIS MCMLXXVII

Contents

Introduction

There can be no doubt that moral theology is the one area today in which change and newer developments in Catholic life and theology have been most acutely felt. All other areas of theology have changed, but their impact on the daily life of Catholics and Christians is not as significant as that of moral theology, which deals precisely with Christian life and actions. Even such important questions as the personality of Jesus do not cause as much disturbance in the Church as questions of daily life and practice such as sexuality, violence, and a more equitable distribution of the goods of creation.

This book does not intend to be impartial in the sense of merely presenting two sides of the discussion. The studies gathered together here present a picture of moral theology which differs in many aspects from the moral theology contained in the manuals previously used in theologates, seminaries, and Catholic colleges. However, the objective weight of the evidence in my judgment calls for a different approach. This does not mean that the newer approaches which have been proposed in the last few years are merely uncritically accepted. Even within the newer approaches there are many differences among different theologians.

Any truly critical renewal of theology must rest on four different sources — the Scriptures, the historical tradition, contemporary understandings, and the eschatological pull of the future. All these sources contribute to the approach proposed in these pages. There is a much greater emphasis on the Scriptures than in the manuals of moral theology, but the hermeneutical problem of the eschatological and cultural conditioning of the Scriptures calls for caution in using the Scriptures. Yes, the Scriptures describe the general aspects of the Christian life, the most significant dispositions and attitudes of the Christian, and the goals and ideals for which we must strive; but on particular questions one must be careful in using an individual Scriptural quotation as a proof text.

Although the approach differs in some points from the manuals of moral theology, the basic methodology and tone are very much within the general Roman Catholic approach to moral theology. Unfortunately, some people too readily identify the tradition with just the manuals of moral theology, but the tradition is much broader and richer than that. This volume is "traditional" in the best sense of that term, for the Catholic tradition has always been willing to accept truth wherever faith and reason find it. Often older Catholic approaches are criticized, and I point out precisely how and why something different is required.

A renewed theology must also give great attention to the contemporary understandings of human and Christian existence. These pages show a dialogue with other Christian thinkers and with contemporary philosophers. There can be no Catholic theology today which is not truly "catholic" in the sense of universal and dialoguing with Protestants, non-Christians, philosophers, and scientists. Non-Catholic Christians will find here not only a contemporary statement of Catholic moral theology but also an approach which has been greatly influenced by the ecumenical times in which we live and, in turn, hopes to make a contribution to ecumenical theology. The eschatological pull of the future does not furnish much data, but it does provide a vision which strives for a greater dynamism, a more self-critical approach, and a greater appreciation of historicity both in moral theology and in the Christian life upon which theology reflects.

The studies gathered together in this book treat themes in fundamental moral theology. These themes form the basic considerations in moral theology and Christian ethics. Even the themes chosen show the close affinity with the Catholic tradition, although the explanation often differs in some respects from the manuals of fundamental moral theology. As befits a discussion of fundamental moral theology, specific content questions as such are not addressed.

A few words of caution are in order. This volume does not pretend to offer a systematic treatise on fundamental moral theology. The book gathers together previously written studies which discuss the most important questions in fundamental moral theology. Six of these studies previously appeared in two different books published by Fides Publishers but now out of print — *A New Look at Christian Morality* and *Contemporary Problems in Moral Theology*. These essays have been somewhat revised to fit into this new context. Chapter 5 appeared in the December 1976 issue of *Concilium* and, like the other essays mentioned above, is included here with the permission of the original publisher. The last chapter on conscience was prepared especially for this volume and attempts to synthesize and concretize many of the ideas presented throughout the volume.

This book emphasizes the social aspect of moral theology. So too the doing of moral theology also has a social dimension. I want to thank all those who have assisted me in my theologizing and writing — students, librarians, friends, and colleagues at the Catholic University and my colleagues in moral theology and Christian ethics both in this country and abroad who by their criticism and support have helped my endeavors. I am grateful to the University of Notre Dame Press and to Mr. John Ehmann for encouraging me to prepare this volume and for publishing it. A special word of thanks goes to Ms. Johann Klodzen, administrative assistant in the Department of Theology of

Catholic University, for her help in preparing this and previous manuscripts.

1: The Relevancy of the Gospel Ethic

Contemporary theology has shifted its gaze from heaven to earth, from God to the human, from the after life to the present life. Human existence and its meaning are the primary problems of contemporary theology. The world today is ageric — the modern person is not a contemplator but a doer. Dogma and speculation for its own sake have very little appeal to people today. Within the Catholic Church some are questioning the primacy attributed to liturgy over life itself. Is liturgy not the celebration of life rather than the font and source of all life? Life is the most important reality.

The Christian Church and the individual Christians are reading the signs of the times. Christians need to speak to the actual life of people today. What does the ethical teaching of Jesus mean for contemporary human existence? But the Church must carefully avoid just talking. Words without deeds are like the Pauline sounding brass or tinkling cymbal. The credibility gap merely widens when the pious mouthings of the Church are contradicted by its own life and actions.

The Christian trying to realize the meaning of human life naturally turns to the ethic of Jesus. The ethical teaching of Jesus is not a detailed blueprint for human activity, but the follower of Jesus at least begins by examining the ethical teaching of the scriptures. Many speculative problems arise from a consideration of biblical ethics and modern existence. Theology today is discussing secularity, the relationship between the immanent and the transcendent, the connection between human progress and the coming of the kingdom, the meaning of history. An older theology struggled with the problems of nature and grace or law and gospel. A thorough consideration of all these issues lies beyond the scope of the present chapter. The essay will merely attempt to indicate the relevancy of the ethic of Jesus for the contemporary Christian.

A very important problem is to determine what is the ethical teaching of Jesus. We know that the gospels are the expression of the faith of the early Church communities and do not give us an exact historical account of the ethical teaching of Jesus. Scripture scholars continually discuss what, if any, are the true sayings of Jesus and what are their original contexts. For our present purposes we will take the ethical teaching as found in the Gospels and refer to it as the ethical teaching of Jesus with the realization that it is the teaching proposed in the early Church.

An Ethic of Love

What is the ethical teaching of Jesus? In general, Jesus calls his followers to live a life in union with God and neighbor. Many theologians summarize the moral teaching of Jesus under the category of love. The three synoptic accounts mention the twofold commandment of love of God and neighbor as the core of the ethical teaching of Jesus (Mark 12:28-34; Matt. 22:34-40; Luke 10:25-37).

Why is the twofold love commandment called a new commandment? Love of God and neighbor was central in the teaching of the Old Testament and in many other religions. One distinctive characteristic of the love ethic of Jesus is the insistence on an indissoluble interior bond between the love of God and the love of neighbor. The followers of Jesus are recognized by their love for others. The judgment scene of Matt. 25 indicates that our relationship to God is known and manifested in our relationship with others. The follower of Jesus cannot claim to love God and yet neglect the neighbor who is hungry, thirsty, naked, alone, or in prison. John says very poignantly that we cannot love the God we do not see if we do not love the neighbor whom we do see (1 John 4:20). The ethic of Jesus does not eschew life in this world; rather, the authentic love of God is found in a loving concern for others. The follower of Jesus can find no excuse (not even worship at the altar) which takes precedence over loving concern and forgiveness for the neighbor.

A second characteristic of the love ethic of Jesus centers on the universality attached to the concept of neighbor. To love friends is easy. To love when one is loved in return requires no self-giving. But the Christian love for others is modeled on the love of Jesus for us. Jesus loved us while we were yet sinners. Jesus' love for us did not depend on what we could give him in return. The love of Jesus is completely disinterested and gratuitous in the sense that his love in no way depends on the loving qualities or the response of creatures. Jesus' love is creative, not responsive; giving, not possessing. Who are the privileged recipients of the love of Jesus? The strong, the influential, the wealthy, the intelligent, the respected? No, the privileged recipients of Jesus' love are the poor, the children, and even sinners. The nonvalue of the recipients of the good news of salvation is a startling fact.

The Christian is called to love just as Jesus has loved. The greatest example of Christian love is love for enemies. The enemy can give the lover nothing in return. In fact, the enemy returns hatred for love. The enemy might react with vengeance and annoyance, but love of enemies remains the great sign of Christian love. Our love for others does not depend on what they can do for us. Since the love of Jesus does not depend on the loving qualities of others, the object of his love is universal. The parable of the good Samaritan illustrates the universality of neighbor in the love ethic of Jesus. The neighbor is the person who is in need. The priest and the levite walk by the man in the road; but the Samaritan, a foreigner and enemy, has compassion on the man in need. Love is not just liking but a loving concern for the neighbor in need.

Perhaps the ethical teaching of Jesus as the complete giving of self to God and neighbor cannot be perfectly expressed in any human formula or concept. There are theological difficulties in reducing the ethic of Jesus even to the twofold commandment of love of God and neighbor. The love of the Christian for God and love for the neighbor are not the same kind of love. Love of God is the adoring gratitude of one who has received all from the giver of life. Love of neighbor is a creative giving and a redemptive forgiving which does not depend on the lovable qualities of the other. The two loves are different. St. Paul seldom speaks of our love for God as *agape* precisely because of the difference between God's love for us and our love for God.

Even our relationship to our neighbor cannot be adequately explained in terms of *agape* — the loving concern which is a total giving independent of the lovable qualities of the other. The human relationship of love does at times require that I love the other precisely because of that person's loving qualities. We each do want to be loved in ourselves and for what we are. Bishop Pike has criticized Professor Fletcher for reducing the entire Christian ethic to *agape*. There are times when *eros* as a responsive and possessive love or friendship as a mutual love are absolutely essential for human well-being. The theologian should be cautious in thinking that one can reduce the ethical teaching of Jesus to any neat human formulae. H. Richard Niebuhr claims that no human virtue as such can adequately explain the ethical teaching of Jesus.

However, all can agree that the ethical teaching of Jesus calls for the giving of self to God and neighbor. The neighbor in need, according to many biblical passages, has the first claim on the love of the Christian. We must examine this ethical teaching in more detail. The most prolonged statement of the ethical teaching of Jesus is found in the composite arranged in Matthew around the literary form of the Sermon on the Mount (Matt. 5-7). Luke brings together much of the ethical teaching of Jesus in his shorter Sermon on the Plain (Luke 6:20-49). Matthew begins the Sermon on the Mount with the Beatitudes. Although Luke employs the Beatitudes in a sapiential perspective and the more primitive form of the Beatitudes was probably a messianic proclamation, Matthew employs the Beatitudes in a catechizing and moralizing way to outline the characteristics which mark the life of the follower of Jesus. Matthew's spiritualization of the Beatitudes (the poor in spirit and the clean of heart) and the peculiar emphasis on justice or righteousness indicate that Matthew is trying to describe the moral life of the follower of Jesus. The Christian is called to be the light of the world and the salt of the earth through love, meekness, mercy, forgiveness, peacemaking, and the pursuit of righteousness.

Matthew then continues to describe the ethical teaching of Jesus as the completion and fullness of the law. Matthew first contrasts (perhaps by way of completion and not antithesis according to W. D. Davies) the ethical teaching of Jesus with that of the Scribes, the theologians of the time. The six antitheses or completions of the ethical teaching of Jesus concern anger, chastity, divorce, oaths, forgiveness and love of enemies. The section ends with a call to be perfect just as our heavenly Father is perfect. The parallel verse in Luke is a call to be merciful or compassionate as our heavenly Father is merciful (Luke 6:36). Matthew begins chapter 6 by comparing the attitude of the Pharisees and the followers of Jesus on the matters of almsgiving, prayer, and fasting. The follower of Jesus is concerned with a true change of heart and not just a rigid external observance. In the final section of the Sermon on the Mount, Matthew outlines other characteristics of the followers of Jesus. Jesus asks for a complete and loving trust in himself which leads to the abandonment of all other persons and things. Thus the literary device of the Sermon on the Mount capsulizes the ethical teaching of Jesus as found throughout the New Testament.

Embarrassing Questions

A meditative reflection on the moral teaching of Jesus raises embarrassing questions. Do the Church and the followers of Jesus really put into practice the ethical teaching of their Lord? Can the Church truly say to Jesus: "When you were hungry, thirsty, naked, lonely, abandoned, and in prison, I was there to comfort you"? Does the average person living today see reflected in the life of the Church the ethical teaching of Jesus? Is the primary concern of the Church the neighbor in need or is the Church more interested in preserving and augmenting its image, status, wealth, and power? Is the Church truly credible when it does raise its voice on particular issues, since so often there is only loud silence on other problems involving the neighbor in need? Has the Church left all to follow Jesus or is it trying to serve two masters? When the hierarchical Church does speak on a particular issue, how often are the words accompanied by appropriate actions even to the giving away of earthly power and possessions? Does the Church really take seriously the ethical teaching of Jesus?

However, one cannot merely point an accusing finger at the Church. How about myself as a Christian? Am I really willing to give all that I possess for my neighbor in need? Am I really willing to forgive my enemies the same way that Christ did? How difficult it remains to speak well of those who have hurt me in the past. Am I always willing to turn the other cheek or to walk an extra mile? How often do I really go out of my way to help others?

There exists an even more embarrassing question: can anyone be expected to live the ethical teaching of Jesus? At first glance, all are compelled to admit the beauty and sublimity of the ethical teaching of Jesus. But the moral demands of Jesus are radical and seemingly impossible.

The disciple of Jesus leaves all things to follow his master. Luke, who is the evangelist of total renouncement, even goes so far as to call for hatred of father and mother, brother and sister (Luke 15:26-33). Can anyone truly live the ethical teaching of Jesus?

The ethic of Jesus seems totally unreal when applied to the particular problems that so often arise in our lives. How can a Christian not worry about what one is going to eat or drink? What minister of God's Word would ever say to an improvident father that he should not worry about food, clothing, and shelter for his family? Can a wife forgive her husband and welcome him with open arms if he constantly beats her and the children? Can I as a Christian stand by and turn the other cheek when other innocent people (e.g., young children) are being attacked? How practical is it not to resist the evil doer? Who can possibly give to everyone who asks? Could the Gospel injunction of turning the other cheek have been an apt solution to the complicated problems of American involvement in Viet Nam? In all wars?

Even the Church does not follow the ethical demands of Jesus. Just after speaking about divorce, Matthew reminds the followers of Jesus never to take any oaths but to restrict their speech to yes and no (Matt. 5:33-37). However, the Roman Catholic Church has insisted on a number of oaths that must be taken by priests and teachers. Even on such a practical matter as judicial processes and matrimonial courts, Church procedure is practically never willing to accept the word of the Christian. The ethic of Jesus might be sublime and beautiful, but the teaching of Jesus seems impossible and irrelevant for the daily life of Christians.

Proposed Solutions

Conscientious Christians have constantly grappled with the problems created by the ethical teaching of Jesus. A true follower of Jesus cannot dismiss his whole ethical teaching as irrelevant and meaningless for daily human existence. Some explain the difficulty connected with the moral teaching of Jesus as arising from the fondness for imagery and exaggeration, which is associated with the oriental mentality. The beam in one's eye, the camel and the eye of the needle, forgiveness seventy times seven times, all these expressions embody overstatement and exaggeration. Undoubtedly Jesus reflected the thought patterns of his own culture, but can the entire moral teaching of Jesus be satisfactorily explained in terms of oriental exaggeration? Within a Lutheran tradition some want to interpret the Sermon on the Mount as *Moyses Moysissimus* — the law of Moses in the nth degree. The important function of law is to bring us to acknowledge our own weakness and sinfulness. The Mosaic Law brought the individual to Christ not by continuous development, but through discontinuity. The Law made people aware that they could find salvation not in the works of the Law but only through faith in Christ Jesus. The radical and impossible demands of the Sermon on the Mount only intensify the function of law which brings Christians to realize their sinfulness and need of redemption through faith in Christ. Although such a solution does serve as a partial explanation of the problem, the *Moyses Moysissimus* solution does not really take seriously the ethical teaching of Jesus.

A few have tried to take literally the ethical teaching of Jesus as universal norms for moral conduct which are always and everywhere binding. Such biblical fundamentalism quickly clashes with the problems of everyday human existence. Common sense and experience remind us that we cannot accept the ethical teachings of Jesus as laws of conduct which are always obliging in similar circumstances.

The Catholic theological tradition has generally ignored the problem created by the radical ethical demands of Jesus. At least on a popular level, Catholic teaching maintained that only a few people were called to perfection. Such people followed the evangelical counsels and generally entered the religious life. The vast majority of Christians living in the world were content with just observing the commandments which are binding on all. Catholic theology thus ignored the problem created by the radical moral teaching of Jesus. However, the consequences of ignoring the problem have been evident in Catholic life and practice. Only with Vatican II does popular Catholic teaching stress the universal vocation of all Christians to perfection. Catholic theology has not developed a theology and spirituality for life in the world because people outside the religious life were content with just obeying the commandments.

Many serious attempts to come to grips with the radical ethical teaching of Jesus hinge on the question of eschatology. Interestingly, contemporary theologians are also calling for a renewed eschatology. The eschatological views see the ethic of Jesus in connection with his mission in proclaiming the reign of God. The ethic of Jesus is above all a religious ethic, intimately connected with the reign that Jesus proclaimed. The reign of God calls for a complete and radical response from the hearer.

Albert Schweitzer well represents the school that labeled the moral teaching of Jesus an "interim ethic." In reacting against liberal Protestantism, Schweitzer stressed the eschatological dimension of Jesus' mission. Jesus expected the kingdom of God to come even before his disciples returned from their first missionary journey. When the kingdom did not come, Jesus went up to Jerusalem to precipitate the coming of the kingdom by his death. The strenuous ethic proposed by Jesus was for the very short interim that would precede the final coming of the kingdom. The ethical teaching of Jesus cannot be lived and sustained over a long period of time. Jesus' ethic is intimately connected with his own mistaken eschatology. Today, most theologians have rejected the opinion proposed by Schweitzer. The reign of God is not all future; to some extent the kingdom of God in Christ is already present and working in the world. Even many who maintain that Jesus believed in a very quick coming of the final stage of the reign of God do not think that Jesus would have preached a different ethic even if he had realized that the final stage of the kingdom would not arrive for a long period of time.

Perhaps the ethic of Jesus was meant only to describe life in the final stage of the reign of God and has no practical meaning for life here and now. Jesus did not propose a moral teaching for life in this world but was merely describing the life in the final coming of the reign of God. Again there is some truth in such an assertion, but the follower of Jesus cannot conclude that the ethical teaching of the master is completely irrelevant for Christians living in the world of today. Even the conflict and troubling situations described by Jesus seem much more applicable to the situation of our own daily lives than to the description of some future state of blessedness.

Eschatological Tension

The ethic of Jesus is closely aligned with his mission in proclaiming the reign of God. The final stage of the reign of God is coming. The reign is already begun but is now hastening toward its conclusion. The eschatological dimension at least adds a sense of urgency to some of the ethical teachings of Jesus (e.g., anger, lust). But there is also a content to the ethic of Jesus which is influenced by the presence and impending fulfillment of the reign of God. The ethical teaching of Jesus is a constant reminder of the absolute claim which the presence of the reign of God makes on the follower of Jesus. Jesus does not propose universal norms of conduct which are obliging for all Christians under all circumstances. Rather, in a very graphic way Jesus pictures the individual before the call of the reign of God's love. The reign of God places an all-engaging claim upon the hearer. Nothing else matters or counts when compared to the reign of God proclaimed and inaugurated by Jesus. Many of the ethical sayings of Jesus confront the individual with the inexorable claim of the presence of God's call. Jesus' graphic descriptions prescind from all other circumstances which might enter the picture. The neighbor in need and the follower of Jesus are placed face to face in a dramatic fashion.

The complexity of human problems is cast aside. Jesus prescinds from all other circumstances and conditions while showing the claim of the reign of God and the neighbor in need upon the individual follower. No mention is made of the binding obligations which a wife might have to her husband or family. Jesus prescinds from all such realities and simply shows in a very stark and dramatic way the radical claim of the reign of God and the needs of the neighbor upon his followers. The Christian, like Jesus himself, should be willing to sacrifice all for others. One can understand better the sayings about turning the other cheek, walking the extra mile, giving to everyone who asks, imitating the lilies of the field, hating father and mother, plucking out an eye or cutting off a hand as illustrative of the radical demands of the presence of the reign of God.

The gift of the reign of God puts an unconditional claim on the believer. But what does such a simplistic view of reality mean for the follower of Jesus who lives amid the complexity of modern human existence? Very often the Christian is confronted by many people in need. The Christian has manifold responsibilities that are always on the horizon. Can a Christian so give self and time to the neighbor in need that one forgets familial obligations? What value is the simplistic evangelical description of the dramatic confrontation between an individual and the call of the kingdom or the neighbor in need?

The radical and seemingly impossible ethical teaching of Jesus is more than rhetoric. Jesus indicates the goal and direction that should characterize the life and actions of his followers. "Give to everyone who asks" is an impossible ethical imperative, but such a demand indicates the constant thrust that characterizes the life of the Christian.

I cannot claim everything I have as my own and dispose of it in any way I want. The Christian realizes that personal talents, treasure, and abilities are in the service of the kingdom and the neighbor in need. There are times when the follower of Jesus might not be able to turn the other cheek; but the model of patience and forebearance, coupled with mercy and not vengeance, always remains meaningful. Occasionally the Christian might deem violence necessary to protect innocent human life (e.g., a young child being attacked by a demented person), but the thrust of the radical teaching of Jesus can never be forgotten.

Eschatological considerations introduce an inevitable tension into Christian ethics. The tension results from the fact that the reign of God in Christ is now present and is going forward toward its fullness. We are living in the times in between the two comings of Jesus. The reign of God is present but not yet fully present. The incipient presence of the eschaton calls for a continual growth and development. The followers of Jesus can never rest content with the present. The eschatological future is to some extent now present and urging the Christian forward. The true follower of the New Law can never say: "All these I have kept from my youth." The ethical teaching of Jesus calls for a continual effort to overcome the obstacles and shortcomings of the present moment.

Deficiencies in the Past

Unfortunately, the recent Catholic tradition has forgotten the eschatological tension both in the life of the individual and in the life of the Church. Theology did not insist upon the radical teachings of Jesus. In popular teaching the Christian ethical demands were reduced to a comparatively few, negative, universal norms which were to be observed by all. Such norms not only gave a negative tone to the Christian life, but comparatively easy norms of conduct robbed the Christian life of its inherent dynamism. The Christian could be content with having observed a comparatively few norms of morality. The Christian found a false sense of security in such norms and occasionally succumbed to a pharisaical attitude. On a wider scale the Church itself suffered from the same defect. The charge of triumphalism rang true in the Conciliar halls of Vatican II. The Church forgot its pilgrim status and lost the dynamic thrust of continual growth and conversion. The radical ethical teaching of Jesus prevents either his Church or his followers from ever remaining content and smug in the present stage of life.

Specifically in the area of moral theology, Catholic teaching has tried to avoid the tension created by the ethics of Jesus. As a result Catholic theology very frequently has lost the eschatological dimension of growth; or, less frequently, has required of all a goal that was not always attainable. The loss of the dynamic thrust in moral theology can be seen in the teaching on the right to life. Catholic theologians have not been in the forefront of those who were arguing for the abolition of capital punishment, the suspension of nuclear testing, the cessation of war. Why not? Catholic teaching over the years developed a very intricate system or theory for dealing with problems of life and death. Direct killing of the innocent is never permitted; but the state has the right to kill malefactors, and individuals may kill others indirectly or in self-defense. However, such a norm, considered only in itself, lacks the dynamic thrust in favor of human life which should always characterize the Christian life. The principles governing the questions of life and death solve complex problems too easily. The follower of Jesus can never be content when forced to take a life. Every taking of life is a falling short of the radical ethic of Jesus. Perhaps at times it is necessary to take human life; but a Christian can take life with only the greatest remorse and reluctance.

Likewise in the question of war, theologians tend to dismiss too easily the deaths of thousands of people because they are only "indirect" killings. There may be times when the follower of Jesus must act according to the principles of indirect killing, but the Christian can never lose sight of the thrust imposed by the radical ethic of Jesus. Personally I cannot be a total pacifist in the sense that at times resorting to violence might be necessary to defend innocent people. However, the follower of Jesus always strives in the direction of pacifism. When killing is deemed necessary it can only be as a reluctant accommodation to the needs of the present time.

In many other areas Catholic theology has too easily accommodated itself to the present moment and forgotten the radical ethical demands of Jesus. Problems of slavery, race and sex immediately come to mind. The Church and the theologians too easily acquiesced to predominant social patterns and structures. The Church cannot be altogether proud of its historical record on behalf of the freedom and dignity of all human beings. Theologians and Church leaders have also been absent from leadership in the fight for the equality of women. The institutional Church seems to have perpetuated a system of colonization rather than fighting for the rights of people to govern themselves. In the ninth century Pope Nicholas I condemned physical constraint and torture; but a few centuries later the Church used torture and violence to further its own dubious goals. Papal teaching on justice and the rights of the worker is a comparatively bright chapter in the history of the Church. But history also reminds us that Karl Marx recognized the problem almost half a century before Leo XIII wrote his encyclicals.

The followers of Jesus and his Church can never forget the radical ethical teaching of the Master. However, the imperfections and sinfulness that characterize the present times will mean that the Christian often falls far short of the goal described by Jesus. Accommodation to the present reality is a necessity at times. But the absolute claim of the reign of God and the needs of our neighbor never allow the Christian to be content when it is necessary to fall short of the radical moral teaching of Jesus. The Christian always possesses an uneasy conscience. Compromise and adaptation to present needs can only be accepted reluctantly. Catholic theology has too often forgotten the uneasy conscience of the Christian in confronting the imperfect and sinful situations of the present time. Jesus calls his followers to be the light of the world and the salt of the earth.

Ideal and Accommodation

On the other side of the paradox, there are times when the universal norms in Catholic theology do not sufficiently take into consideration the reluctant but necessary possibility of not fully accomplishing the moral demand of Jesus. Perhaps the universal norm absolutizes what is a radical demand of Jesus which is not always achievable. The biblical teaching on divorce furnishes an example. (Naturally one cannot settle the teaching of the Catholic Church on divorce merely from biblical evidence, but the solution proposed according to the biblical understanding may very well be applicable to the present understanding of divorce in the Church.) In the Sermon on the Mount in Matthew the two verses on divorce follow the radical maxim of plucking out an eye or cutting off a hand if the eye or the hand lead one astray. The divorce passage is followed by the saying of Jesus that his true followers will never take any oaths but will be content to make their speech a plain "yes" or "no." In Matthew 19 the matter of divorce is approached in the context of the two opposing opinions existing among the rabbis. Jesus definitely upholds the indissolubility of marriage. Jesus explains the permission given by Moses in the Old Testament on the grounds of the hardness of the heart of the people. However, there is in Matt. 19:9 the puzzling exception clause ("except for unchastity" — *porneia*) which also appears in Matt. 5:32.

Within the New Testament times there are accommodations in the teaching of absolute indissolubility. The famous Pauline privilege represents a falling short of the ideal proposed by Jesus. Paul, according to some exegetes, allowed converts to the faith to marry a new wife if their heathen wife wanted a separation (1 Cor. 7:12-16). Exegetes have developed many different theories for the famous incisions in the Gospel of Matthew. Although scripture scholars disagree on the exact meaning of such exceptions, many would agree that the exceptions were probably added to the primitive statements by the early Church. The exceptions may well represent some type of accommodation within the early Church to the radical ethical demands of Jesus. The accommodations made in New Testament times, whatever they may have been, are not the only possible accommodations that the Church and Christians might have to make in the course of time.

The radical ethic of Jesus, although seemingly impossible, is relevant precisely because the presence of the reign of God tending toward its eschatological fulfillment places an absolute claim upon the follower of Jesus. Even when the Christian must fall short of the radical demand of Jesus, he cannot rest content with the accommodation to the needs and imperfections of present reality. The dangers in any ethic of pure accommodation are manifold. The collaboration of citizens with the war aims and activities of their governments is perhaps the most painful and obvious example for the modern Christian. The conscience of the Christian can never rest content with any type of accommodation, but always seeks new ways to pursue the direction and goal pointed out in the radical ethics of Jesus. The ethic of Jesus for the contemporary Christian involves a creative tension between the present and the final stage of the reign of God.

Unfortunately, Christians find such tension difficult to live with. Some eliminate the tension by forgetting about the future and the continual call to growth and development. Others overthrow the tension by naively forgetting the present reality. Until very recently Catholic theology and life dissolved the tension and the frustration by forgetting about the radical ethics of Jesus and the consequent call for continual growth and even revolution. Absolute norms capable of being observed to the letter provided us with a false sense of security. Catholics acted as if we had all the answers to the problems confronting the world. The certitude and the security of the Church were a rock against the shifting sands of human existence. Various types of security were built into the system in addition to the watered down ethical demands which gave a reassuring sense of security to those who obeyed them. Indulgences, First Fridays, and First Saturdays were all means of providing assurance of eternal salvation. The Church itself did not know doubt, confusion, growth, pain, and tension.

Catholic life and theology in the post Vatican II era no longer claim to have the security and certitude that characterized Catholic life and teaching just a few short years ago. However, there is still a tendency to avoid the doubts, growing pains, and frustrations of a pilgrim people and a pilgrim Church. For Catholic life today the older securities and certitudes are gone forever; but many still look, somewhat naively, for a false sense of security. In opening up the Church to the world, in opening up ourselves to others, we reveal our own uncertainties, frustrations and weaknesses. In the midst of such frustration people easily seek a false sense of security. Postconciliar life in the Church has seen a number of new Messiahs appear on the horizon with great expectations, but the hopes of their followers are quickly dashed against the realities of human existence in the times in between. Many pinned their hopes on the liturgy in English or lately on an entirely new liturgy, but experience shows that the liturgy will never become the new Messiah. Many other Messiahs have appeared — ranging from Martin Buber to Harvey Cox to the scriptural renewal. But the eschaton has not yet come. Perhaps the pessimism of Sartre serves as an excellent reminder of the naive personalism and optimism of many today.

Some Catholics have abandoned a triumphalism in the Church only to embrace a triumphalism of the world or the secular city. I firmly believe that the mission of the Christian and the Church is in service of the world, but the present state of the world is not entirely salvific. There is too much suffering and inequality in our own country, let alone in a world blighted by injustice, ignorance, and hunger, for the Christian to be content with the present situation. Professor Charles West of Princeton Theological Seminary, in describing the meeting on Church and Society sponsored by the World Council of Churches in Geneva in the summer of 1966, remarked about the opposition to the theological advocates of the secular city. West claims that the majority of theologians from the underdeveloped countries were "theological guerrillas" who saw revolution as the only way of shaking off the shackles of contemporary political and social structures. The "theological technocrats" of the secular city were amazed at the vehemence of the revolutionaries.

To live with the eschatological tension is difficult. The Christian too experiences doubt, frustration, opposition, and resistance to any growth. One who realizes the difficulties in breaking away from one's own selfishness and sinfulness also understands the slowness of growth in the structures of human existence. To become resigned to the present is just as inadequate a solution as to expect miraculous progress without opposition or frustration. For the Christian the virtue of hope allows one to live the eschatological tension. Hope constantly beckons in the direction of the final stage of the kingdom of God. The follower of Jesus can never rest content with the present situation of one's own change of heart or the present situation of humanity. But hope also strengthens the follower of Jesus against the frustrations and opposition that accompany any growth. Hope makes the Paschal Mystery of Christ a reality. Only by dying does the Christian rise in the newness of life.

Despair looms all too easily on the horizon for one who

expects the eschaton to come too easily or too quickly. The greatness of God's gift to us is the fact that we have a role to play in bringing about the new heaven and the new earth. The radical ethic of Jesus could very easily bring one to despair because of the impossibility that it entails. However, the ethic of Jesus is both gift and demand. My inability to live according to the strenuous moral teaching of Jesus is a constant reminder of my need for God's mercy and forgiveness. At the same time the radical ethical demand serves as a constant reminder to the Christian to open oneself ever more to the call of God and neighbor. The Christian creatively tries to make oneself and one's world. All the old securities and certitudes are gone. There are no false props that the Christian can use. Christian maturity demands that the follower of Jesus stand on one's own feet and carve out one's human existence despite all the frustrations and doubts of life. The Christian as a pilgrim traveling to the new heaven and the new earth never has the luxury and the security of one who has already arrived at the final destination. In the insecurity of the journey only hope in the Word and Work of God gives the courage to continue. Hope is the virtue that allows the Christian to live the tension of the reign of God present but not yet fully here.

There are tendencies in the evangelical ethic to abandon entirely life in this world. However, the contemporary Christian realizes that the needs of his neighbor can and must be met at the present time. The Christian's hope in the final coming of the reign of God does not provide any blueprint for human development and growth. Only a naive biblicism would expect to find in the scriptures the solutions to the problems confronting society today. The ethical teaching of Jesus urges his followers to creatively find solutions to come to the aid of the neighbor in need.

Like the individual Christian, the Church too must take seriously the moral teaching of Jesus and the virtue of hope. The primary concern of the Church should be the neighbor in need. The Church constantly needs to rethink the ways in which it tries to accomplish its primary purposes. The tendency to seek security in the means that were helpful in the past is all too tempting. There is also the temptation to seek security in other things and not in the Word of God in Christ. For a long time the Church tried to find its security in the protection of the State. Now the temptation seems to be for the Church to find its security in brick and mortar institutions. Structures and institutions will always be necessary, but they only serve to help the Church be faithful to the mission and teaching of Jesus which puts primary emphasis on the neighbor in need. The Church should not seek false security in status, wealth or power. The pilgrim Church finds its only security in the promise of its founder.

The relevancy of the Gospel ethic of Jesus is the challenge and vocation given to the followers of Jesus and his Church.

BIBLIOGRAPHY

Bruce C. Birch and Larry L. Rasmussen, *Bible and Ethics in the Christian Life* (Minneapolis: Augsburg Publishing House, 1976). Surveys different approaches to the use of the Scriptures in Christian ethics and then develops an approach emphasizing the Church as the proper community setting for relating Bible and ethics.

W. D. Davies, *The Sermon on the Mount* (Cambridge: Cambridge University Press, 1966). Davis answers both yes and no to the question: Has Matthew departed from the mind of Jesus by making the words of Jesus in the Sermon on the Mount into "the new law"?

C. H. Dodd, *Gospel and Law* (Cambridge: Cambridge University Press, 1951). Four essays originally given as the Bampton Lectures at Columbia University in 1950. The radical ethical sayings of Jesus are interpreted in the third essay as showing the goal and direction toward which the Christian strives and also serving as a reminder of our constant need for forgiveness.

Victor Paul Furnish, *Theology and Ethics in Paul* (Nashville: Abingdon Press, 1968) and *The Love Command in the New Testament* (Abingdon Press, 1972). In these two books Furnish provides a critical study of important aspects of biblical ethics from a Protestant perspective.

Richard H. Hiers, *Jesus and Ethics: Four Interpretations* (Philadelphia: Westminster Press, 1968). Hiers considers the approach of Harnack, Schweitzer, Bultmann, and Dodd to the question of the ethical teaching of Jesus. He strongly rejects Dodd's realized eschatology and stresses the eschatological coloring of the ethics of Jesus.

J. L. Houlden, *Ethics and the New Testament* (New York: Penguin Books, 1973). A short consideration of the writers and some questions of New Testament ethics (divorce, political obedience, wealth, and toleration). Against Schnackenburg and others Houlden insists that the ethical teaching of Jesus should not come at the beginning but only at the end of New Testament ethics, for the writers interpret Jesus in different ways.

John Knox, *The Ethic of Jesus in the Teaching of the Church* (New York: Abingdon Press, 1961). A somewhat popular and very readable summary of the different solutions to the problem of the radical ethic of Jesus.

Nöel Lazure, O.M.I., *Les Valeurs morales de la théologie johannique* (Paris: J. Gabalda, 1965). One of the few studies devoted exclusively to the moral teaching of John.

Norman Perrin, *The Kingdom of God in the Teaching of Jesus* (Philadelphia: Westminster Press, 1963). A fine, scholarly summary of the discussion about the nature of the kingdom and its relationship to ethics from Schleiermacher to the present.

Jack T. Sanders, *Ethics in the New Testament* (Philadelphia: Fortress Press, 1975). Sanders comes to the "overwhelmingly negative conclusion" that neither Jesus nor the early Church nor the New Testament can or should furnish the basis for a contemporary Christian ethic because of the eschatological influence.

Rudolf Schnackenburg, *The Moral Teaching of the New Testament* (Freiburg: Herder, 1964). A one-volume summary and synthesis of the moral teaching of the entire New Testament.

Ceslaus Spicq, O. P., *Agape in the New Testament*, 3 vols. (St. Louis: B. Herder, 1963, 1965, 1966). An exegetical and scriptural study of *agape* in the New Testament without the very complete footnotes found in the original French volume.

Ceslaus Spicq, O. P., *Théologie morale du Nouveau Testament*, 2 vols. (Paris: J. Gabalda, 1965). A comparatively complete and analytical treatment (there is no attempt made at synthesis of the teaching) of the different moral themes and teachings in the New Testament. The footnotes with very complete bibliographies are most valuable.

2: Natural Law

Pope Paul's encyclical *Humanae Vitae* explicitly employs a natural law methodology to arrive at its particular moral conclusions on the licit means of regulating births. The encyclical admits that the teaching on marriage is a "teaching founded on natural law, illuminated and enriched by divine revelation" (*H. V.* n. 4). The papal letter then reaffirms that "the teaching authority of the Church is competent to interpret even the natural moral law" (*H. V.* n. 4). Recently, Catholic moral theologians have been reappraising the notion of natural law.[1] The sharp response to the papal letter indicates there is a great divergence between the natural law methodology employed in the encyclical and the methodology suggested by recent studies in moral theology. The natural law approach employed in the encyclical raises two important questions for moral theology: the place of natural law in the total understanding of Christian ethics; the concept of natural law itself.

I. Natural Law in the Total Christian Perspective

The recent papal pronouncement realizes that natural law forms only a part of the total horizon of moral theology. The Apostles and their successors have been constituted "as guardians and authentic interpreters of all the moral law, not only, that is, of the law of the Gospel, but also of the natural law, which is also an expression of the will of God" (*H. V.* n. 4). The encyclical admits there is a source of ethical wisdom and knowledge for the Christian apart from the explicit revelation of the Scriptures, so that Christians and the Church do learn ethical wisdom from non-Christians and the world.

There have been many theologians especially in the more strict Protestant tradition who would tend to deny any source of ethical wisdom and knowledge which Christians share with all mankind.[2] Such theologians based their position on the uniqueness and self-sufficiency of the scriptural revelation, the doctrine of justification, and an emphasis on sin as corrupting whatever exists outside the unique revelation of Jesus Christ.[3] However, contemporary Protestant theologians generally maintain the existence of some ethical wisdom apart from the explicit revelation of God in the Scriptures and in Christ Jesus, even though they may avoid the term natural law.[4] Protestant theologians in the last few decades have employed such concepts as the orders of creation (Brunner), the divine mandates (Bonhoeffer), love and justice (Reinhold Niebuhr), love transforming justice (Ramsey), common ground morality (Bennett), and other similar approaches.

The natural law theory as implied in the encyclical has the theological merit of recognizing a source of ethical wisdom for the Christian apart from the explicit revelation of God in Christ Jesus. This recognition remains a most important and lasting contribution of Catholic thought in the area of theological ethics. The difficult question for Christian theology centers on the relationship between the natural law and the distinctively Christian element in the understanding of the moral life of the Christian. The same basic question has been proposed in other terms. H. Richard Niebuhr describes five different models of the relationship between Christ and culture.[5] An older Catholic theology spoke about the relationship between nature and grace, between the natural and the supernatural. Niebuhr has described the typical Catholic solution to the question of Christ and culture in terms of "both-and" — both culture and Christ.[6] Such an approach corresponds with an unnuanced understanding of the relationship between nature and grace. The two are neither opposed nor identical; but they exist side by side. Grace adds something to nature without in any way destroying it. A simplistic view of the supernatural sees it as something added to the natural. But the natural retains its own finality and integrity as the substratum to which the supernatural is added.[7]

In such a perspective the natural tends to be seen as something absolute and sufficient in itself to which the supernatural is added. The natural law thus exists as a self-contained entity to which the law of the gospel or revelation is then added. *Humanae Vitae* seems to accept such a "both-and" understanding of the relationship between natural law and the gospel or revelation. "All the moral law" is explained as "not only, that is, of the law of the Gospel, but also of the natural law, which is also an expression of the will of God . . ." (*H.V.* n. 4). The papal letter calls for an anthropology based on "an integral vision of man and his vocation, not only of his earthly and natural, but also his supernatural and eternal, vocation" (*H.V.* n. 7). The "both-and" relationship appears again in paragraph 8 which refers to "the entire moral law, both natural and evangelical."

Not only the wording of the encyclical but the methodology presupposed in the argumentation employs a "both-and" understanding of the relationship of natural law and evangelical law. Msgr. Lambruschini, who explained the encyclical at a press conference, said that purposely no mention was made of scriptural arguments, but the entire reasoning was based on natural law.[8] Bernard Häring has criticized the encyclical because it does not even mention the admonition of St. Paul that husband and wife should "not refuse each other except by mutual consent, and then only for an agreed time, to leave yourselves free for prayer;

then come together again in case Satan should take advantage of your weakness to tempt you" (1 Cor. 7:5).[9] The
Pastoral Constitution on the Church in the Modern World
did take heed of Paul's admonition. "But where the inti-
macy of married life is broken off, it is not rare for its
faithfulness to be imperiled and its quality of fruitfulness
ruined" (n. 51). However, the primary criticism is not the
fact that there is no reference to any particular scriptural
text, but the underlying understanding that the natural law
is something totally integral in itself to which the evangelical or supernatural law is added.

Christian ethics cannot absolutize the realm of the natural as something completely self-contained and unaffected
by any relationships to the evangelical or supernatural.
Christian theology derives its perspective from the Christian faith commitment. The Christian views reality in the
light of the total horizon of the Christian faith commitment — creation, sin, incarnation, redemption, and parousia. Natural law itself is thus Christocentric.[10] The doctrine
of creation forms the theological basis for natural law, and
Christ as logos is the one in whom all things are created
and through whom all things are to be returned to the
Father. Natural law theory has taken seriously the implications of the incarnation through which God has joined
himself to the human, the worldly, and the historical.
However, nature and creation form only a part of the total
Christian view. The reality of "the natural" must always be
seen in the light of sin, redemption, and the parousia. Nature and creation are relativized by the transforming Christian themes of redemption and final resurrection destiny
of all creation. The natural law theory is theologically
based on the Christian truths of creation and incarnation,
but these aspects are not independent and unrelated to the
full horizon of the Christian view of reality. The Christian
situates natural law in the context of the total history of
salvation which transforms and criticizes what is only "the
natural." Thus in the total Christian perspective there is a
place for the "natural," but the natural remains provisional

and relativized by the entire history of salvation.

The full Christian view of reality also takes account of the existence of sin and its effects on human existence. However, the natural law theory as illustrated in *Humanae Vitae* does not seem to give sufficient importance to the reality and effect of human sinfulness. In section III under "Pastoral Directives" the papal letter speaks about the compassion of Christ and the Church for sinners. "But she [the Church] cannot renounce the teaching of the law which is, in reality, that law proper to a human life restored to its original truth and conducted by the Spirit of God" (*H. V.* n. 19). The implication remains that the disruptive force of sin has already been overcome by the grace of God. Such an approach has definite affinities with a simplistic view of sin as depriving the Christian of the supernatural gift of grace, but not affecting the substratum of nature. However, in the total Christian horizon the disrupting influence of sin colors all human reality.

Humanae Vitae does recognize some effects of sin in human beings. Sin affects the will, but the help of God will strengthen our good will (*H. V.* n. 20). Sin affects the instincts, but ascetical practices will enable the reason and will to achieve self-mastery (*H. V.* n. 21). Sinfulness also makes itself felt in some aspects of the social environment, "which leads to sense excitation and unbridled customs, as well as every form of pornography and licentious performances" (*H. V.* n. 22). But no mention is made of the fact that sin affects reason itself and the very nature on which natural law theory is based. Sin relativizes and affects all reality. How often has reason been used to justify human prejudice and arrogance! Natural law has been appealed to in the denials of human dignity and of religious liberty. The just war theory has been employed to justify wars in which one's own nation was involved.[11] History shows the effect of sin in the very abuses which have accompanied natural law thinking.

Recently, I have proposed the need for a theory of compromise in moral theology precisely because of the existence of sin in the world.[12] The surd brought about by human sinfulness is so oppressive that occasionally we cannot overcome it immediately. The presence of sin may force a person to do something one would not do if there were no sin present. Thus in sin-filled situations (notice all the examples of such situations in the current literature) the Christian may be forced to adopt a line of action which one would abhor if sin were not present. A theory of compromise does not give us a blank check to shirk our Christian responsibilities. However, there are situations in which the value sacrificed is not proportionate to the demand asked of the Christian. Protestant theology has often adopted a similar approach by saying that in some circumstances the Christian is forced to do something sinful. The sinner reluctantly performs the deed and asks God for mercy and forgiveness.[13] At times Protestant theology has overemphasized the reality of sin, but Catholic theology at times has not paid enough attention to the reality of sin.

The recent papal encyclical presupposes a natural law concept that fails to indicate the relative and provisional character of natural law in the total Christian perspective. Critics have rightly objected to a theory which tends to absolutize what is only relative and provisional. Take, for example, the teaching in Catholic theology on the right of private property. The modern popes have approached the question of private property in a much more absolute way than Thomas Aquinas. The differences of approach are instructive for the moral theologian. The popes, especially Leo XIII, stressed private property as the right of every individual stemming from the dignity of the human person, the person's rational nature, labor, the need to provide for self and family, and the need to overcome the uncertainties of life.[14] Thomas gave greater importance to the social function of all property and the reality of human sinfulness. Perhaps Thomas was influenced by the often-cited opinion of Isidore of Seville that according to the natural law all things should be held in common.[15] Thomas ultimately sees the sin of human beings as the reason for the existence of private property. Society would not have peace and order unless everyone possessed his or her own goods. Likewise, Thomas pointed out that earthly goods are not properly cared for if they are held in common.[16] Thomas maintained there would be no need for private property in the world of original justice.

There are other indications that private property is not as absolute a right of man as proposed in some papal encyclicals. With his understanding of a more absolute right of private property, Leo XIII spoke of the obligation of the rich to share their goods with the poor as an obligation of charity and not justice.[17] However, a very respectable and long tradition in the medieval Church maintained that the rich had an obligation in justice to share their goods with the poor.[18] Even in our own day one can ask if private property is the best way to protect the dignity and freedom of the human person. The great inequalities existing in society today at the very least must modify and limit the concept of the right of private property. In our historical circumstances we are much more conscious of the social aspect of property than was Leo XIII.[19] The teaching on private property well illustrates the dangers of a natural law approach that is not relativized by the whole reality of salvation history.

The natural law theory suggested in, and employed by, the encyclical *Humanae Vitae* has the advantage of affirming the existence of a source of ethical wisdom apart from the explicit revelation of God in Christ in the Scriptures. However, such a concept of natural law tends to absolutize what the full Christian vision sees as relative and provisional in the light of the entire history of salvation. The "natural" does not and never has existed as such. All of creation must be seen and understood in the light of redemption and resurrection destiny.

II. A Critique of Natural Law

The debate over the condemnation of artificial contraception in *Humanae Vitae* indicates a basic dissatisfaction with the natural law methodology employed in the encyclical. The encyclical uses a notion of natural law which has generally been found in the classical textbooks and manuals of moral theology, but precisely this concept of natural law is subject to severe negative criticism. This section will point out three major weaknesses in that concept of natural law: (1) a tendency to accept natural law as a monolithic philosophical system with an agreed upon body of ethical content which is the source for most, if not all, of Catholic moral teaching; (2) the danger of physicalism which identifies the human act with the physical or biological structure of the act; (3) a classicist worldview and methodology.

Not a Monolithic Philosophical System

The first defect will only be summarized here, since it is treated at greater length elsewhere. Natural law remains a very ambiguous term.[20] The first section of this study used the concept of natural as distinguished from supernatural; in addition, it has been pointed out that the word nature had over twenty different meanings in Catholic thinking before Thomas Aquinas. The word law is also ambiguous, since it tends to have a very legalistic meaning for most people today; whereas for Thomas law was an ordering of reason. Natural law ethics has often been described as a legalistic ethic, that is, an ethic based on norms and laws; but in reality for Thomas natural law is a deliberative ethic which arrives at decision not primarily by the application of laws, but by the deliberation of reason. Many thinkers in the course of history have employed the term natural law, but frequently they defined natural law in different ways. Thinkers employing different natural law approaches have arrived at different conclusions on particular moral topics. Natural law in the history of thought does not refer to a monolithic theory, but tends to be a more generic term which includes a number of different approaches to moral problems. There is no such thing as *the* natural law as a monolithic philosophical system with an agreed upon body of ethical content existing from the beginning of time.

Many erroneously believe that Catholic theology is committed to a particular natural law approach to moral problems. In practice, however, the vast majority of Catholic teaching on particular moral questions came into existence even before Thomas Aquinas enunciated his theory. Likewise, contemporary Catholic theology recognizes the need for a pluralism of philosophical approaches in the Christian's quest for a better understanding of man and his reality. There is no longer "one Catholic philosophy."

The Danger of Physicalism

Ethical theory constantly vacillates between two polarities — naturalism and idealism. Naturalism sees the human being in perfect continuity with the nature about him. Nature shapes and even determines the individual. Idealism views the human being completely apart from nature and as completely surpassing nature. Even Thomistic philosophy, the main Catholic proponent of natural law theory, knows an ambivalence between nature and reason.

The Thomistic natural law concept vacillates at times between the order of nature and the order of reason.[21] The general Thomistic thrust is towards the predominance of reason in natural law theory. However, there is in Thomas a definite tendency to identify the demands of natural law with physical and biological processes. Thomas, too, is a historical person conditioned by the circumstances and influences of his own time. These influences help explain the tendency (but not the predominant tendency) in Thomas to identify the human action with the physical and biological structure of the human act. A major influence is Ulpian, a Roman lawyer who died in 228.

Ulpian and Thomas. Ulpian defined the natural law as that which nature teaches all the animals. Ulpian distinguished the natural law from the *ius gentium*. The *ius naturale* is that which is common to all animals, whereas the *ius gentium* is that which is proper to humans.[22] Albert the Great rejected Ulpian's definition of the natural law, but Thomas accepted it, and even showed a preference for such a definition.[23] In the *Commentary on the Sentences*, for example, Thomas maintains that the most strict definition of natural law is the one proposed by Ulpian: *ius naturae est quod natura omnia animalia docuit.*[24]

In his *Commentary on the Nichomachean Ethics*, Thomas again shows a preference for Ulpian's definition. Aristotle has proposed a twofold division of *iustum naturale* and *iustum legale*, but Ulpian proposed the threefold distinction of *ius naturale, ius gentium* and *ius civile*. Thomas solves the apparent dilemma by saying that the Roman law concepts of *ius naturale* and *ius gentium* both belong under the Aristotelian category of *iustum naturale.* The human being has a double nature. The *ius naturale* rules that which is proper to both humans and the animals, such as the union of the sexes and the education of offspring; whereas the *ius gentium* governs the rational part of human beings which is proper to humans alone and embraces such things as fidelity to contracts.[25]

In the *Summa Theologiae* Thomas cites Ulpian's definition on a number of occasions.[26] In the classification of natural law again Thomas shows a preference for Ulpian's definition. Thomas accepts the division proposed by Isidore of Seville, according to which the *ius gentium* belongs to the category of human law and not the category of divine law. Thomas uses Ulpian's definition to explain Isidore's division. The natural law pertains to the divine law because it is common to humans and to all the animals.[27] In a sense, the *ius gentium* does pertain to the category of human law because humans use reason to deduce the conclusions of the *ius gentium*.

Thomas thus employs Ulpian's definition of natural law as opposed to what reason deduces (the *ius gentium*) to defend the division of law proposed by Isidore. The same question receives somewhat the same treatment later in the *Summa.*[28] The texts definitely show that Thomas knew and even accepted the definition of natural law proposed by Ulpian.

Ulpian's Concept of Natural Law. Ulpian is important for the understanding of natural law morality. The natural law for Ulpian is defined in terms of those actions which are common to humans and all the animals. There results from this the definite danger of identifying the human action with a mere animal or biological process. "Nature" and "natural" in Ulpian's meaning are distinguished from that which is specifically human and derived by reason. Traditional theology has in the past definitely employed the words "natural" and "nature" as synonymous with animal or biological processes and not as denoting human actions in accord with the rational, human nature.

Moral theology textbooks even speak of sins according to nature. The manuals generally divide the sins against the sixth commandment into two categories — the sins against nature (*peccata contra naturam*) and sins in accord with nature (*peccata secundum naturam*). "Nature" is thus used in Ulpian's sense, as that which is common to humans and all the animals. In matters of sexuality (and Ulpian himself uses the example of the sexual union as an illustration of the natural law), humans share with the animal world the fact of the sexual union whereby male seed is deposited in the vas of the female. Sins against nature, therefore, are those acts in which the animal or biological process is not observed — pollution, sodomy, bestiality, and contraception. Sins according to nature are those acts in which the proper biological process is observed but something is lacking in the sphere which belongs only to rational beings. These include fornication, adultery, incest, rape, and sacrilege.[29]

The classification of sins against chastity furnishes concrete proof that "nature" has been used in Catholic theology to refer to animal processes without any intervention of human reason. Many theologians have rightly criticized the approach to marriage and sexuality used by Catholic natural law theoreticians because such an approach concentrated primarily on the biological components of the act of intercourse. The personal aspects of the sexual union received comparatively scant attention in many of the manuals of moral theology. Ulpian's influence has made it easier for Catholic natural law thinking to identify the human act simply with the physical structure of the act.

Ulpian's Anthropology. Ulpian's understanding of the natural law logically leads to disastrous consequences in anthropology. The distinction between two parts in humans — that which is common to humans and all the animals, and that which is proper to humans — results in a two-layer version of human beings. A top layer of rationality is merely added to an already constituted bottom layer of animality. The union between the two layers is merely extrinsic — the one lies on top of the other. The animal layer retains its own finalities and tendencies, independent of the demands of rationality. Thus the individual may not interfere in the animal processes and finalities. Note that the results of such an anthropology are most evident in the area of sexuality.

A proper understanding of the human should start with that which is proper to humans. Rationality does not just lie on top of animality, but rationality characterizes and guides the whole person. Animal processes and finalities are not untouchable. Our whole vocation, we have come to see, is to bring order and intelligence into the world, and to shape animal and biological finalities toward a truly human purpose. Ulpian's concept of natural law logically falsifies the understanding of the human and tends to canonize the finalities and processes which humans share with the animal world.

A better anthropology would see the distinctive in human beings as guiding and directing the totality of one's being. For Thomas rationality constituted what is distinctive and characteristic in humans. Modern philosophers differ from Thomas on what is distinctively human. Phenomenologists tend to view the individual being as a symbolic person; while personalists look upon the human as an incarnate spirit, a "thou" in relation to other "you's." However, all would agree in rejecting an anthropology that absolutizes animal finalities and tendencies without allowing any intervention of the specifically human rational aspect of human beings.

I am not asserting that Thomas always identified human actions with animal processes or the physical structure of the act. In fact, the general outlines of the hylomorphic theory, by speaking of material and formal components of reality, try to avoid any physicalism or biologism. Nevertheless, the adoption of Ulpian's understanding of "nature" and "natural" logically leads to the identification of the human act itself with animal processes and with the mere physical structure of the act. Such a distorted view of the human act becomes especially prevalent in the area of medical morals, for in medical morality one can more easily conceive a moral human action solely in terms of the physical structure of that action.

Likewise, Ulpian's notion of nature easily leads to a morality based on the finality of a faculty independent of any considerations of the total human person or the total human community. One must, of course, avoid the opposite danger of paying no attention to the physical structure of the act or to external actions in themselves. However, Catholic theology in its natural law approach has suffered from an oversimple identification of the human action with an animal process or finality.

Marriage and Sexuality. Ulpian's understanding of natural law logically has had another deleterious effect on Catholic moral theology. Until the last decade magisterial pronouncements frequently spoke of the primary and secondary ends of marriage.[30] The latest statements of

Pope Paul and the Pastoral Constitution on the Church in the Modern World (*Gaudium et Spes*) happily avoid this terminology.[31] However, such a distinction has obviously influenced Catholic teaching on marriage and sexuality. Many people have questioned the distinction as being contradicted by the experience of married couples.

The distinction logically follows from Ulpian's concept of the natural law and the human, although I do not claim that Ulpian is the source of such a distinction. "Primary" is that which is common to humans and all the animals. Ulpian, and Thomas in citing Ulpian, use the union of the sexes and the procreation and education of offspring as examples of that which is common to humans and all the animals. "Secondary" is that which is proper to humans. Since only humans and not animals have sexual intercourse as a sign and expression of love, the love union aspect of sexuality remains proper to humans and therefore secondary. The former teaching on the ends of marriage is logically connected with Ulpian's understanding of the human being and natural law. Thus the teaching of Ulpian on natural law has a logical connection with the inadequate understanding of a human action as identified with an animal process.

A More Primitive Attitude. Another historical factor based on the conditions of a primitive culture has also influenced the tendency to make the processes of nature inviolable. Stoic philosophy well illustrates a more general historical factor that tends to identify the human action with its physical or natural structure. One should avoid too many generalizations about the Stoics because Stoic philosophy included a number of different thinkers who covered a comparatively long span of years. In addition, Stoic philosophers invoked the natural law to justify practices that contemporary natural law theoreticians brand as immoral.[32] However, there is a common thrust to the ethical doctrine proposed by the Stoics.

Ethics considers human beings and their actions. We

humans want to find happiness. What actions should we perform to find happiness and fulfillment? A more primitive and less technical society will come to conclusions different from those reached by a more technically and scientifically developed society. Primitive people soon realize that they find happiness in conforming to the patterns of nature.

Primitive people remain almost helpless when confronted with the forces of nature. The forces of nature are so strong that the human individual is even tempted to bow down and adore. One realizes the futility in trying to fight them. Happiness will come only by adjusting oneself to nature.

Nature divides the day into light and dark. When darkness descends, there is little or nothing that humans can do except sleep. When the hot sun is beating down near the equator, one will find happiness only by avoiding work and overexposure in the sun. In colder climates, one will be happy only when using clothing and shelter as protection against nature. If one wants to be happy, one will stay under some form of shelter and avoid the rain and snow. If there is a mountain in one's path, the wise person will walk around the mountain rather than suffer the ardors of trying to scale the peak. For people living in a primitive society (in the sense of nonscientific and nontechnical), happiness is found in conforming self to nature.

Stoic philosophy built on this understanding of life in a nontechnical society. As Greeks, the Stoics believed in an intelligible world. They made the universe as a whole — the cosmos — their principle of intelligibility. Stoic philosophy held that reason governed the order of nature. Human happiness consisted in conforming to reason, that is, in conforming to the order of nature. Reason rather easily became identified with the order of nature. The primary norm of morality, therefore, was conformity to nature.[33]

We who live in a scientific and technological society will have a different view of human life and happiness. Modern people do not find happiness in conforming to nature. The whole ethos and genius of modern society is different. Contemporary humans make nature conform to them rather than vice-versa. Through electricity we can change night into day. There are very few things that moderns cannot do at night now that it is illuminated by electricity.

We contemporary people use artificial heat in the winter and air conditioning in the summer to bring nature into conformity with our needs and desires. Nature did not provide us with wings to fly; in fact, the law of gravity seems to forbid flying. However, science has produced the jet plane and the rocket, which propel us at great speeds around the globe and even into the vast universe. When a mountain looms up as an obstacle, we either level the mountain with bulldozers or tunnel under the terrain. We could never tolerate a theory which equates human happiness with conformity to nature. We interfere with the processes of nature to make nature conform to us.

But a word of caution is in order. In the last few years the ecological crisis has made us aware of the danger of not giving enough importance and value to the physical aspects of worldly existence. We are not free to interfere with nature any way we see fit. Just as it is wrong to absolutize the natural and the physical, so too it is wrong to give no meaning or importance to the natural and the physical.

These few paragraphs have not attempted to prove the influence of Stoic philosophy on St. Thomas. Rather, Stoic philosophy was used to illustrate how the conditions existing in a nontechnological society will influence the philosophical understanding of anthropology and ethics. Thomas too lived in an agrarian, nonscientific world. The nontechnological worldview would be more prone to identify the human act with the physical process of nature itself.

Reality or Facticity. A more primitive society also tends to view reality in terms of the physical and the sensible. The child, unlike the adult, sees reality primarily in terms of externals. The tendency to identify the human action with the physical structure would definitely be greater in a more primitive society. For example, the importance that Catholic theology has attached to masturbatory activity, especially the overemphasis since the sixteenth century, seems to come from viewing it purely in terms of the physiological and biological aspects of the act. Modern psychology, however, does not place that great importance on such activity.

Theologians must incorporate the findings of modern science in trying to evaluate the human act of masturbation. To view it solely in terms of the physical structure of the act distorts the total reality of this human action. Contemporary theologians cannot merely repeat what older theologians have said. Today we know much more about the reality of the human act of masturbation than, say, St. Alphonsus or any other moral theologian living before the present century.[34]

It would be erroneous to say that Catholic theology has identified the human act with the brute facticity of natural processes or just the physical structure of the act itself. In the vast majority of cases, moral theology has always distinguished between the physical structure of the action and the morality of the action. The moral act of murder differs from the physical act of killing. The physical act of taking another's property does not always involve the moral act of stealing. However, in some areas of morality (for example, contraception, sterilization, direct effect) the moral act has been considered the same as the physical structure of the act itself.

The Morality of Lying. Another area in which Catholic theologians are moving away from a description of the human act in purely physical or natural terms is lying. The contemporary theological understanding of lying serves as a salutary warning to the natural law concept found in the manuals of theology because the morality of lying cannot be determined merely by examining the faculty of speech and its finality, apart from the totality of the human person speaking and the community in which one speaks.

The manuals of moral theology traditionally define lying as *locutio contra mentem*. The faculty of speech exists to express what is in the mind. When human speech does not reflect what is in the mind there is a perversion of the faculty. The perverted faculty argument is based on the finality of the faculty of speech looked at in itself. Accordingly, a lie exists when the verbal utterance does not correspond with what is in the mind. Theologians then had to face the problem created by the fact that at times the speaker simply could not speak the truth to his hearer or questioner (for example, in the case of a committed secret). A casuistry of mental reservations arose to deal with such situations.[35]

Today most contemporary Catholic theologians accept the distinction between a lie and a falsehood. A falsehood involves an untruth in the sense that the external word contradicts what is in the mind. However, the malice of lying does not consist in the perversion of the faculty of speech or the lack of conformity between the word spoken and what is in the mind. The malice of lying consists in the harm done to society and the human community through the breakdown of mutual trust and honesty. Thus, some theologians distinguish between a lie as the denial of truth which is due to the other and falsehood which is a spoken word not in conformity with what is in the mind.

The distinction between lying and falsehood obviates the rather contrived casuistry associated with broad and strict mental reservations.[36] But what does the more contemporary understanding of lying indicate? The new definition denies the validity of the perverted faculty argument. It is not sufficient merely to examine the faculty of speech and determine morality solely from the purpose of the faculty in itself. Likewise, the malice of lying does not reside in the lack of "physical" conformity between word and thought.

To view the faculty of speech apart from the total human situation of the person in society seems to give a distorted view of lying. The faculty of speech must be seen and judged in a human context. One can interfere with the physical purpose of the faculty for a higher human need and good. Perhaps in a similar vein, the notion of "direct" in the principle of the double effect cannot be judged merely from the sole immediate effect of the physical action itself, apart from the whole human context in which the act is placed. The morality must be viewed in a total human context, and not merely judged according to the physical act itself and the natural effect of the act seen in itself apart from the whole context.

The influence of Ulpian and the view of primitive society tend to identify the total human action with the natural or biological process. A better understanding of such historically and culturally limited views should help the ethician in evaluating the theory of natural law as understood in *Humanae Vitae*. I have not proved that the human act never corresponds with the physical structure of the act. However, I think it is clear that ethicians must be very cautious that older and inadequate views of reality do not influence their contemporary moral judgments. It does seem that the definition of Ulpian and the general views of a more primitive society have a logical connection with what seem to be erroneous conclusions of the natural law theory of the manuals.

A Changed Worldview

A third major weakness with the theory of natural law presupposed in the Encyclical stems from the classicist worldview which is behind such a theory of natural law. Bernard Lonergan maintains that the classicist worldview has been replaced by a more historically conscious worldview.[37] In the same vein, John Courtney Murray claimed that the two different theories on Church and State represent two different methodologies and worldviews.[38] And today, other more radical Catholic thinkers are calling for a change from a substantive to a process metaphysics.[39] At the least, all these indications point to an admission by respected Catholic scholars that the so-called classicist worldview has ceased to exist.

The following paragraphs will briefly sketch the differences in the two approaches to viewing reality. There are many dangers inherent in doing this. There is really no such thing as *the* classical worldview or *the* historically conscious worldview — there are many different types of historical mindedness. By arguing in favor of an historically conscious worldview, I by no means intend to endorse all the theories and opinions that might be included under such a heading.

Since this section of the chapter will argue against a classical worldview, a reader might conclude that I am denying to past thinkers the possibility of any valid insights into the meaning of reality. Such a conclusion is far from true. There are even those (for example, Lonergan and Murray) who would argue that a moderate historically conscious methodology is in continuity with the best of Thomistic thought. We must never forget that some of the inadequacies in the classical worldview stem from the poor interpretation of St. Thomas by many of his so-called followers.

Two Views of Reality. The classicist worldview emphasizes the static, the immutable, the eternal, and the unchanging. The Greek column symbolizes this very well. There is no movement or dynamism about a Doric or Ionic column; the simple Greek column avoids all frills and baroque trimmings. The stately Greek column gives the impression of solidity, eternity, and immutability. Its majestic and sober lines emphasize an order and harmony which appear to last forever. This classical worldview speaks in terms of substances and essences. Time and history are "accidents" which do not really change the constitution of reality itself. Essences remain unchangeable and can only go through accidental changes in the course of time. Growth, dynamism, and progress therefore receive little attention.

The Platonic world of ideas well illustrates this classical

worldview. Everything is essentially spelled out from all eternity, for the immutable essences, the universals, exist in the world of ideas. Everything in this world of ours is a participation or an accidental modification of the subsistent ideas. We come to know truth and reality by abstracting from the accidents of time and place, and arriving at immutable and unchangeable essences. Such knowledge based on immutable essences is bound to attain the ultimate in certitude.

The more historically conscious worldview emphasizes the changing, developing, evolving, and historical. Time and history are more than mere accidents that do not really change essential reality. Individual and particular differences receive much more attention from a correspondingly more historically conscious methodology. The classical worldview is interested in the essence of human beings, which is true at all times in history and in all civilizations and circumstances. A historically minded worldview emphasizes the individual traits that characterize the individual. Moderns differ quite a bit from primitives precisely because of the historical and individual traits that an individual has acquired today.

In the more historical worldview the world is not static but evolving. Progress, growth, and change mark the world and all reality. Cold, chaste, objective order and harmony are not characteristic of this view. Blurring, motion, and subjective feeling are its corresponding features, as in the difference between modern art and classical art. Modern art emphasizes feeling and motion rather than harmony and balance. It is not as "objective" as classical art. The artists impose themselves and their emotions on the object.

Perhaps modern art is telling the theologian that the older distinction between the objective and the subjective is no longer completely adequate. Music also illustrates the change that has occurred in our understanding of the world and reality. Classical measure and rhythm are gone; free rhythm and feeling mean very much to the modern ear. What is meaningful music to the ear of the modern is only cacophony for the classicist. Changes in art and music illustrate the meaning of the different worldviews and also show graphically that the classical worldview is gone.

Two Methodologies. The two worldviews created two different theological methodologies. The classicist methodology tends to be abstract, *a priori*, and deductive. It wants to cut through the concrete circumstances to arrive at the abstract essence which is always true, and then works with these abstract and universal essences. In the area of moral theology, for example, the first principles of morality are established, and then other universal norms of conduct are deduced from these.

The more historical methodology tends to be concrete, *a posteriori*, and inductive. The historical approach does not brush by the accidental circumstances to arrive at the immutable essences. The concrete, the particular, and the individual are important for telling us something about reality itself. Principles are not deduced from other principles. Rather, the modern person observes and experiences and then tentatively proceeds to conclusions in a more inductive manner. Note that the historical consciousness as a methodology is an abstraction, but an abstraction or theory that tries to give more importance to particular, concrete, historical reality.

As we have noted above, John Courtney Murray claims that the different views on Church and State flow from the two different methodologies employed.[40] The older theory of the union of Church and State flows from a classicist methodology. It begins with the notion of a society. The definition of a society comes from an abstract and somewhat *a priori* notion of what such a society should be. The older theory then maintains that there are two perfect societies, and deduces their mutual duties and responsibilities, including their duties and obligations vis-à-vis one another. The theory concludes that the *cura religionis*, as it was then understood, belongs to the State. The State has the obligation of promoting the true faith.

What happens when the older theory runs headlong into

a *de facto* situation in which the separation of Church and State is a historical fact? The older solution lies in a distinction between thesis and hypothesis, which roughly corresponds to the ideal order which should exist and the actual order which can be tolerated because of the presence of certain accidental historical circumstances. Notice the abstract and ahistorical characteristics of such a theory.

The newer theory of Church and State as proposed by Murray employs a more historically conscious methodology. Murray does not begin with an abstract definition of society and then deduce the obligations and rights of Church and State. Rather, Murray begins from a notion of the State derived from his observations of states in contemporary society. The modern State is a limited, constitutional form of government.

Its limited role contrasts with the more absolute and all-embracing role of the State in an earlier society. It does not interfere in matters that belong to the private life of individuals, such as the worship of God. Murray's theory has no need for a distinction between thesis and hypothesis, since he begins with the concrete historical reality. His conclusions then will be in harmony with the present historical situation.[41] Using a historical methodology, he can even admit that in the nineteenth century the older opinion might have been true, but in the present historical circumstances separation of Church and State is required.[42]

A classicist mentality is horrified at the thought that something could be right in one century and wrong in another. Note, however, that the historical methodology employed by Murray and Lonergan insists on a continuity in history and rejects any atomistic existentialism which sees only the uniqueness of the present situation without any connection with what has gone before or with what will follow in history.

A New Catholic Perspective. Theologians and philosophers are not alone in speaking of the changed perspective. In the documents of Vatican II the bishops do not officially adopt any worldview or methodology. But Vatican II definitely portrays reality in terms of a more historical worldview, and also employs a historically conscious methodology. The fact that the council has chosen to call itself a "pastoral" council is most significant; but "pastoral" must not be understood in opposition to "doctrinal." Rather, pastoral indicates a concern for the Christian faith not as truths to be learned but as a life to be lived.

The pastoral orientation of the council reflects a historical worldview. The bishops at the council also acknowledged that the Church has profited by the history and development of humanity. History reveals more about human beings and opens new roads to truth. The Catholic Church must constantly engage in an exchange with the contemporary world.[43]

Gaudium et Spes frequently speaks of the need to know the signs of the times. The introductory statement of this constitution asserts the need for the Church to know them and interpret them in the light of the Gospel (n. 4). The five chapters of the second section of the constitution begin with an attempt to read the signs of the times. The attention given to what was often in the past dismissed as accidental differences of time and history shows a more historical approach to reality. The constitution does not begin with abstract and universal ideas of Church, society, state, community, and common good, but rather by scrutinizing the signs of the times. *Gaudium et Spes* thus serves as an excellent illustration of the change in emphasis in Church documents from a classicist methodology to a more historically conscious approach.

The teachings on the Church as contained in the Constitution on the Church (*Lumen Gentium*) and the other documents of Vatican II also reflect a more historical approach and understanding. Previously Catholics pictured the Church as a perfect society having all the answers, and as the one bulwark of security in a changing world. However, *Lumen Gentium* speaks often and eloquently of the pilgrim Church. The charge of triumphalism rang true in

the conciliar halls of Vatican II. A pilgrim Church, however, does not pretend to have all the answers.

A pilgrim Church is ever on the march towards its goal
of perfect union with Christ the spouse. A pilgrim Church
is constantly striving, probing, falling, rising, and trying
again. A pilgrim is one who is constantly on the road and
does not know there the security of one's own home. So
too the pilgrim Church is a church always in need of
reform (*ecclesia semper reformanda*). Change, development, growth, struggle and tension mark the Church of
Christ in this world. The notion of the pilgrim Church,
even in language, differs very much from the perfect society of the theological manuals.

The conciliar documents underscore the need for the
Catholic Church to engage in dialogue — dialogue with
other Christians, dialogue with Jews, dialogue with other
non-Christians, dialogue with the world. Dialogue is not
monologue. Dialogue presupposes that Catholics can learn
from all these others. The call for dialogue supposes the
historical and pilgrim nature of the Church, which does
not possess all the answers but is open in the search for
truth. The need for ongoing dialogue and ongoing search
for truth contrasts sharply with the classicist view of reality
and truth.

Lumen Gentium rebuilds ecclesiology on the notion of
the Church as the people of God and points out the various functions and services which exist in the Church (chapter 2). Hierarchy is one form of service which exists in it.
Another office is prophecy. The prophetic function exists
independently of the hierarchy (n. 12). The hierarchical
Church can learn, and has learned, from the prophetic
voice in the Church. History reminds us that in the Church
change usually occurs from underneath. Vatican Council II
brought to fruition the work of the prophets in the biblical,
liturgical, catechetical and ecumenical movements.

Thank God for Pope John and the bishops at Vatican II,
we can say, but there never would have been a Vatican II if
it were not for the prophets who went before. Many of

them were rejected when they first proposed their teaching, but such has always been the lot of the prophet. The pilgrim Church, with the prophetic office, will always know the tension of trying to do the truth in love. The Church sorely needs to develop an older notion of the discernment of the Spirit, so that the individual and the total Church will be more open and ready to hear its true voice while rejecting the utterances of false prophets.[44]

The Church portrayed in Vatican II is a pilgrim Church which does not have all the answers but is constantly striving to grow in wisdom and age and grace. Thus the conciliar documents reflect a more historical view of the Church, and even employ a historically conscious methodology.

Theological Consequences

A historical worldview and a more historically conscious methodology will have important consequences when applied to the field of moral theology, for the manuals of moral theology today definitely reflect the classicist approach. In fact, there is a crisis in moral theology today precisely because such theology seems out of touch with the contemporary understanding of reality. Of course I do not claim that every modern view about reality is correct, but then not everything in the classicist worldview was correct.

Sin infects the reality we know, and the Christian thinker can never simply accept as is whatever happens to be in vogue. However, the God of creation and redemption has called us to carry on his mission in time and space. The Christian, then, is always called upon to view all things in the light of the gospel message, but whatever insights we may gain into reality and the world of creation can help us in our life.

Change and Development. The first important consequence of this new worldview and methodology affects our attitude towards change and development. The classical worldview, as we have seen, had little room for change. Only accidental changes could occur in a reality that was already constituted and known in its essence. Naturally such a view rejected any form of evolutionary theory because it was most difficult to explain evolution in such a system. On the other hand, the new worldview emphasizes the need for change. Change and growth do not affect merely the accidental constitution and knowledge of reality.

Human beings thirst for truth and constantly try to find it. The human person is never satisfied with the knowledge one has at any given moment. The contemporary person is continually probing to find out more about reality. The growth and progress of modern society demonstrate that development is absolutely necessary. The classicist methodology, on the other hand, claims a comparatively absolute and complete knowledge. Change naturally becomes a threat to the person who thinks that she or he already possesses truth. Of course, we recognize that not all change is good and salutary. There will be mistakes on the way, but the greatest error would be not to try at all.

Let us take as an example the dogmatic truth about the nature of Christ. The early christological councils proposed the formula of one person and two natures in Christ, a formula that is not present in the Scriptures. At the time there was an agonizing decision to go beyond the language of the Scriptures. But why does change have to stop in the fifth century? Might there not be an even better understanding of the natures and person of Christ today? Modern people might have different — and better — insights into the reality of Christ. Who can say that the fifth century was the final point in the development of our understanding?

When the classical worldview does speak of development, it places much emphasis on the fact that the truth always remains the same but it is expressed in different ways at different times. The same essential truth wears different clothing in different settings. However, does not the truth itself change and develop? There is more involved than just a different way of stating the same essential reality. Even in such sacrosanct dogmatic teachings there is room for real change and development.

The historical worldview realizes the constant need for growth and development, and also accepts the fact that mistakes and errors will always accompany such growth. But the attitude existing towards theology on the part of many Catholic priests in this country epitomizes the older worldview. As seminarians, they learned all the truths of the Christian faith. There was no need, in this view, to continue study after ordination, since the priest already possessed a certain knowledge of all the truths of the Christian faith.

Such an attitude also characterized the way in which theology was taught. Very little outside reading was done. The student simply memorized the notes of the professor which contained this certain knowledge. But the new methodology will bring with it a greater appreciation of the need for change and development in all aspects of the life and teaching of the Church.

Theology and Induction. Theology must adopt a more inductive methodology. Note that I am not advocating a unilaterally inductive and *a posteriori* approach for theology. However, in the past theology has attached too much importance to a deductive and somewhat *a priori* methodology. (Of course, as we shall see, with a more inductive approach moral theology can never again claim the kind of certitude it once did. At best, in some areas of conduct the ethician will be able to say that something clearly appears to be such and such at the present time.)

The classical methodology was a closed system, whereas a more historically conscious methodology proposes an open and heuristic approach. It will always remain open to new data and experience. Nothing is ever completely solved and closed, for an inductive methodology is more tentative and probing.

An inductive approach recognizes the existence of mistakes and errors, and even incorporates the necessary mechanism to overcome them. The building and manufacture of the Edsel automobile illustrates the possibility of error in a more inductive approach. Obviously, elaborate and expensive tests were run beforehand to see if there was a market for a car in the class of the projected Edsel. The decision to market the car was made on the best possible evidence. However, experience proved that the Edsel was a failure. A few years later, after similar exhaustive testing, the same company produced the Mustang, which has been a great success.

Theology, of course, is not the same as the other sciences. Progress and growth are much more evident in the area of the empirical sciences. However, the historicity of the gospel message and the historicity of human beings and the world demand a more historical approach in theology and the integration of a more inductive methodology. A more inductive approach in theology, especially in moral theology, will have to depend more on the experience of Christian people and all people of good will. The morality of particular actions cannot be judged apart from human experience. History seems to show that the changes which have occurred in Catholic morality have come about through the experience of all the people of the community. The fact that older norms did not come to grips with reality was first noticed in the experience of people.

Changes have occurred in the areas of usury, religious liberty, the right to silence, the role of love as a motive for marital relations, and other areas.[45] Certainly the rigorism of the earlier theologians on the place of procreation in marriage and marital intercourse has been modified by the experience of Christian people — for example, they held that marriage relations without the express purpose of procreation was at least venially sinful. And when the older theory of Church and State did not fit in with the historical circumstances of our day, John Courtney Murray showed that the living experience of people in the United States was more than just a toleration of an imperfect

reality. In each case, experience showed the inadequacy of
the older theory.

The older casuistry of mental reservation never set well
with the experience of Christian people. The dissatisfaction
with such casuistry played an important part in the understanding of lying now accepted by most contemporary theologians. Of course, just as theological methodology can
never become totally inductive (the theologian always begins with the revelation of God in Christ), so too experience can never become the only factor in the formation of
the Christian ethic. However, experience has a very important role to play. Since the experience of Christian people
and all people of good will is a source of moral knowledge,
an ethician cannot simply spell out in advance everything
that must be done by the individual. Contemporary theology should enlarge upon and develop the concept of prudence which was an important experiential factor in the
thought of Aquinas.

The Empirical Approach. Since a more historical methodology emphasizes the individual and the particular and
employs a more inductive approach to knowing reality,
Catholic theology will have to work much closer with the
empirical and social sciences. It is these sciences that help
human beings to pursue their goals and guide their development. A classicist approach which emphasized universals
and essences was content with an almost exclusively deductive approach.

The Catholic Church in America today still reflects the
fact that an older worldview did not appreciate or understand the need for the empirical and social sciences. The
Catholic Church is probably the only very large corpora-
tion in America — I am here using "church" in the sense
of a sociological entity and its administration — which
does not have a research and development arm. How long
could other corporations stay in existence without devot-
ing huge sums to research and development? Heretofore,

the Catholic Church has not realized the importance of change and growth.

Perhaps the crisis the Church faces today stems from a clinging to older forms of life when newer forms are required. However, without research and experimentation, who can determine which new forms are needed? The answers are not all spelled out in the nature of things.

Certitude. As we have already seen, a changed theological methodology must necessarily result in a different attitude towards certitude. The classicist methodology aimed at absolute certitude. It was more easily come by in the classical approach, for this method cut through and disregarded individual, particular differences to arrive at immutable, abstract essences. In a deductive approach the conclusion follows by a logical connection from the premise. Provided the logic is correct, the conclusion is just as certain as the premise. Since circumstances cannot change the essences or universals, one can assert that the conclusion is now and always will be absolutely certain. There is no room for any change. A deductive methodology can be much more certain than an inductive approach.

The penchant for absolute certitude characterized the philosophical system which supports the concept of natural law as found in theology manuals. Science, in this view, was defined as certain knowledge of the thing in its causes. Science, therefore, was opposed to opinion and theory. However, modern science does not aim at such certitude. Science today sees no opposition between science and the hypothetical; in fact, scientific opinion and scientific theory form an essential part of the scientific vocabulary.

Absolute certitude actually would be the great enemy of progress and growth. Once absolute certitude is reached, there is no sense in continuing research except to clear up a few peripheral matters.[46] In the Thomistic framework there was really no room for progress in scientific fields.

And there was little or no room for development within the sciences, so conceived, because the first principles of the science itself were already known. The revolutionary approaches within the modern sciences show the fallacy in the Thomistic understanding of science.[47]

A more historically conscious methodology does not pretend to have or even to aim at absolute certitude. Since time, history, and individual differences are important, they cannot be dismissed as mere accidents which do not affect essential truth. This approach does not emphasize abstract essences, but concrete phenomena. Conclusions are based on the observations and experience gleaned in a more inductive approach. Such an approach can never strive for absolute certitude.

Modern science views reality in this more historical manner and consequently employs this more inductive approach. Scientific progress demands a continuing search for an even better way. An inductive methodology can never cease its working. It constantly runs new experiments and observations, for modern science aims at the best for the present time, but realizes that new progress must be made for the future.

Positive Law. A more historically conscious approach and a greater emphasis on the person attribute a much changed and reduced role to positive law. Canon law exists primarily to preserve order and harmony in the society of the people of God, and not to serve as a guide for the life of the individual Christian.[48] Nor are civil laws primarily a guide for moral conduct. Civil law as such is not primarily interested in the true, the good, and the beautiful. Civil law has the limited aim of preserving the public order.[49]

Society functions better not when law dictates to everyone what is to be done, but rather when law tries to create the climate in which individuals and smaller groups within the society can exercise their creativity and development for the good of the total community.[50] No longer is society under a master plan minutely controlled by the rules of the society. Rather, modern society's progress and growth come from the initiative of people within the society. Thus, the more historically minded worldview has a different perspective on the meaning and role of law in human life. Natural and human laws are no longer seen as detailed plans which guide and direct all human activity.

The Nature of Reality. A classicist worldview tends to see reality in terms of substances and natures which exist in themselves apart from any relations with other substances and natures. Every substance has its own nature or principle of operation. Within every acorn, for example, there is a nature which directs the acorn into becoming an oak tree. The acorn will not become a maple tree or an elm tree because it has the nature of an oak tree. The growth and "activity" of the thing is determined by the nature inscribed in it. Growth is the intrinsic unfolding of the nature within the substance.

Notice how such a view of reality affects morality. Human action depends upon the human nature. Human action is its intrinsic unfolding in the person. Nature, therefore, tells what actions are to be done and what actions are to be avoided. To determine the morality of an action, one must study its nature. The above description, although a caricature of Thomas' teaching, does represent the approach to morality of the kind of unilaterally substantialist view of reality generally assumed in the manuals.

The contemporary view sees reality more in terms of relations than of substances and natures. The individual is not thought of as a being totally constituted in the self, whose life is the unfolding of the nature already possessed. There seemingly can be no real human growth and history when future development is already determined by what is present here and now. This is the point of difference between a naturalist view and a historicist view.[51]

According to a more contemporary, relational view, reality does not consist of separate substances existing completely independent of each other. Reality can be understood only in terms of the relations that exist among the individual beings. A particular being can never be adequately considered in itself, apart from its relations with other beings and the fullness of being. An emphasis on relations rather than substances surely cannot be foreign to Catholic thinking, since theologians have spoken of the persons of the Trinity as relations.

Human experience also reminds us of the importance of relationship even in constituting ourselves as human persons. A relational understanding of reality will never see morality solely in terms of the individual substance or nature. Morality depends primarily not on the substance viewed in itself but on the individual seen in relationship to other beings. Unfortunately, the so-called traditional natural law approach frequently derives its conclusions from the nature of a faculty or the physical causality of an action seen only in itself and not in relationship with the total person and the entire community.

A brief defense of Aristotle is necessary here to avoid false impressions. Aristotle did not have a static view of reality. Nature itself was a principle of operation that tended toward a goal, but the goal was specific rather than individual. The emphasis was on the species of oak tree, that is, and not on the individual oak as such. But Aristotle did not conceive of the human person as he did of lesser life.

As an acute observer of the human scene, he realized that most individuals do not achieve their goal of happiness and self-fulfillment. The person, he thought, does not possess an intrinsic dynamism which necessarily achieves its goal. The human being's happiness, consequently, depends not on an intrinsic tending to perfection according to the demand of nature, but rather one's happiness depends on extrinsic circumstances.

The individual person has no intrinsic orientation (a nature) necessarily bringing about personal perfection; rather, according to Aristotle, one depends more on the contingent and the accidental. The person needs freedom, health, wealth, friends, and luck to find fulfillment.[52] Notice that Aristotle himself constructed an anthropology that answers some of the strictures made against textbook natural law theories today.

The classicist worldview of the manuals tends to arrange the world in a very detailed pattern. The function of the individual is to correspond to this structure (the "natural law") as minutely outlined. One puts together the different pieces of human behavior much like one puts together the pieces of a jigsaw puzzle. The individual finds the objective pieces already existing and just fits them together. The more historical-minded worldview, on the other hand, sees the human being as creating and shaping the plan of the world. The person does not merely respect the intrinsic nature and finalities of the individual pieces of the pattern. Rather, one interferes to form new pieces and new patterns.

A different worldview, as we have seen, affects our understanding of reality. The older stressed the objectivity of reality. In this view truth consists in the mind's grasp of the reality itself. A clear distinction exists between the object and the subject. Meaning exists in the objective reality, and the subject perceives the meaning already present in reality. Modern thought and culture stress more the creative aspects (both intellectual and affective) of the subject. Modern art reveals the feelings and emotions of the subject rather than portraying an objective picture of reality. The modern cinema confronts the viewer with a very subjective view of reality that calls for imagination and perceptivity on the part of the viewer. Catholic theologians are now speaking in somewhat similar terms of a transcendental methodology in theology.

Karl Rahner has observed that natural law should be approached in this way.[53] A transcendental methodology talks about the conditions and structure in the subject necessary for it to come to know reality, for this very structure is part of the knowing process. Bernard Lonergan speaks about meaning in much the same way.[54] Human meaning can change such basic realities as community, family, state, etc. Meaning involves more than just the apprehension of the objective reality as something "out there."

A note of caution is necessary. Although Lonergan, for example, espouses a more historical consciousness and a transcendental method, at the same time he strongly proclaims a critical realism in epistemology. Lonergan definitely holds for propositions and objective truth, and truth as a correspondence. However, for Lonergan human knowing is a dynamic structure; intentionality and meaning pertain to that objectivity. He reacts against a "naive realism" or a "picture book" type of objectivity.

The problem in the past was that the objectivity of knowledge was identified with the analogy of the objectivity of the sense of sight. "Objective" is that which I see out there. Such a concept of objectivity is false because it identifies objectivity with just one of the properties of one of the operations involved in human knowing. Lonergan rejects both a naive realism and idealism.[55] It seems, however, that the objectivity talked about in manuals of moral theology is often a naive, picture-book objectivity.

The concept of natural law presupposed in Catholic theology manuals definitely reflects a classicist worldview, which sees a very precise and well-defined pattern existing for the world and man's moral behavior. This ordering and pattern is called the natural law. Natural law reigns in the area of the necessary.

Within the area marked out by the pattern showing the absolute and the necessary is the contingent and the changing. Just as natural law governs the human life in the area of the principles common to all, so positive law, both civil and ecclesiastical, governs the human life in the contingent and the changing circumstances of life. The plan for the world is thus worked out in great detail in the mind of the creator, and the individual's whole purpose is to conform to the divine plan as made known in the natural and positive laws. (Despite the classical worldview of his day, in his system Thomas did leave room for the virtue of prudence and the creativity of the individual. However, the place later assigned to prudence in textbooks was drastically reduced, and thus Thomas' teaching was distorted.)

But a more historical-minded worldview does not look upon reality as a plan whose features are sketched in quite particular detail according to an unchanging pattern. Human moral life does not primarily call for conformity to such a detailed and unchanging plan. One looks upon existence as a vocation to find the meaning of human existence creatively in one's own life and experience. The meaning of human life is not already given in some pre-existing pattern or plan.

A historically conscious methodology must avoid the pitfall of a total relativism which occasionally creeps into Christianity in various forms of cultural Christianity. One needs to understand the ontological foundations of historical development; the Christian needs to understand all things in the light of the uniqueness of the once-for-all event of Christ Jesus. Both contemporary Protestant (for example, Macquarrie, Ogden) and Catholic (Rahner, Lonergan) scholars are addressing themselves to this problem.

Perhaps the characterization of the two worldviews in this chapter tends to be oversimplified. For one thing, the points of difference between them have been delineated without any attempt to show the similarities. The differences in many areas of morality — for example, the understanding and living of the evangelical norm of love and forgiveness — would be minimal. The reasoning developed in this section has prescinded, as well, from the question of growth and development in human values and morals. However, in the modern world, characterized by instant communication, rapid transportation, and changing sociological patterns, it is clear that the individual needs a more historical worldview and a more historically conscious methodology than the person who lived in a comparatively static and closed society.

III. Physicalism and a Classicist
Methodology in the Encyclical

The encyclical on the regulation of birth employs a natural law methodology which tends to identify the moral action with the physical and biological structure of the act. The core practical conclusion of the letter states: "We must once again declare that the direct interruption of the generative process already begun, and above all directly willed and procured abortion, even if for therapeutic reasons, are to be absolutely excluded as licit means of regulating birth" (*H. V.* n. 14). "Equally to be excluded . . . is direct sterilization. . . . Similarly excluded is every action which, either in anticipation of the conjugal act, or in its accomplishment, or in the development of its natural consequences, proposes, whether as an end or as a means, to render procreation impossible" (*H. V.* n. 14). The footnotes in this particular paragraph refer to the Roman Catechism and the utterances of more recent popes. Reference is made to the Address of Pius XII to the Italian Catholic Union of Midwives in which direct sterilization is defined as "that which aims at making procreation impossible as both means and end" (n. 13, *AAS* 43 [1951], 838). The concept of direct is thus described in terms of the physical structure and causality of the act itself.

The moral conclusion of the encyclical forbidding any interference with the conjugal act is based on the "intimate structure of the conjugal act" (*H. V.* n. 12). The "design of God" is written into the very nature of the conjugal act; the person is merely "the minister of the design established by the Creator" (*H. V.* n. 13). The encyclical acknowledges that "it is licit to take into account the natural rhythms immanent in the generative functions." Recourse to the infecund periods is licit, whereas artificial contraception "as the use of means directly contrary to fecundation is condemned as being always illicit" (*H. V.* n. 16). "In reality there are essential differences between the two cases; in the former, the married couple make legitimate use of a natural disposition; in the latter, they impede the development of natural processes" (*H. V.* n. 16). The natural law theory employed in the encyclical thus identifies the moral and human action with the physical structure of the conjugal act itself.

Humanae Vitae in its methodology well illustrates a classicist approach. The papal letter admits that "changes which have taken place are in fact noteworthy and of varied kinds" (*H. V.* n. 2). These changes give rise to new questions. However, the changing historical circumstances have not affected the answer or the method employed in arriving at concrete conclusions on implementing responsible parenthood. The primary reason for rejecting the majority report of the Papal Commission was "because certain criteria of solutions had emerged which departed from the moral teaching on marriage proposed with constant firmness by the teaching authority of the Church" (*H. V.* n. 6).

The encyclical specifically acknowledges the fact that there are new signs of the times, but one wonders if sufficient attention has really been paid to such changes. The footnotes to the encyclical are significant even if the footnote references alone do not constitute a conclusive argument. The references are only to random scriptural texts, one citation of Thomas Aquinas, and references to earlier pronouncements of the hierarchical magisterium. A more inductive approach would be inclined to give more importance and documentation to the signs of the times. The footnote references contain no indication of any type of dialogue with other Christians, non-Christians and the modern sciences. When the letter does mention social consequences of the use of contraception, no documentation is given for what appear to be unproven assumptions. Since the methodology describes the human act in physical terms, the practical moral conclusion is the absolute condemnation of means of artificial birth control. The encyclical thus betrays an epistemology that has been rejected by many Catholic theologians and philosophers today.

IV. Different Approaches with Different Conclusions

Natural law theory has traditionally upheld two values that are of great importance for moral theology: (1) the existence of a source of ethical wisdom and knowledge which the Christian shares with all mankind; (2) the fact that morality cannot be merely the subjective whim of an individual or group of individuals. However, one can defend these important values for moral theology without necessarily endorsing the particular understanding of natural law presupposed in the encyclical. In the last few years Catholic thinkers have been developing and employing different philosophical approaches to an understanding of morality. One could claim that such approaches are modifications of natural law theory because they retain the two important values mentioned above. Others would prefer to abandon the term natural law since such a concept is very ambiguous. There is no monolithic philosophical system called the natural law, and also the term has been somewhat discredited because of the tendency among some to understand natural in terms of the physical structure of acts. We can briefly describe three of the alternative approaches which have been advanced in the last few years — personalism, a relational and communitarian approach, a transcendental methodology. As mentioned above, these three approaches emerge within the context of a more historically conscious worldview and understand anthropology and moral reality in a way that differs from the concept of anthropology and moral reality proposed by the classical methodology. All these approaches would deny the absolute conclusion of the papal encyclical in condemning all means of artificial birth control.

A more personalist approach has characterized much of contemporary ethics. For the Christian, the biblical revelation contributes to such an understanding of reality. A personalist approach cannot be something merely added on to another theory. A personalist perspective will definitely affect moral conclusions, especially when such conclusions have been based on the physical structure of the act itself. Personalism always sees the act in terms of the person placing the act. The Pastoral Constitution on the Church in the Modern World realized that objective standards in the matter of sexual morality are "based on the nature of the human person and his acts" (n. 51). An essay by Bernard Häring shows how a personalist perspective would not condemn artificial contraception as being always immoral.[56]

Classical ethical theory embraces two types or models of ethical method: the teleological and the deontological. H. Richard Niebuhr has added a third ethical model — the model of responsibility. The moral agent is not primarily a maker or a citizen but a responder. There are various relationships within which the responsible self exists. "The responsible self is driven as it were by the movement of the social process to respond and be accountable in nothing less than a universal community."[57] Robert Johann in developing his understanding of anthropology acknowledges a great debt to Niebuhr.[58]

In the particular question of contraception, a more relational approach would not view the person or a particular faculty as something existing in itself. Each faculty exists in relationship with the total person and other persons within a universal community. Morality cannot merely be determined by examining a particular faculty and its physical structure or a particular act in itself. The changed ethical evaluation of lying well illustrates the point. Both Johann and William H. van der Marck (who embraces a more phenomenological starting point) have employed a more relational approach to argue for the licitness of contraception in certain circumstances.[59]

A third philosophical approach espoused by a growing number of Catholic thinkers today is a theory of transcendental method. Transcendental methodology owes much to the neo-Thomist Joseph Marechal and is espoused today in different forms by Bernard Lonergan, Karl Rahner, and Emerich Coreth.[60] In general, transcendental method goes beyond the object known to the structures of the human knowing process itself. According to Lonergan, "the intrinsic objectivity of human cognitional activity is its intentionality."[61] Lonergan's ethics is an extension of his theory of knowing. Moral value is not an intrinsic property of external acts or objects; it is an aspect of certain consciously free acts in relation to my knowledge of the world. The moral subject must come to examine the structures of the knowing and deciding process.[62]

Lonergan uses as a tool the notion of horizon analysis. Basic horizon is the maximum field of vision from a determined standpoint. This basic horizon is open to development and even conversion. Lonergan posits four conversions which should transpire from the understanding of the structures of human knowing and deciding — the intellectual, the moral, the religious, and the Christian. Ethics must bring people to this Christian conversion so that they can become aware of their knowing and doing and flee from inauthenticity, unreasonableness, and the surd of sin. Thus Christian ethics is primarily concerned with the manner in which an authentic Christian person makes ethical decisions and carries them out. However, such a meta-ethics must then enter into the realm of the normative, all the time realizing the provisional value of its precepts which are limited by the data at hand.[63] One commentator has said of Lonergan's ethic as applied to moral theology: "The distinct contribution of the moral theologian to philosophical ethics would consist in clarifying the attitudes which are involved in man's responding in faith to the initiative of a loving God who has redeemed man in Christ."[64] Thus a transcendental method would put greater stress on the knowing and deciding structures of the authentic Christian subject. Such a theory would also tend to reject the encyclical's view of anthropology and of human generative faculties.

There has been even among Catholic theologians a sharp negative response to the practical conclusions of the papal encyclical on the regulation of birth. This essay has tried to explain the reason for the negative response. The concept of natural law employed in the encyclical tends to define the moral act merely in terms of the physical structure of the act. In contemporary theology such an understanding of natural law has been severely criticized. Newer philosophical approaches have been accepted by many Catholic thinkers. Such approaches logically lead to the conclusion that artificial contraception can be a permissible and even necessary means for the regulation of birth within the context of responsible parenthood.

V. Application to the Situation Ethics Debate

In the last few years moral theology and Christian ethics have been immersed in a controversy over situation ethics. The controversy tends to polarize opinions and fails to show the huge areas of agreement existing among Christian moralists. There are, nevertheless, many real differences in approaches and in some practical conclusions. The principal areas of practical differences between some situationists and the teaching found in the manuals of moral theology are the following: medical ethics, particularly in the area of reproduction; conflict situations solved by the principle of the indirect voluntary, especially conflicts involving life and death, e.g., killing, abortion; sexuality; euthanasia; and divorce.

These major points of disagreement have one thing in common. In these cases, the manuals of Catholic moral theology have tended to define the moral action in terms of the physical structure of the act considered in itself apart from the person placing the act and the community of persons within which he lives. A certain action defined in terms of its physical structure or consequences (e.g., euthanasia as the positive interference in the life of the person; male masturbation as the ejaculation of semen) is considered to be always wrong. I have used the term "negative, moral absolutes" to refer to such action described in their physical structure which are always wrong from a moral viewpoint. Thus the central point of disagreement in moral theology today centers on these prohibited actions which are described primarily in terms of their physical structure.

In the area of medical ethics certain actions described in terms of the physical structure of the act are never permitted or other such actions are always required. Artificial insemination with the husband's semen is never permitted because insemination cannot occur except through the act of sexual intercourse.[65] Contraception as direct interference with the act of sexual intercourse is wrong. Direct sterilization is always wrong. Masturbation as the ejaculation of semen is always wrong even as a way of procuring semen for semen analysis.[66] Frequently in such literature the axiom is cited that the end does not justify the means. However, in all these cases the means is defined in terms of the physical structure of the act. I believe in all the areas mentioned above there are circumstances in which such actions would be morally permissible and even necessary.

Catholic moral theology decides most conflict situations by an application of the principle of the indirect voluntary. Direct killing, direct taking of one's life, direct abortion, direct sterilization are always wrong. However, the manuals of theology usually define direct in terms of the physical structure of the act itself. Direct killing according to one author "may be defined as the performance (or the omission of) an act, the primary and natural result of which is to bring about death."[67] According to the same author "direct abortion is the performance of an act, the primary and natural effect of which is to expel a nonviable fetus from its mother's womb." In these cases direct refers to the physical structure and consequences of the act itself. One exception in the manuals of theology to the solution of conflict situations in terms of the principle of the indirect voluntary is the case of unjust aggression. The physical structure of the act is not the determining factor in such a conflict situation.

In general a Christian ethicist might be somewhat suspicious of conflict situations solved in terms of the physical structure of the act itself. Such a solution seems too facile and too easily does away with the agonizing problems raised by the conflict. Likewise, such an approach has tended to minimalize what is only an indirect effect, but the Christian can never have an easy conscience about taking the life of another even if it is only an indirect effect.

The case of "assisted abortion" seems to illustrate the inherent difficulties in the manualistic concept of direct and indirect. For example, the best available medical knowledge indicates that the woman cannot bring a living child to term. If the doctor can abort the fetus now, he or she can avert very probable physical and psychological harm to the mother from the pregnancy which cannot eventually come to term. The manuals indicate that such an abortion would be direct and therefore immoral. However, in the total context of the situation, it does not seem that such an abortion would be immoral. The example of assisted abortion illustrates the impossibility of establishing an absolute moral norm based on the physical description of the action considered only in itself apart from the person placing the action and the entire community. It seems that the older notion of direct enshrines a prescientific worldview which is somewhat inadequate in our technological age. Why should the doctor sit back and wait for nature to take its course when by interfering now he can avoid great harm to the mother? In general, I do not think that conflict situations can be solved merely in terms of the physical structure and consequences of the act.

Perhaps the approach used in conflict situations of unjust aggression would serve as a better model for the solution of other conflict situations. In unjust aggression the various values at stake are weighed, and the person is permitted to kill an unjust aggressor not only to save one's life but also to protect other goods of comparable value, such as a serious threat to health, honor, chastity, or even material goods of great importance.[68] (I believe that in some cases the older theologians went too far in equating the defense of these values and the life of the aggressor.) Thus in the question of abortion there seem to be cases when it is moral to abort to save the life of the mother or to preserve other very important values. I am not proposing that the fetus is an unjust aggressor but rather that the ethical model employed in solving problems of unjust aggression avoids some of the problems created by the model of direct and indirect effects when the direct effect is determined by the physical structure of the act itself.

The present discussion about the beginning of human life centers on the criteria for identifying human life. Are the physical criteria of genetics and embryology sufficient? Or must other criteria of a more psychological and personalistic nature be employed for discerning the existence of human life? What then would be the difference between the fetus in the womb and the newborn babe who is now existing outside his mother's womb? There are many complicated problems in such a discussion. For many, the biological and genetic criteria are the only practical way of resolving the problem.[69] I am merely pointing out that the problem exists precisely because some people will not accept the biological and genetic considerations as establishing an adequate criterion for determining the beginning of human life.

Chapter 7 will consider the question of sexuality which has been distorted in the Catholic theological tradition for many reasons including an overemphasis on the physical structure of sexual actuation. In the question of euthanasia, Catholic and other theistic ethicists generally approach the problem in terms of the limited dominion which the individual has over his or her own life. Today even Christians claim a greater power over their own existence both because of scientific advances and because of better understanding of participation in the Lordship of Jesus. However, in one important aspect in the area of euthanasia the question of dominion over one's life is not primary. Catholic thinking has maintained that the patient does not have to use extraordinary means to preserve life. In more positive terms, there is a right to die. Many Catholic theologians remind doctors they have no obligation to give intravenous feeding to a dying cancer patient. Likewise, a doctor may discontinue such feeding with the intent that the person will thus die. But the manuals of theology would condemn any positive action on the part of the doctor — e.g., injection of air into the bloodstream — under the same circumstances.[70]

At the particular time when death is fast approaching, the primary moral question does not seem to revolve explicitly around the notion of one's dominion over life. The problem centers on the difference between not giving something or the withdrawal of something necessary for life and the positive giving of something to bring about death. Is the difference between the two types of action enough to warrant the total condemnation of positively interfering? I do not think so; Catholic theologians should explore the possibility of interfering to hasten the dying process, a notion similar to the concept of assisted abortion mentioned above. But the theologian would also have to consider the possibility of a general prohibition based on the societal effects of such interference.

The problem of describing moral reality in terms of the physical description of an act viewed in itself apart from the person also manifests itself in the question of divorce. According to Catholic teaching a consummated marriage between two baptized persons is indissoluble. But consummation is defined in solely physical terms. Thus the notion of consummation as found in the present law of the Church is inadequate.[71] Moreover, divorce in general qualifies as a negative moral absolute in the sense described above. A particular action described in nonmoral terms (remarriage after a valid first marriage) is always wrong. The entire question of divorce is too complex to be considered adequately in the present context since it involves biblical, historical, conciliar, and magisterial aspects. But the concept of "the bond of marriage" adds weight to the arguments against divorce. The bond becomes objectivized as a reality existing apart from the relationship of the persons which is brought into being by their marriage vows. All Christians, I believe, should hold some element transcending the two persons and their union here and now. But can this bond always be considered totally apart from the ongoing relationship between the two who exchanged the marital promises?

Thus a quick overview shows that the critical, practical areas of discussion in contemporary moral theology and Christian ethics center on the absolute moral prohibition of certain actions which are defined primarily in terms of the physical structure of the act. Moral meaning is not necessarily identical with the physical description of an act. Modern anthropology is in a much better position than medieval anthropology to realize that fact. The underlying problem is common to every human science — the need to clearly differentiate the category of meaning as the specific data of any science involving human reality. Historians of ideas would be familiar with this problem from the nineteenth century differentiation of Dilthey between the *Geisteswissenchaften* and *Naturwissenchaften.*[72] In the Anglo-American context, Matson has recently published an informative survey of the present status of this same differentiation involving the notion of human behavior.[73]

A word of caution is in order. It appears that some proponents of situation ethics have not given enough importance to the bodily, the material, the external, and the physical aspects of reality. On the other hand, contemporary theory is less prone to accept the physical and the biological aspects of reality as morally normative. An analysis of the current scene in moral theology and Christian ethics in a broad ecumenical view indicates that the primary point of dispute centers on the existence of negative moral absolutes in which the moral action is described in physical terms. It would be unwarranted to conclude that the moral act is never identified with the physical structure and description of the act. However, one can conclude that an ethical theory which begins with the assumption that the moral act is identified with the physical structure and consequences of the act will find little acceptance by contemporary theologians.

NOTES

1. E.g., *Light on the Natural Law,* ed. Illtud Evans, O.P. (Baltimore: Helicon Press, 1965); *Das Naturrecht im Disput,* ed. Franz Böckle (Dusseldorf: Patmos, 1966); "La Nature fondement de la morale? " *Supplément de la Vie Spirituelle* 81 (May 1967), 187–324; *Absolutes in Moral Theology?* ed. Charles E. Curran (Washington: Corpus Books, 1968).

2. Edward LeRoy Long Jr., *A Survey of Christian Ethics* (New York: Oxford University Press, 1967); Thomas G. Sanders, *Protestant Concepts of Church and State* (Garden City, N.Y.: Doubleday Anchor Books, 1965).

3. Such emphases can still be found, although not in an absolute sense, in the writings of Niels H. Söe. See Söe, "Natural Law and Social Ethics," in *Christian Social Ethics in a Changing World,* ed. John C. Bennett (New York: Association Press, 1966), pp. 289-309. The same article with a response by Paul Ramsey appeared in *Zeitschrift für Evangelische Ethik,* 12 (March 1968), 65-98.

4. John C. Bennett, "Issues for the Ecumenical Dialogue," in *Christian Social Ethics in a Changing World,* pp. 377, 378.

5. H. Richard Niebuhr, *Christ and Culture* (New York: Harper Torchbook, 1956).

6. Niebuhr actually describes the Thomistic approach as "Christ above culture." He goes on to explain that "Thomas also answers the question about Christ and culture with a 'both-and'; yet his Christ is far above culture, and he does not try to disguise the gulf that lies between them" (p. 129).

7. One cannot simplistically condemn the nature-grace and natural-supernatural distinctions. In their original historical contexts such distinctions tried with considerable success to describe and synthesize this complex reality. Although such distinctions do have some meaning today; nevertheless, many Catholic theologians realize the need to reinterpret such distinctions in the light of different metaphysical approaches. See the three articles by Bernard Lonergan, S.J., which appeared in *Theological Studies* 2 (1941), 307-324; 3 (1942), 69-88, 375-402. For an exposition of the thought of Karl Rahner on this subject, see Carl J. Peter, "The Position of Karl

Rahner Regarding the Supernatural," *Proceedings of the Catholic Theological Society of America* 20 (1965), 81-94.

8. A wire release of N. C. News Service with a Vatican City dateline published in Catholic papers in this country during the week of August 4, 1968.

9. Bernard Häring, C.SS.R., "The Encyclical Crisis," *Commonweal* 88 (September 6, 1968), 588-594.

10. Joseph Fuchs, S.J., *Natural Law*, trans. Helmut Reckter, S.J., and John Dowling (New York: Sheed and Ward, 1965).

11. Christian Duquoc, O.P., *L'Eglise et le progrès* (Paris: Editions du Cerf, 1964), pp. 68-117. The author considers the past teaching in the Church on slavery, the freedom of nations, the dignity of women, Church and State, torture, and questions of war and peace.

12. "Dialogue with Joseph Fletcher," *Homiletic and Pastoral Review*, 67 (1967), 828, 829.

13. Helmut Thielicke, *Theological Ethics I: Foundations*, ed. William Lazareth (Philadelphia: Fortress Press, 1966), 622ff.

14. Pope Leo XIII, *Rerum Novarum*, n. 7-14; Pope Pius XI, *Quadregesimo Anno*, n. 44-52.

15. Thomas explicitly cites Isidore in *I-II*, q. 94, a. 2, ob. 1. In *II-II*, q. 66, a. 2, Thomas gives the opinion proposed by Isidore without a direct reference. Thomas explains that reason has called for the right of private property not as something against natural law, but as something added to natural law.

16. The reasons adduced by Thomas in *II-II*, q. 66, a. 2, indicate that human sinfulness is a very important factor in the argument for the right of private property.

17. *Rerum Novarum*, n. 22.

18. Hermenegildus Lio, O.F.M., "Estne obligatio justitiae subvenire pauperibus?" *Apollinaris* 29 (1956), 124-231; 30 (1957), 99-201.

19. Leo XIII was conscious of the social aspect of property (*Rerum Novarum*, n. 22), but he did not emphasize it. The subsequent Popes down to Paul VI have put increasingly more emphasis on the social aspects of property. The concentration on such social aspects explains the many discussions about the notion of socialization in the encyclicals of Pope John XXIII.

20. See note 1; also my treatment of this precise question in *A New Look at Christian Morality* (Notre Dame, Ind.: Fides Publishers, 1968), pp. 74-89.

21. Jean Marie Aubert, "Le Droit Naturel: ses avatars historiques et son avenir," *Supplément de la Vie Spirituelle* 81 (1967), especially 298 ff.

22. *The Digest* or *Pandects of Justinian*, Book 1, t. 1, nn. 1-4.

23. Odon Lottin, *Le Droit Naturel chez Saint Thomas d'Aquin et ses prédécesseurs*, 2nd ed. (Bruges: Charles Beyaert, 1931), p. 62.

24. *In IV Sent.* d. 33, q. 1, a. 1, ad 4.

25. *In V Ethic.*, lect. 12.

26. *I-II*, q. 90, a. 1, ob. 3; q. 96, a. 5, ob. 3; q. 97, a. 2; *II-II*, q. 57, a. 3, ob. 1, and *in corp.*

27. *I-II*, q. 95, a. 4.

28. *II-II*, q. 57, a. 3. For a detailed analysis of Thomas's teaching that comes to the same conclusion, see Michael Bertram Crowe, "St. Thomas Aquinas and Ulpian's Natural Law," in *St. Thomas Aquinas, 1274-1974: Commemorative Studies*, vol. 1 (Toronto, Canada: Pontifical Institute of Medieval Studies, 1974), pp. 261-282.

29. E.g., H. Noldin et al., *Summa Theologiae Moralis: De Castitate*, 36th ed. (Oeniponte: F. Rauch, 1958), pp. 21-43.

30. Decree of the Holy Office on the ends of marriage, April 1, 1944, *AAS*, 36 (1944), 103. Also various addresses of Pius XII: *AAS*, 33 (1941), 422; 43 (1951), 835-854.

31. Regis Araud, S.J., "Évolution de la théologie du marriage," *Cahiers Laënnec*, 27 (1967), 56-71; W. van der Marck, O.P., "De recente ontwikkelingen in de theologie van het huwelijk," *Tijdschrift voor Theologie* 7 (1967), 127-140. English summary on page 140.

32. Gerard Watson, "The Early History of Natural Law," *The Irish Theological Quarterly* 33 (1966), 65-74.

33. John L. Russell, S.J., "The Concept of Natural Law," *The Heythrop Journal* 6 (1965), 434-438; Pierre Colin, "Ambiguïtés du mot nature," *Supplément de la Vie Spirituelle* 81 (1967), 253-255.

34. Charles E. Curran, "Masturbation and Objectively Grave Matter: An Exploratory Discussion," *Proceedings of the Catholic Theological Society of America* 21 (1966), 95-109; also chapter 7.

35. H. Noldin et al., *Summa Theologiae Moralis*, vol. 2: *De Praeceptis* (Oeniponte: F. Rauch, 1959), pp. 553-560; E. F. Regatillo, S.J., and M. Zalba, S. J., *Theologiae Moralis Summa*, vol. 2 (Matriti: Biblioteca de Autores Cristianos, 1953), 1000-1018.

36. J. A. Dorszynski, *Catholic Teaching about the Morality of Falsehood* (Washington: Catholic University of America Press, 1949); Francis J. Connell, C.SS.R., *More Answers to Today's Moral Problems*, ed. Eugene J. Weitzel, C.S.V. (Washington: Catholic University of America Press, 1965), p. 123, 124. Augustine had at one time accepted the distinction between falsehood and lying, but he later changed his opinion.

37. Bernard Lonergan, S.J., *Collection* (New York: Herder and Herder, 1967), pp. 252-267; Lonergan, "A Transition from a Classicist Worldview to Historical Mindedness," in *Law for Liberty: The Role of Law in the Church Today*, ed. James E. Biecher (Baltimore: Helicon Press, 1967). Lonergan along with other theologians such as Marechal, Rahner, and Metz maintains that although Thomas Aquinas reflected a classical worldview, the followers of Thomas distorted his teaching especially in such areas as the emphasis on a

deductive methodology and a nonrelational understanding of being.

38. John Courtney Murray, S.J., "The Declaration on Religious Freedom," *Concilium* 15 (May 1966), 3-16.

39. Eulalio R. Baltazar, *Teilhard and the Supernatural* (Baltimore: Helicon Press, 1966); Leslie Dewart, *The Future of Belief* (New York: Herder and Herder, 1966). Lonergan espouses historical mindedness but strenuously opposes the approach of Dewart. See Lonergan, "The Dehellenization of Dogma," *Theological Studies* 28 (1967), 336-351.

40. Murray, Declaration of Religious Freedom," pp. 11-16.

41. John Courtney Murray, S.J., *The Problem of Religious Freedom* (Westminster, Md.: Newman, 1965).

42. John Courtney Murray, S.J., "Freedom, Authority, Community," *America* (December 3, 1966), 735.

43. *Gaudium et Spes* (The Pastoral Constitution on the Church in the Modern World), n. 44. For a competent one-volume translation of the documents of Vatican II, see *The Documents of Vatican II*, ed. Walter M. Abbot, S.J. (New York: America Press and Association Press, 1966).

44. Karl Rahner, S.J., *The Dynamic Element in the Church* (New York: Herder and Herder, 1964).

45. Daniel C. Maguire, "Moral Absolutes and the Magisterium," *Absolutes in Moral Theology?*, pp. 57-107.

46. Herbert Butterfield, *The Origins of Modern Science, 1300-1800* (New York: Macmillan, 1951); Lonergan, *Collection*, p. 259 ff.

47. Andreas van Melsen, "Natural Law and Evolution," *Concilium* 26 (June, 1967), 49-59.

48. *Law for Liberty: The Role of Law in the Church Today*, passim.

49. *Documents of Vatican II*, p. 686, n. 20. The footnote on the role of civil law was written by John Courtney Murray.

50. Thomas B. McDonough, "Distribution of Contraceptives by the Welfare Department: A Catholic Response," in *The Problem of Population*, vol. 2 (Notre Dame: University of Notre Dame Press, 1964), pp. 94-118.

51. Douglas Sturm, "Naturalism, Historicism, and Christian Ethics: Toward a Christian Doctrine of Natural Law," *The Journal of Religion* 44 (1964), 40-51. Note again that some Catholic thinkers see in the excessive emphasis on *res in se* apart from any relational consideration a distortion of the understanding of St. Thomas.

52. Russell, "Concept of Natural Law," pp. 434-438.

53. Karl Rahner, S.J., "Theology and Anthropology," in *The Word in History*, ed. T. Patrick Burke (New York: Sheed and Ward, 1966), pp. 1-23; Rahner, "Naturrecht," *Lexikon für Theologie und Kirche*, vol. 7, pp. 827-828.

54. Lonergan, "Dimensions of Meaning," *Collection*, pp. 252-267.

55. Lonergan, *Collection*, pp. 221-239; *Theological Studies* 28 (1967), 337-351.

56. Bernard Häring, "The Inseparability of the Unitive-Procreative Functions of the Marital Act," *Contraception: Authority and Dissent*, ed. Charles E. Curran (New York: Herder and Herder, 1969), pp. 176-192.

57. H. Richard Niebuhr, *The Responsible Self* (New York: Harper and Row, 1963), p. 88.

58. Robert O. Johann, S.J., *Building the Human* (New York: Herder and Herder, 1968), pp. 7-10.

59. Robert O. Johann, S.J., "Responsible Parenthood: A Philosophical View," *Proceedings of the Catholic Theological Society of America* 20 (1965), 115-128; William H. van der Marck, O.P., *Toward a Christian Ethic* (Westminster, Md.: Newman Press, 1967), pp. 48-60. Note that Germain G. Grisez in his *Contraception and the Natural Law* (Milwaukee: Bruce, 1964), argues against artificial contraception although he explicitly denies the "perverted faculty" argument. However, Grisez seems to accept too uncritically his basic premise that the malice of contraception "is in the will's direct violation of the procreative good as a value in itself, as an ideal which never may be submerged."

60. For a succinct exposition of transcendental philosophy, see Kenneth Baker, S.J., *A Synopsis of the Transcendental Philosophy of Emerich Coreth and Karl Rahner* (Spokane: Gonzaga University, 1965).

61. Lonergan, *Collection*, p. 228.

62. In addition to the bibliography of Lonergan's which has already been mentioned, see Bernard J. F. Lonergan, S.J., *Insight* (New York and London: Longmans, Green, and Co., 1964); Donald H. Johnson, S.J., "Lonergan and the Redoing of Ethics," *Continuum* 5 (1967), 211-220; and John P. Boyle, "Lonergan's *Method in Theology* and Objectivity in Moral Theology," *The Thomist* 37 (1973), 589-601.

63. David W. Tracy, "Horizon Analysis and Eschatology," *Continuum* 6 (1968), 166-179.

64. Johnson, "Lonergan and the Redoing of Ethics," 219, 220.

65. Pope Pius XII, Address to the Fourth World Congress of Catholic Doctors, Rome, September 29, 1949, *A.A.S.* 41 (1949), 560; Pope Pius XII, Address to the Italian Catholic Union of Midwives, October 29, 1951, *A.A.S.* 43 (1951), 850; Pope Pius XII, Address to the Second World Congress of Fertility and Sterility, May 19, 1956, *A.A.S.* 48 (1956), 472.

66. Pope Pius XII, *A.A.S.* 48 (1956), 472; Pope Pius XII, Address to the Italian Urologists, October 8, 1953, *A.A.S.* 45 (1953), 678; Decree of the Holy Office, August 2, 1929, *A.A.S.* 21 (1929), 490.

67. John McCarthy, *Problems in Theology II: The Commandments* (Westminster, Md.: Newman Press, 1960), pp. 159, 160. The author mentions other current definitions of direct killing (e.g., an act which aims, *ex fine operis,* at the destruction of life) earlier on pp. 119-122.

68. Marcellinus Zalba, S.J., *Theologia Moralis Summa II; Theologia Moralis Specialis* (Madrid: Biblioteca de Autores Cristianos, 1953), pp. 275-279.

69. Such an approach is adopted by Paul Ramsey who claims that at least from blastocyst the fetus must be considered as a human being. For further developments in Ramsey's thought and my own critique, see Charles E. Curran, *Politics, Medicine and Christian Ethics: A Dialogue with Paul Ramsey* (Philadelphia: Fortress Press, 1973), pp. 110-131.

70. Gerald Kelly, S.J., *Medico-Moral Problems* (St. Louis: Catholic Hospital Association, 1957), pp. 128-141.

71. For a fuller critique of the notion of consummation, see Dennis Doherty, "Consummation and the Indissolubility of Marriage," *Absolutes in Moral Theology?,* pp. 211-231.

72. Wilhelm Dilthey, *Pattern and Meaning in History* (New York: Harper Torchbook, 1967).

73. Floyd W. Matson, *The Broken Image* (Garden City, N.Y.: Doubleday Anchor Books, 1966).

3: Church Law

The consideration of the relationship between Church law and conscience will embrace three areas of investigation: (1) the concept of positive law in the Church; (2) the relationship between law and sin; (3) the observance of positive law in the life of the Christian. In the following discussion Church law or canon law always refers to the purely positive laws of the Roman Catholic Church and not to the restatement of other obligations.

The Concept of Positive Law in the Church

In his Epistle to the Romans, Paul explains the freedom of the Christian as a freedom from sin, death, and the law. St. Paul does not merely say that the Christian is freed from the ceremonial and juridical aspects of the law. Paul apparently uses law to mean, in this particular case, the entire Mosaic law insofar as the Mosaic law is an example of a general economy of law. The Christian is freed from living under an economy of law in the sense that salvation would depend upon the observance of certain laws or precepts. Salvation comes through faith in Christ Jesus. Freedom from law, however, does not mean that the Christian can now do whatever one pleases. Through the gift of the Spirit the Christian has received the new life in Christ Jesus. The Christian must now produce in life the fruits of the Spirit and walk according to the Spirit. The primary law for the Christian is the Spirit who dwells in the hearts of the just. The law of the Spirit is a law of freedom precisely because its demands are not imposed upon us from outside. The love of God is poured into our hearts by the Holy Spirit. The Spirit gives us the new heart which then directs all the activities of the Christian. The Spirit becomes the vital principle of Christian life and activity. The primary law for the Christian is "the law of the Spirit giving life in Christ Jesus" (Rom. 8:2).

Since the primary law of the new covenant is the Spirit who dwells in the hearts of the just, canon law and Church law necessarily assume a secondary and ancillary role. Too often in the past, the prevailing attitude has given too much importance to the role of positive law in the life of the Church. Canonical legislation should not occupy the primary role in the living of the Christian life. In discussions about eliminating Friday abstinence, some people objected that the changes are doing away with all mortification in Christian life. Such objections betray a mentality that equates the Christian life with the observance of the positive laws of the Church. The greatest mortification remains always the attempt to live out the Paschal Mystery in everyday life. The attitude of some Catholics in the past implied that laws make people holy. A proliferation of laws in many religious communities seems to bear out that understanding of law. However, the notion that more and better laws make people holy is totally inadequate. St. Paul reminds us that laws only provoke more transgressions. History indicates that positive laws have come into existence when the ebb of Christian life was already low. As long as Christians maintained a real understanding of the Eucharist, there was no need to make a law about receiving communion once a year. Positive laws are neither the source of Christian life nor an adequate sign of vitality in the Christian community.

However, there is a need for positive law in the Church. Since the Church strives to be a community of love in this world, positive law will always have its place in the life of that community. Although the community owes its continued existence primarily to the Spirit, positive law plays a secondary role in the life of the Church. Positive law is a necessity in any community for the well being of the community itself and the individuals who comprise the community. Life in a community demands a certain amount of order which positive law seeks to obtain. If just two or three people are living together, they can decide among themselves what they intend to do; but when there is a large community, there is need for established order within which the community lives and functions.

The positive law of the Church, like all other externals in the Church, has a sacramental character. The law must be a sign of the inner reality of the Church, which is above all the community of love. The whole purpose of the law of the Church must be to build up the Body of Christ in truth and love. Canon law should strive to create the climate in which the Church and its individual members can better respond to the call of the Spirit.

Law in the Church cannot be considered in exactly the same way as law in any other society, for the Church is a unique community. Naturally, there are many analogies between the Church and other communities, but the law of the Church must always manifest the unique character of the community of salvation. Church law has the somewhat negative function of preserving the necessary order in the Church so that the community and individuals can best accomplish their God-given destiny. At the same time Church law should also exercise a more positive function in pointing out some of the demands of the Spirit for the community and the individual Christian. In its more positive and even creative function, Church law must be careful not to stifle the freedom which it is trying to promote. Unfortunately, in the past positive law played too dominant a role and stifled rather stimulated the life of the Church.

Roman Catholic theological tradition has embraced two divergent understandings of positive law. The Thomistic concept defines law as the *rationis ordinatio ad bonum commune, ab eo qui curam communitatis habet, promulgata* (*I.II.*q. 91,a. 4). In the Thomistic tradition law is primarily an ordering of reason. There is another school which is more voluntaristic and is represented by Scotus and Suarez. In the voluntaristic concept, law is primarily an act of the will of the legislator. The speculative differences about the concept of law have very practical consequences. In a Thomistic understanding, something is commanded because it is good in itself. In the voluntaristic viewpoint, something is good precisely because it is commanded.

The first practical consequence concerns the obliging force of law. A voluntaristic concept derives the obliging force of law primarily from the will of the legislator. The Thomistic understanding of law derives the moral obligation of law from the ordering to the common good of the society. Notice the realism present in the Thomistic approach. The law must correspond to the reality of the situation and not just to the will of the legislator.

A second practical consequence concerns the role and function of the legislator. In a voluntaristic understanding the will of the legislator is supreme. Everything depends on the will of the legislator. Such a concept of positive law certainly represented the sociological situation of feudal and monarchical society. The legislator was supreme, and the will of the legislator determined what was right. As an example, note the axiom — *cuius regio, eius religio*. In a more Thomistic interpretation, the will of the legislator is not the last word. The legislator must conform to the needs of the society here and now. In my application of the Thomistic teaching today, I am not understanding the *ordinatio rationis* in the same sense as St. Thomas did. Nor did St. Thomas see the role of the legislator in the same way that I am envisioning the legislator today. However, Thomas has established the basic principle of realism — the law must reflect the needs of the community here and now. Consequently, the legislator is not the last word. The legislator must conform to the needs of the community and the ordering required for the common good.

An examination of the old axiom — "the will of the superior is the will of God" — will help focus the conflicting viewpoints. A voluntaristic understanding of law can accept that axiom as being true. However, a more realistic understanding must reject such an axiom. The will of the superior is not the will of God. I am not denying that the superior in some way takes the place of God. But the superior takes the place of God not in the function of willing a law, but in the function of ordering for the needs of the community. The sad lessons of history remind us that we cannot identify the will of the superior with the will of God.

The role of the legislator or superior in a realistic understanding of law corresponds very well with the biblical description of authority. Jesus emphasized the difference between the rulers of this world and his own apostles. The rulers of this world lord it over their subjects and make all subjects feel the weight of their authority. But, whoever has authority among the apostles must become the servant and the slave of all, for Christ himself came not to be served but to serve and give his life as a ransom for many (Mark 10:42-45). The legislator does not rule supreme because his or her law is the last word on the subject. Rather, as the humble servant of the community, the legislator tries to unite the service and love of all the members so they can work together for their own fulfillment and the fulfillment of the whole community.

The legislator in the Church must always see that role as the servant of the community trying to order the life of the community according to its own needs and purposes. In addition, the legislator in the Church is the servant of the Spirit. The Spirit and the law of the Spirit must always remain supreme in the Church. The legislator must always conform the will of the legislator to the call of the Spirit. The legislator can never proceed arbitrarily as if the will makes something right or wrong. The legislator rather must conform to the call of the Spirit and the needs of the community. The legislator in the Church, as well as all authority in the Church, remains always the servant of the Spirit and the servant of the community. The servant role of the legislator corresponds with the necessary but secondary role of law in the life of the Church. A Thomistic or realistic understanding of law reemphasizes the biblical notion of law and authority in the Church.

The Relationship between Law and Sin

Can Church law bind under penalty of mortal sin? On this specific point, the Code of Canon Law has been much more accurate than the teaching of some theologians. Actually, the Code of Canon Law is very discreet and does not talk in terms of sin. But too frequently, on a popular level, one hears, for example, not simply that it is a "grave matter" but that all Catholics are obliged under pain of mortal sin to participate in the Eucharist on Sunday. Sin, however, should never be conceived as a penalty for the violation of Church law. Sin is not primarily a penalty or a punishment. Rather, sin is the reality of the creature's breaking the relationship of love with God. If the Christian has not broken that relationship with God, the Church cannot say that the relationship is broken. The Church has no right to use sin as a penalty for its own laws.

The idea of sin as a penalty for the infringement of Church laws probably owes its origins to an overly slavish imitation of an earlier secular society and authority. Secular society uses penalties as threats to bring about observance of the law. The Church in the past has succumbed to the temptation to use sin as a penalty and a threat to insure the observance of a Church law. But in so doing, the Church has acted more like secular society and not in accord with her own true nature. I am not saying that Church law cannot deal with sanctions, but purely Church law can never use sin as a penalty or a punishment. Sin is the reality of one's breaking one's relationship with God and is not just an extrinsic penalty which the Church can attach to particular actions.

Can mere positive Church law propose that certain actions are mortal sins? For example, it is a mortal sin to miss the breviary or it is a mortal sin to miss Mass on Sunday. Church law should not speak in terms of sin. Church law must consider the need for certain actions to be done or others to be avoided. The commission of certain actions or the omission of others might be a sin for this particular person here and now, but the Church cannot speak about the action itself as being a sin. The manuals of moral theology mention three conditions that are required for mortal sin: (1) grave matter, (2) advertence to the gravity of the matter, and (3) perfect consent of the will. (Personally I believe that mortal sin ultimately consists in the involvement of the subject in a particular action. Mortal sin involves a fundamental option of the person in the particular choice which he makes. The three conditions mentioned above for mortal sin are presumptive guidelines and not the ultimate explanation of mortal sin. (This notion of sin will be explained later in greater detail.) Church law only speaks about the matter itself and does not consider advertence or consent. Consequently, Church law cannot speak in terms of sin. Church law can only speak about the greater or lesser importance of a particular action for the life of the community. And this is precisely what the Code of Canon Law does. It speaks about the relative importance of a particular matter in the life of the community and the individual. The expressions, "grave matter" or "light matter", refer precisely to the greater or lesser importance which the Church attaches to a particular action.

However, the Church in this time of renewal must ask if any one particular action is really that important a matter. For example, it was commonly taught by theologians that it was grave matter to omit even a smaller hour of the breviary. Any realistic understanding must conclude that missing the recitation of the breviary is not an important matter. There are so many important matters in the world today that the Church exposes herself to ridicule by maintaining that such things are that important. In considering the importance attached to praying the breviary daily, one can see quite clearly at work the attitude that has used sin or the threat of sin to bring about compliance with the law. But the Church can never use sin as a penalty or a threatened penalty. Participation in the Eucharistic banquet is certainly an important matter for the Christian; but I think that the importance of participation every single Sunday has been exaggerated by most theologians and canonists.

By speaking merely in terms of the greater or lesser importance of certain actions, the Church can do much in the proper formation of Christian consciences. The final judgment and application in a particular situation will be left up to the individual. Unfortunately, in the past the observance of the laws of the Church has become the infallible criterion of Christian life for many Catholics. Legalism has had an adverse effect not only on the formation of individual consciences but also on the attitude of the Church as a whole. Legalism easily leads to a mediocrity that stifles all creativity and initiative.

The overemphasis on the law serves as a crutch which saves the teaching Church from exerting all its necessary efforts. It is so much easier to say that missing Mass on Sunday is a mortal sin than it is to show by our celebration that we believe the Eucharist to be an important matter in the life of the Christian. The temptation to become administrators and just cite the law has often usurped the teaching office and function in the Church. Legalism also leads to a smugness, a sterility, and an unwillingness to see the need for necessary change. I believe that for too long pastors and teachers have relied on the Sunday obligation to coerce people to "hear Mass." I am convinced that if we had to meet open competition in presenting the meaning of the Eucharist to Christian people, somewhat as a soap commercial on TV has to meet competition openly, we would not have left our presentation completely unchanged for the past four centuries. How long would an announcer last in the competitive field of TV advertising if he spoke in a foreign language, mumbled the lines, and kept his back turned to the people? Legalism has made us all a bit lazy. Yes, law will always be necessary in the Church, but its function is always secondary and dependent on the law of the Spirit.

The Observance of Positive Law in the Life of the Christian

In any society there will be a tension between the laws of the community and the rights of the individual. The Church experiences these tensions not only because it is a society like others but even because of its own peculiar nature. The fundamental law for the Christian and for the Church is the law of the Spirit, which is primarily an internal law. There is a need for external law in the Church, but this external law must be in conformity with the demands of the internal law. Obviously, here is the first source of tension in the life of the Church. The external law might not always correspond to the demands of the Spirit here and now. The external law of the Church might say that religious vows are by their very nature permanent, but for the good of an individual here and now such vows may become a positive hindrance. The Church law prescribes a certain formulary of prayers for her religious and clerics in major orders. However, perhaps the prescribed prayer does not meet the needs of a particular individual.

A second source of tension comes from the unique nature of the Church itself as the pilgrim Church. Precisely because the Church has not yet arrived at its final goal and perfection, there will always be the possibility of conflicting demands. The pilgrim Church must constantly change its laws, but actual change might lag behind the changes that have already occurred in the life of the community itself. For example, today there are very few who abide by the canonical restrictions on the buying and selling of church property.

A third source of tension is common to all societies and communities — the tension between the individual and the society itself. Such a tension exists because the individual is not completely subordinated to the society. Totalitarianism or collectivism demands the total subordination of the individual to society. On the other hand, only anarchy would maintain that the individual is completely independent of the demands of society. Society and the individual are going to exist in a constant state of tension precisely because they are neither totally independent of nor totally dependent on one another. A true Christian communitarianism should avoid the extremes of collectivism, on the one hand, and, on the other hand, anarchy. In this tension one finds the theological defense of so-called civil disobedience. When the law interferes with the inalienable rights of individuals, then it can no longer be a binding law.

A fourth source of tension is the very nature of positive law itself. Most Catholic theologians teach with St. Thomas that positive law admits exceptions. Positive law obliges *ut in pluribus*. Since positive law is not based on immutable essences but on changing circumstances, the legislator cannot possibly foresee all the different circumstances that might arise in a particular case. There are times when the letter of the law can become an injustice for an individual. In fact, the very imperfection of positive law appears more readily in the Church than it does in many secular societies and states. Nations are more homogeneous groupings of people than the Church. For example, here in the United States, people enjoy the same type of climate, the same basic culture of a technological civilization, a high degree of education, a common history and heritage. Consider the difficulties involved in framing laws for people living all over the globe, in completely different climates, with opposing cultural formations, with no common heritage, with differing languages and customs. A law enacted for a greater number of people living in very disparate circumstances will necessarily admit more exceptions than a law made for a more homogeneous grouping of people. Any revision of Canon Law must take into account the principle of subsidiarity, but existing legislation which tries to be at one and the same time rather minute and adaptable for all people in the Church must admit of a greater number of exceptions than most existing civil laws.

A fifth source of tension comes from the possibility of human error. Our nation has already admitted that prohibition was a mistake and has repealed the law. Is it possible for the Church with the guidance of the Holy Spirit to be led astray by human error? The Apostolic Constitution, *Veterum Sapientia,* which required theology courses in seminaries to be taught in Latin, is an excellent example of error on the part of the lawmaker in the Church.

The rapidly changing sociological conditions of modern life merely accentuate the inherent tensions in human law, and consequently, in Church law. In rather stable and immobile times, the tensions might not be apparent. However, the tensions existing in Church law today are also aggravated by a problem peculiar to the life of the Church here and now. The law of the Church as it exists in the Code of Canon Law reflects a period of life, both in the Church and in secular society, which gave much more emphasis to the place of law in the life of the person. Even in considerations of secular society many Catholic theoreticians have not realized the shrinking place that law occupies in civil society. Catholic theologians frequently speak of law as existing for the common good of society. However, it seems that the function of law is geared for the public order, which is much more limited than the concept of the common good.

There are many and different groups within society which must work for the common good. Law today does not have the function of controlling and directing most of the life within the community. Rather, the role of law is limited to assuring that all these other smaller societies and institutions can make their contribution towards the common good. The role and place of law in the secular society today is much less than it was in medieval society. The recent Church-State and religious liberty controversies point up the changed role of law and government in modern society. Law provides the framework within which the individuals and the different institutions within society can make their contribution for the common good. Perhaps the predominant role given to law in the life of the Church reflected the secular societies of the medieval period; but society and the role of law in society have greatly changed since that time.

The biblical teaching on law and the contemporary theological understanding of the Church show that law has only an ancillary role in the life of the Church. However, the Church is currently living under a legislative system which reflects an epoch in which law played a more predominant role. As the emphasis swings from conformity to creativity, the tensions created by law in the Church are only going to increase. The present Code of Canon Law does not reflect the current theological understanding of the role of law in the Church; nor does it reflect the role of law in modern civil societies.

However, moral theology has always taught that there are built-in safeguards to deal with the possible sources of tension relating to law in the Church. Manuals of moral theology spend a great number of pages discussing excusing causes, dispensations, privileges, etc. However, there is one built-in safeguard which requires greater emphasis today — *epikeia*.

Catholic moral teaching embraces two different notions of *epikeia*. Most manuals of theology actually adopt a very restricted and Suarezian understanding of *epikeia*. *Epikeia* has usually been surrounded with many precautions and safeguards. If the obliging force of law comes from the will of the legislator, then *epikeia* must be seen in terms of the will of the legislator. In any given situation an individual must have recourse to the will of the legislator to determine if the particular law is still obliging. If in an individual situation it is impossible to approach the legislator, then the individual may act according to the presumed will of the legislator. *Epikeia* is looked upon with some suspicion because it goes against the letter of the law.

The Thomistic teaching on *epikeia* is quite different. Thomas makes the flat assertion that *epikeia* is a virtue (*II. II*. q. 120. a.l.). Despite the objections that *epikeia* might foment anarchy, cause dissensions, or harm the common good, Thomas still asserts that *epikeia* is a virtue. The Thomistic teaching maintains that *epikeia* is a part of the virtue of justice precisely because of the inherent imperfections of human law. *Epikeia* for Thomas is not a lazy attempt to escape from certain obligations, but rather *epikeia* is the response to a higher law, the law of justice. *Epikeia* has been called the crown of legal justice and the virtue of the spirit of the law. For the Christian, *epikeia* cannot be merely the wish to free oneself from a particular obligation, but rather *epikeia* must be a demand of the higher law — the law of the Spirit.

The question naturally arises about the need to have recourse to the legislator before using *epikeia*. A voluntaristic notion of law and *epikeia* stresses the need to have recourse to the will of the legislator. Since in this view the obligation stems from the will of the legislator, the individual should have recourse to the will of the legislator to see if the obligation is still existing. *Per se* the Thomistic notion of *epikeia* does not demand recourse to the legislator. A realistic interpretation of law puts the obliging force of law in the ordering for the common good (better: the public order). If the law does not contribute to the common good in these circumstances, then it no longer obliges. Thomas' own teaching on *epikeia* does at times demand the need for the determination of the ruler. Thomas maintains that in doubtful matters there is need for interpretation, and in these cases it is not permitted to go against the letter of the law without the determination of the ruler (*principis*). But in obvious cases, there is no need for interpretation, but only for execution.

I believe that the Thomistic understanding of *epikeia* is valid today with some adjustments because of the changed sociological circumstances. It is important to realize in the Thomistic understanding that *per se epikeia* does not require recourse to the will of the legislator. Thomas demands recourse only for interpretation in doubtful cases. I contend that today even in doubtful cases the interpretation of the legislator is not the last word. Certainly, the presumption must always stand for the justice of the particular law, but the presumption must cede to the truth in particular cases. The role of the individual in society has changed greatly since Thomas' time. Today both in the Church and in secular society the stress is on the freedom and responsibility of the individual. People in secular society are citizens and not subjects. The whole structure of modern society depends upon the creative contributions of individuals and institutions within society. Law contributes only a small part to the common good of society. Thomas knows only a society which is structured from the top down — everything must come from the command and word of the ruler. (The very word *princeps* used by Thomas indicates that he is not talking about the same type of society that we know.) Less than a century ago, Pope Leo XIII could refer to subjects as the unlettered masses. This is not true in modern society. Society has changed, and the role of the legislator and the individual member in society has changed since the thirteenth century. Consequently, even for interpretation, recourse to the legislator is not required. In many circumstances today such recourse would be virtually impossible.

Our present understanding of law in the Church also shows that interpretation does not demand recourse to the legislator with the final outcome depending on the legislator. The primary law for the Christian is the law of the Spirit. Every other law is secondary. The Christian is entrusted by God with the responsibility of listening to the voice of the Spirit. External law is necessary, the presumption is always with the legislator; but the ultimate decision in the particular case rests with the individual.

The twelfth chapter of Matthew's gospel offers a good illustration of the virtue of *epikeia*. Christ himself justifies the breaking of the letter of the Sabbath law to heal the person with a withered arm. Christ reminds his hearers that they too would break the letter of the law even to free a sheep that may have fallen into a ditch. Notice that no recourse for interpretation is required in these cases. Christ also recalls the story from the Old Testament in which David and his men ate the sacred loaves which according to the law could be eaten only by the priests. In cases of emergency, obviously the letter of the law is no longer binding.

The objection immediately comes to mind — *epikeia* ultimately leads to anarchy. By stressing the need for the individual to make the final decision, *epikeia* results in pure subjectivism and anarchy. However, the objection is not valid if one has a proper understanding of the virtue of *epikeia*. *Epikeia* does require that ultimate responsibility rests with the individual, but such a concept does not lead to anarchy.

First, *epikeia* is a part of the virtue of justice. *Epikeia* does not mean license and the possibility of following personal whims and selfishness. Some authors have called *epikeia* the crown of justice, for at times a literal interpretation of the law would violate justice.

Second, *epikeia* is closely connected with the virtue of prudence. Prudence is probably the most forgotten virtue in the manuals of moral theology. Prudence is basically an art. No one can really teach prudence to another, and yet all have an obligation to learn prudence in their daily life. In the past, moral theology has tried to do away with the virtue of prudence by an exaggerated casuistry that tried to solve in advance every conceivable type of problem. Today, many people are calling for prudence. However, prudence, according to St. Thomas, is always a virtue of action. Prudence does not mean an unwillingness to act, rather prudence is the virtue that is present in every risk and decision in the Christian life.

Third, *epikeia* is always a demand of the higher law, the law of the Spirit. *Epikeia* is not a mere sneaking out from some positive obligation. The law of the Spirit is the ultimate criterion in the use of *epikeia*. One is trying one's best to hear the call of the Spirit in a particular situation. Openness to the Spirit is completely incompatible with irresponsibility and a selfish seeking of the easiest way out in a given situation. Contemporary theology needs to develop the treatise on the rules for the discretion of spirits. The discernment of the Spirit is a most important factor in the moral life of the contemporary Christian.

Fourth, *agape* remains always the fundamental attitude of the Christian. Perhaps too often today one speaks of the law of love and the law of the Spirit without realizing the concrete demands of love in a given situation. *Agape* includes the willingness to give oneself for others. The attitude of the Christian toward the laws of the Christian community must be a meditation of love. Christian love demands the willingness to make personal sacrifices for the good of others. Christians must even see the inherent imperfections in Church law as an opportunity to live the Paschal Mystery in the dying to self in the service of others. *Epikeia* in the context of *agape* can never lead to selfishness and egoistic individualism.

What about abuses? There will be abuses, even glaring abuses. However, the old theological axiom remains true: *abusus non tollit usum. Epikeia* is the great virtue of Christian 'freedom and Christian responsibility. The Christian must stand on his or her own two feet and make the decisions with regard to the obligations of Church laws in particular circumstances. Naturally, one will be guided by the counsel and actions of others in the Christian community. However, the ultimate decision rests with the individual. The freedom and responsibility entailed in the proper understanding of *epikeia* are the same freedom and responsibility which the free call of God in Christ presupposes.

God could have corralled all people into salvation, but he chose to freely call human beings to a life of community with himself and all others. The divine plan of salvation has tried to safeguard personal responsibility and freedom. Sin is the terrible abuse of human freedom, and yet God was willing to accept the horrible consequences of sin rather than do away with human responsibility. The abuses connected with *epikeia* can never constitute a sufficient reason to deny the need for *epikeia* in the life of the Christian.

Why all the stress on *epikeia* today? There are many reasons contributing to the greater need for the virtue of *epikeia* today. As already mentioned, the tensions between the individual and the community are much greater today than in the past. Likewise, theology now realizes the ancillary role of law in the Church, but much of the present legislation reflects a mentality that practically equates life in the Christian community with the observance of positive law. Also, the stress on individual responsibility is being recognized in all of theology. When people were truly the unlettered masses, they were not able to make their own decisions. Just a few centuries ago, all life was structured from the top down. The individual person who lacked adequate knowledge and education always looked to the authorities to find out what one should do. In such circumstances, the greatest stress was put on dispensations, privileges, and recourse to the will of the legislator. Today, privileges and dispensations have no real meaning when they concern laws that affect only individuals. In fact, some of the privileges connected with certain organizations are a source of scandal, especially today. If membership in a certain society gives me the privilege of not praying the breviary under certain conditions, there is no reason why as a mature Christian I cannot make the judgment that in particular situations I am not bound to the canonical law of praying the breviary.

The complexity and responsibility which characterize modern life require that the individual Christian make the final decision in a particular situation involving a positive law of the Church. The individual Catholic must respect and follow the laws of the Church, but a true understanding recognizes the provisional and imperfect nature of Church law. The virtue of *epikeia* moderates the literalness and inapplicability of the law in the face of the very real Christian demands in a concrete situation. *Epikeia* is a virtue of Christian maturity and responsibility. A true understanding of *epikeia* should avoid false extremes of legalism and anarchy. *Epikeia* is the practical functioning of the law of the Spirit, the primary law of the Christian life, in the context of the positive law of the Church.

4: Ethical Methodology and Church Teaching

In the recent debates in Roman Catholic moral theology, two important areas of consideration — ethical methodology and the teaching role of the Church in moral matters — have come to the fore. The ecumenical aspect of theological ethics is illustrated by the fact that in Protestant ethics these same two topics have also assumed a great significance.[1] This chapter will consider both of these questions. Since chapter 2 criticized Catholic natural law theory and proposed some different approaches, this chapter will discuss the shortcomings of some other methodologies. The chapter following will present an in depth discussion of utilitarianism, consequentialism, and contemporary developments in Christian ethics. The second part of this chapter will discuss the controversial question of the teaching authority and role of the Church in moral matters.

Ethical Methodology

The moral methodology presented in the manuals in the Roman Catholic tradition is not the only source of difficulties in contemporary thinking in Christian ethics. I personally am in basic agreement with the thrust of the Catholic tradition which has constantly maintained that there is a source of ethical wisdom and knowledge existing apart from the explicit revelation of God in the Scriptures and that through reason human beings can come to some understanding of their destiny. But the older approach of the manuals did not properly understand the theological and philosophical limitations of human reason, did not properly relate the natural with the supernatural, and also fell into the ahistorical error of identifying reason with just one philosophical understanding (Thomist philosophy) which despite all its merits remains culturally and historically limited and unable in its totality to claim the title of the perennial philosophy. Many difficulties and errors have also surfaced in some of the contemporary responses and approaches to Christian ethics.

A first difficulty arises from a Christian vision or horizon which is too exclusive. The Christian posture or stance, a most important component in any theological ethics, looks at reality in terms of the total Christian mystery of creation, sin, incarnation, redemption, and resurrection destiny.[2] Christian thought in the past has frequently succumbed to extreme temptations of either an eschatological irresponsibility which has not given enough importance and value to the reality of the present or of an uncritical acceptance of the present and a naively optimistic feeling that humanity can bring about the new heaven and the new earth by its own efforts in the very near future. The eschatological aspect of Christianity confirms the incompleteness and limitations of the present; the Christian view of sin reminds us that sin affects all human reality.[3] Christian theological ethics must avoid the danger of a denial of transcendence resulting in an overly immanent approach. Transcendence reminds the Christian that there is something beyond the present situation and the present life, but if properly understood in terms of eschatology also reminds the Christian of the call to cooperate in bringing about the new heaven and the new earth. Symptoms of this denial of transcendence can be illustrated by the failure of some contemporary theology to discuss certain topics; e.g., prayer, suffering, death.

Those who forget the transcendent aspect easily fall into a naive triumphalism which paradoxically shows itself in two almost diametrically opposed forms. On the one hand, there is a tendency to unquestionably and smugly accept the present and the social structures of the present as almost perfect mirrors of the reign of God and to resist and resent any efforts to change the present. On the other hand, those who rightly perceive the great limitations and sinfulness of the present sometimes live in the naive hope that by their efforts within a very short span of time they will usher in the new millennium. Both approaches suffer from the same basic triumphalism. The limitations and sinfulness of the present call for constant conversion which at times is truly revolution and rebellion against the present, but which will never perfectly succeed. The Christian living in the era of redemption and looking forward to the fullness of resurrection destiny knows that the follower of Jesus is called upon to overcome the limitations and sinfulness of the present but with the realization that the final stage of the kingdom will come only at the end of time. The present efforts to change one's heart and the world with its frustrations, setbacks, and sufferings make the Christian ever more conscious of belonging to a covenant people living in the hope of the promise that God in Christ will bring to completion the work he has begun.

A second source of erroneous approaches stems from a too exclusive emphasis on a particular aspect of what have been the traditional dichotomies or emphases in Roman Catholic and Protestant theologies. Today there is a general tendency toward convergence on these matters, but at times some of the older emphases appear in an exaggerated way.[4] Protestant theology has traditionally given more importance to faith, whereas Catholic theology has stressed the importance of works. Protestant theology has emphasized the transcendence of God and his freedom, whereas Catholic theology has upheld the goodness of the nature and of human reason. Protestant theology has underscored the freedom of the transcendent God and the Christian freedom of the believer, while Catholic theology has always emphasized order and the positive function of law as a guide or norm for conscience. Catholic theology has thus developed a natural theology and a natural law, whereas Protestantism with its emphasis on the transcendence of God and the Scriptures as the sole norm of truth has downplayed and even opposed the rational and the philosophical. The earlier chapters have pointed out the errors in the extreme emphasis in Catholic theology which too often has embraced Pelagianism, legalism, and an unwarranted trust in the goodness of human reason especially as this was authoritatively interpreted by the Church.

In some contemporary Protestant ethical approaches, the traditional Protestant emphases lead to a dangerous theological actualism. This is true of the ethical theory of Barth and Bonhoeffer as well as of Paul Lehmann in this country.[5] In the Barthian tradition there is a severe critique of ethics as such, since ethics looks for goodness in human beings and in human reason; but James M. Gustafson points out that "the critique of ethics is never as drastic as the language in which it is made would sometimes lead one to think."[6] In theological ethics of this type there exists a tendency to play down the notion of obligation and the imperative as exemplified by Paul Lehmann, who speaks of the indicative rather than the imperative and phrases the ethical question in terms of what God is doing and not in terms of what the human person ought to do.[7] For Barth, command becomes permission because God enables us to do freely and thankfully what he requires us to do.

Above all Barthian theology insists that the response of the Christian is always concrete and particular. God acts in singular concrete actions, and we must respond to these actions. Although the theological ethics of this approach are much more complex than some would believe, nonetheless, such ethics are ultimately too simplistic. This coincides with the judgment made on Barthian ethics by James Gustafson: "The moral actor faces exasperation if he turns

to the ethics of Christ the Redeemer-Lord for some objective, authoritative answer to the question, 'What ought I to
do in my situation?' "[8]

Ethicians must develop other criteria for trying to determine what God is doing in the world here and now. These
other criteria developed through faith and reason will not
usually furnish absolute certitude, but they should form
part of the necessary process by which the ethician considers the way in which Christians make their ethical decisions. Thus in Barthian ethics, which is still present in
some ethical approaches, there lurks the danger of a theological actualism which tries to perceive the concrete will
of God here and now without giving enough importance to
the other criteria, including those of a rational nature
which the Christian must employ in trying to discern his
response. As already pointed out, rational criteria in the
form of norms will not often give that specific an ordering
to our concrete actions, but such criteria at least can be
helpful in eliminating some possibilities and establishing
the area in which the concept of prudence and the role of
the particular discernment of the Spirit begin to operate.

This theological actualism often brings with it an unwarranted specificity about the will of God in particular
situations which reminds one of the Puritan spirit of old.
Paul Ramsey has criticized statements of Protestant
Churches and Protestant theologians especially in the area
of social ethics for making too specific judgments about
particular actions and not leaving enough room for prudence.[9] A theological actualism is logically connected with
such a specific approach. This type of Protestant approach
shares with an older Catholic approach the same triumphal-
istic spirit of claiming to know with too great a certitude
what the precise will or design of God is in this particular
situation. There are not only theological and philosophical
problems but also ecclesiological problems connected with
such specificity in the area of social ethics according to
Ramsey, since there is the danger of saying that someone
is acting in an unchristian way when there is no Christian

criterion for making that judgment. Ramsey believes that the Churches instead of making such specific moral judgments on complex, particular problems — e.g., the war in Viet Nam — should rather concentrate on those criteria or norms, if you wish, on which all Christians can share agreement and leave the practical decisions in the area to the matter of prudence. A theological actualism easily leads to the conclusion that Christians and the Churches can easily arrive at the most complex moral decisions. Also the *ad hoc* problem-solving technique so often followed in statements by Church groups tends to concentrate on the need for very precise and particular solutions.

One can appreciate the problems connected with such a theological actualism without totally agreeing with the approach of Ramsey. Ramsey seems to argue for a distinction between "Christian moral judgments on the one hand and particular political, legal, and military judgments on the other";[10] but such a distinction is unacceptable. From a theological viewpoint all our truly human decisions (not, for example, the purely mathematical decision) are ultimately moral and Christian decisions. Morality cannot be relegated to a limited sphere in human existence which does not include the political, legal, and military. From a practical viewpoint we have experienced the real problems created when the military or legal areas are withdrawn from the sphere of the moral.[11] Individual Christians must make very precise decisions in human life; nations and governments are called upon to make such choices. Christian theologians and the Churches should not shirk from making such judgments, but such judgments must be made in the light of more general criteria by which one moves from the very general notion to the particular decision and with the realization that such particular judgments may be wrong but seem to be the best possible response within the Christian perspective. The problem with theological actualism is the danger of coming to a very specific decision without the help of more general criteria which mediate the ultimate Christian understandings and of proclaiming such specific judgments with an unwarranted certitude which at times is reminiscent of the crusading spirit itself.

Consequentialism appears as another very real difficulty in some Christian ethics today. Paul Ramsey has accused Joseph Fletcher of being a consequentialist, for according to Fletcher morality is ultimately determined by weighing the consequences of our actions.[12] Two reasons have often been adduced in philosophical circles to show the inadequacies of pure consequentialism: no one can know beforehand all the consequences of an action, and there always remains the problem of appraising the hierarchical importance of the various consequences involved. Consequentialism appears to be a rather congenial approach in a highly technological society which is accustomed to measure success in the exclusive terms of results and consequences. Just as society must resist a purely technological approach, so too theological ethics must point out the shallowness and ultimate "a-human" character of consequentialism.

Consequentialism in an overly simplistic manner reduces all reality to the model of means and ends, but not all human reality can be made into mere means to be manipulated for various ends. Human persons, for example, cannot be treated as mere means employed and manipulated for the sake of other ends. For the Christian the thrust of consequentialism runs counter to certain basic Christian assumptions. The relationship between God and us is revealed in the Scriptures in terms of the covenant, but the love of God for us depends only on God's goodness and faithfulness. Despite the chosen people's refusal and sins, Yahweh remains ever faithful to his commitment which is thus in no way dependent upon the consequent response of human beings. Likewise the value that Christianity attributes to the human individual in no way depends upon the individual's works, successes or failures. The fact that the privileged people in the reign of God are not the rich and the powerful but the poor, outcasts, children, and sinners emphasizes the fact that human worth and value do not ultimately depend on one's deeds and above all are independent of one's successes. The technological and managerial spirit may judge persons exclusively in terms of what they do or accomplish, but such a judgment can never be the ultimate judgment for the Christian. Consequentialism as a success-oriented posture too easily forgets about the fact that frustration, suffering, tragedy, and ultimately death itself are important elements in the Christian understanding of human existence. The Paschal Mystery of Christ remains for the Christian the salutary reminder that immediately successful consequences are not the most important values in human existence. It is true that one could avoid the dangers of consequentialism mentioned in these paragraphs by emphasizing the Paschal Mystery and the Pauline strength in weakness, joy in sorrow, and life in death; but as a matter of fact consequentialist approaches in Christian ethics do not seem to follow such a course. There appears to be a real connection between the denial or underemphasis on the transcendent aspects of Christianity and an exclusive consequentialism.

Consequentialism accepts the fact that the end does justify the means, but the end cannot always justify the means precisely because all reality cannot be reduced to the one model of means-ends. Catholic theology, however, has erred in the past by defining the means in terms of the physical structure of the act itself and by failing to realize that in certain circumstances the end does specify the means. An example of such an erroneous approach on the part of consequentialism is the justification of the dropping of the atomic bomb as a means of bringing the war to a quicker conclusion.[13]

Such problems raise the more basic question of the proper way of describing the human act. An older theology rightly stressed the importance of three elements: moral object, end, and circumstances. Consequentialism seems to forget about everything except the end. In somewhat the same way an extrinsicist or voluntaristic approach to ethics likewise overstresses the aspect of intention or end and fails to give enough importance especially to the moral object. Thus one may rightly point out that the dropping of the atomic bomb cannot be described in terms of an act of winning the war and reducing loss of life. In the last few years there has been a growing discussion about consequentialism in Christian ethics. The following chapter will discuss in detail and assess this debate.

These considerations suggest another dangerous emphasis in some contemporary theological ethics of failing to give enough importance to the physical and material aspects of reality. It is true that an older Catholic theology erred by identifying the moral object with the physical structure of the act itself, but the opposite danger of not paying enough attention to the physical and the material aspects of reality appears in some approaches today. This contemporary neo-dualism or neo-angelism overlooks the importance of the physical and the material world, since all morality comes from outside the object itself. A Christian ethic, however, must stress more than just intention, for what we do, and not merely why we do it, remains a necessary ethical consideration. Christians are called upon to build up the new heaven and the new earth by their actions which means that good intentions alone are not sufficient. The complex ethical problems facing our modern society such as the concept and use of power, redistribution of wealth, international trade relations, equality of educational opportunity for all the people in our own country and in the world cannot be solved merely by good intentions, since there are some ways more appropriate than others for solving these problems.

Many of these erroneous approaches illustrate the trend in some situation ethics (note the many different ways in which this term can be used) which fails to give enough importance to the societal aspect of reality. A narrow situationalism often fails to go beyond the two persons involved in a particular action and the very immediate consequences of their actions. Catholic theology has not given enough importance in the past to the human person and individual subjective development, but a narrow personalism is really only an exaggerated individualism. The model of I-thou relationship has been emphasized with many important contributions in recent theological literature, but there remains a great danger in reducing all moral reality to the model of I-thou relationships. The model of ethical thinking must include all the aspects of reality including an individual's relationships to all other people, institutions, and the cosmos itself as well as connections with the past and responsibilities for the future.[14] It is interesting to note that the fascination with the situation ethics debate has waned in the last few years precisely because all today realize the greater importance attached to problems of social ethics, whereas situation ethics generally considered questions of an individual morality. Theological ethics needs a methodology which can deal effectively with both social and individual ethics.

Another danger existing today concerns the very concept of obligation and "ought" in moral theology. An older Catholic theology overemphasized obligation especially in the forms of Pelagianism and legalism which viewed the Christian life almost exclusively in terms of the model of obedience to the laws of God — the divine law, natural law, and positive law. In overreacting to the past there is a danger of completely forgetting the aspect of obligation and speaking only in the indicative and not in the imperative. The Christian has received the new life in Christ Jesus and has the obligation to grow in the Christian life which is summarized in the death-to-life transition of the Paschal Mystery. There is truly no growth or development without implying the concept of obligation, for continual conversion remains both a gift and a demand for the Christian.

Chapter 2 called for an historically conscious methodology in approaching moral problems which avoids the difficulties in the classicist approach, but there is an erroneous tendency today of adopting a sheer existentialism which is a philosophical actualism with some affinities to the theological actualism mentioned above. A sheer existentialism emphasizes the present moment with no connection to what has gone before and no connection with the future and without considering the horizontal relationships of the present that bind people to one another and to their commitments. Such an existentialism so highlights the singularity of the present that there are no adequate criteria for judging the present. Theological ethics has learned from its history the danger of uncritically accepting and baptizing the present moment, since everything in the present moment is not good. Theological ethics needs criteria by which it can judge and properly criticize the present. Any methodology which so concentrates on the present that it cannot stand back to critically judge the present cannot be an adequate approach. The classicist approach erred by establishing many universal norms to which the individual had to conform, but sheer existentialism errs by not being able, even in principle, to establish some criteria for judging the present.

Many of the erroneous approaches in theological ethics as in other sciences do not arise from positive error but rather from an overly simplistic approach which fails to take into consideration elements which are important and necessary. The danger of over-simplification can be seen in some contemporary stresses on the function of love in the life of the Christian. No one can deny the centrality and importance of love in the Christian life, but it is overly simplistic to go immediately from love to the solution of complex human problems. There appears again an unwillingness to grapple with the criteria by which one assesses the demands of love in concrete situations. H. Richard Neibuhr pointed out the impossibility of adequately describing Jesus and his ethics in terms of love or any other single virtue.[15] The critical reaction to Joseph Fletcher's insistence on love also illustrates the error in reducing all Christian ethics to love in an overly simplistic way. The late Bishop Pike criticized Fletcher's concept of love as *agape* precisely because it did not give enough importance to the notion of love as *eros*. *Agape* signifies a love for the other which is independent of the person's own merits or goodness, but Pike rightly points out that at times a person needs to be loved precisely for what one is in oneself and not merely because of the love of God.[16] James Gustafson has criticized in Fletcher's work his confusing concept of love which takes on many different meanings: "It is the *only* thing which is intrinsically good; it *equals* justice; it is a formal *principle*, it is a *disposition*, it is a *predicate* and not a property, it is a ruling *norm*."[17] Donald Evans has likewise pointed out the different and conflicting notions of love in the theory of Fletcher.[18] Since Fletcher reduces ethical theory only to love and the concrete situation, it is obvious that love must take on many different and ultimately conflicting meanings. Again the complex problems of social ethics argue against such an oversimplistic approach to Christian ethics.

A very unfortunate aspect of the situation ethics debate has been the tendency to view the Christian life almost exclusively in terms of law and its application, for the total moral phenomena include much more than just laws. Ethical considerations must also consider the person, the dispositions which characterize the person, and his or her multiple relationships. Also the goals and ideals of the Christian life are most important. As the role of law or norms rightly becomes less in the life of the Christian, these other aspects such as the dispositions and virtues, as well as the general horizon or outlook of the Christian on human reality, will take on even greater importance. There will always be some place for norms and principles in the Christian moral theory (although I have denied the existence of absolute norms in the form of negative, moral absolutes in which the moral act is described solely in terms of the physical structure of the act itself), but Christian thinkers have consistently emphasized that the primary "law" for the Christian is the internal "law of the Spirit." The external law remains always secondary and relative insofar as it points out some of the demands and criteria for recognizing the call of the Spirit.

The Teaching Function of the Church

The most immediate problem raised by the widespread negative reaction to the papal encyclical on birth control obviously concerns the function and role of the teaching office in the Church. Also, Protestants and Roman Catholics have discussed the teaching role of the Church in social questions such as war, civil rights, and international relations.

The recent debate has brought to light the fact that theology and the hierarchical magisterium did recognize in the past that Catholics could dissent from authoritative, noninfallible papal teaching when there are sufficient reasons for such dissent.[19] Theologians today are also reconsidering the entire concept of infallibility, but this aspect of the question lies beyond the scope of the present consideration. There has never been an infallible pronouncement or teaching on a specific moral matter; the very nature of specific moral actions makes it impossible, in my judgment, to have any infallible pronouncements in this area. The hierarchical magisterium has taught in the area of specific moral questions with an authentic or authoritative noninfallible magisterium. Even the terminology "authentic" or "authoritative" must be properly understood, for authentic does not necessarily mean that this teaching is always true. Such terminology is of comparatively recent origin, appearing for the first time in documents of the hierarchical magisterium in 1863.[20] The very term "noninfallible," no matter how it is interpreted, still signifies that this particular teaching is fallible. In the light of these and other considerations, what is the future of the teaching office or function in the Roman Catholic Church?

Should the Roman Catholic Church and other Christian Churches speak out on the moral problems facing human beings and society today? I believe that the Christian Churches have a responsibility to speak out on the issues, for the Church cannot withdraw from the reality and complexity of daily life in the world. The Church exists today in the service of life in the world and can no longer exist merely in sacred times and sacred places. The basic insight behind the theological position affirming the existence of natural law was the fact that our daily life in the world is somehow meaningful and important, but the older approach with its dichotomy between the natural and supernatural did not adequately express the relationship between daily life in the world and the kingdom of God. Also in an older theological pattern the Church was looked upon as more important than the world and as controlling the world in some way, but contemporary theology stresses the importance and independence of the world. The Church can no longer dominate the world, but it must respect the integrity of the world and try to be of service in the world, which is constantly marked by the struggle against human limitation and sinfulness, in trying to cooperate in bringing about the new heaven and the new earth which will be in some continuity with the present but also in some discontinuity with the world and history.

How does the Church carry out its teaching function and mission in the world today? First of all, it is important to point out that the teaching function and role of the Church belong to the whole Church and not just to the hierarchical and papal teaching office in the Church. A Roman Catholic admits the hierarchical and papal teaching office, but there has been a danger in the past of identifying the whole magisterial function of the Church with these offices. The ecclesiology ratified in Vatican II has pointed out that the Church is the whole People of God and not just the hierarchy; now ecclesiology is pushing forward with the realization that the teaching function of the Church, like the Church itself, cannot be restricted to and identical with the hierarchical teaching office. This realization appears in a seminal way in some of the emphases of Vatican II, which point out the many different ways in which the Church teaches and learns. There exists a prophetic voice in the Church which is not the same as the hierarchical teaching office (Constitution on the Church,

n. 12). The Declaration on Religious Liberty in the opening paragraph recognizes a desire for religious liberty arising
in the consciousness and experience of people and declares
these desires "to be greatly in accord with truth and justice." The truth of religious liberty did not come into existence merely when the conciliar magisterium published a
decree, but obviously had been true before that time. A
familiarity with the many areas of change in Catholic
teaching points out the importance of the prophetic voice
in the Church and the role of the experience of people.[21]
The emphasis on dialogue in Vatican II — dialogue with
other Christians, with non-Christians, with atheists, with
the world — reminds us that the Roman Catholic Church
does not have all the answers to the problems of contemporary existence. Again history points out the many times
in which the Church has learned from other Christians and
non-Christians: for example, religious liberty, interest on
loans, the needs of the working person, and lately in our
own country the importance of peace and the rights of the
poor.

Theologically, the fact that the teaching mission of the
Church cannot be restricted to the hierarchical teaching office stems from a number of accepted teachings in the
Catholic Church. The primary teacher in the Church remains the Holy Spirit who dwells in the hearts of the faithful and in all people of good will, so that no one person
has a monopoly on the Spirit. The Spirit is well characterized by the biblical expression of blowing where it wills. A
theology of baptism also illustrates that the whole Church
is magisterial. The liturgical renewal in the Church is based
on the fact that through baptism every Christian participates in the priestly office of Jesus Christ and thus all are
called upon to actively participate in the eucharistic life
and worship of the Church. However, through baptism the
Christian not only participates in the priestly function of
Jesus but also in his prophetic or teaching and ruling function.[22] Just as the priestly function of all believers is not
incompatible with the ministerial priesthood, so too the

magisterial character of all Christians is not irreconcilable with the hierarchical teaching office in the Church. Thus theology supports the contention that the whole Church is magisterial. Catholic theology and practice can no longer simply identify the magisterium of the Church with the hierarchical magisterium, for the hierarchical magisterium is just one aspect of the total teaching mission of the Church.

One of the primary difficulties with the encyclical *Humanae Vitae* is the insistence on identifying the teaching function of the Church with the hierarchical teaching office. With the exception of somewhat general citations from Sacred Scripture and one reference to Thomas Aquinas, all the references cited in this document are to previous statements of the hierarchical magisterium. In fact, the primary reason for not accepting a different approach to the practical question of contraception was the previous teaching of the hierarchical magisterium (*H.V.*, n. 6). This papal document like many others in the past relies almost totally on past teachings of the hierarchical magisterium, and thus is guilty of an intellectual incest. The "papal predecessors of happy memory" have made many important and correct statements in the past, but such teaching on these matters is subject to error and also needs to be relativized in the light of the full teaching function of the Church. A number of overly simplistic approaches should be avoided in this context. The magisterial function of the Church can never be reduced to a mere consensus or majority rule, since the criteria for discerning the Spirit are much more complex than that. Likewise, one cannot merely dismiss papal teaching. Religious assent is the technical term used by the theologians in the past to indicate the respect that must be given to such teaching with the realization, however, that such teaching could be wrong and not call for an intellectual assent. Precisely because the teaching function of the Church is not perfectly identical with the hierarchical teaching office there will always remain this tension which cannot be resolved in an overly simplistic fashion either by maintaining that the pope can never be wrong or by saying that the pope is just another theological voice in the Church.

In the future, theological understanding of the relationship between the hierarchical teaching office in the Church and the whole Church as magisterial in a certain sense must change the methodological approach to the way in which papal teachings are studied and proposed. There was a tremendous difference between the methodological approach in the writing of the Pastoral Constitution on the Church in the Modern World and the methodological approach to *Humanae Vitae*. The Pastoral Constitution was written after consultations with leading experts, theologians, and only after years of debate and consultation with all the bishops of the world. A papal commission was called into existence to help the Pope on the matter of birth control, but obviously *Humanae Vitae* was not written with their help and collaboration. The noncollegial character of the methodology employed in writing *Humanae Vitae* is evidenced by the small and nonrepresentative group of theologians who actually worked on the composition of the encyclical.[23] Future papal teachings must realize better in practice the magisterial function of the whole Church and be elaborated in greater consultation and collegiality with the whole Church so that they speak in a more complete and adequate manner for the whole teaching Church. Even then, though, such teachings on specific moral matters will never enjoy an absolute certitude.

Theology today is much more conscious than it was in the past that teachings on specific matters cannot enjoy an absolute certitude. In the past a number of factors contributed to a greater insistence on certitude in the teaching of the Church although the older theologians recognized in a somewhat guarded way that such noninfallible, authoritative teaching did not insure an absolute certitude which excluded the possibility of error. From a theological perspective, an authoritarian and overly hierarchical understanding of the Church together with a juridical understanding of

teaching authority tended to give an authoritarian certitude to the pronouncements and teachings of the hierarchical magisterium. Better theological approaches in these
areas obviously show the more conditional aspect of such
hierarchical teaching, but even more importantly theologians and philosophers today are much more aware of
human limitations in arriving at certitude than they were
in the past. The more historically minded methodology
calls for a more inductive approach which by its very
nature can never achieve the certitude of a more deductive
approach. All sciences today reflect the changed scientific
ideal which no longer even strives for an absolute certitude
which would in reality be the enemy of any true progress
in knowledge and science. Thinkers today are aware of the
imperfections of human language in attempting to articu-
late and express our understandings of reality. These three
aspects which are intimately connected with a more historically conscious methodology show the impossibility of
arriving at absolute certitude on specific moral matters
especially those affecting complex social problems. Above
we have discussed the reasons against the truth, let alone
the certitude, of negative moral absolutes described as
actions in which the moral act is considered solely in terms
of the physical structure of the act itself.

The fact that the teaching of the Church on such specific matters cannot claim absolute certitude follows from
the incarnational nature of the Church with all its inherent
human limitations which are not overcome by its union
with Christ. The pilgrim nature of the Church and the insistence on the dialogical quest for truth also argue against
the possibility of such certitude. It seems to me that the
very ideal or goal of such absolute certitude itself remains
an obstacle in the Church's carrying out its prophetic and
teaching mission. If one aspires to certitude in statements
and teaching, then one is condemned either to speaking in
platitudes or to speaking long after the critical problems
have arisen and been faced. If the teaching function of the
Church — both in the eyes of its members and others — is

freed from the shackles of absolute certitude in the area of specific moral problems, then it can raise its voice in a way to help the world as it faces so many complex problems today. The complexity of problems and the swiftly changing aspects of contemporary life show the impossibility of any absolute certitude in these matters. However, the Church cannot merely stand back and say nothing, since the Christian Church does have a function in assisting all of God's people to do their important but limited work in bringing about the new heaven and the new earth.

The Church must raise its voice on particular issues facing the world and society today with the understanding that it does not speak with an absolute certitude but proposes what it thinks to be the best possible Christian approach with the realization that it might be wrong. The Church should avoid the dangers of theological and philosophical actualism by showing the various criteria and principles which enter into its judgment in this particular case. Many times the whole Church or the hierarchical magisterium with more certitude will be able to point out in a negative fashion approaches which should not be taken. As the Church or anyone else comes closer to concrete, particular decisions the danger of error becomes greater. The entire Church in its teaching must continue to do two things: to express constantly and continually develop the various criteria, principles, goals, and ideals which the individual Christian incorporates into his or her decision-making process and at the same time, but in a more hesitant manner, propose some concrete solutions for the manifold problems of contemporary existence.

In discussing the teaching mission of the Church it is most important to underscore the analogous concept of the very term "teaching." The dangers of understanding the teaching role in an overly authoritarian and juridical way have already been pointed out. The concept of teaching authority itself opens the door to a voluntaristic and extrinsic concept of teaching which downplays the fact that the truth is the ultimate authority of teaching. Today and in the future one cannot discuss the teaching and prophetic function of the Church without understanding the different interpretations of "teacher." In the past the teacher was the person who packaged knowledge and handed it over in easily digestible form to students who tended in a passive way to absorb this data. The teacher today is not primarily the person who imparts knowledge in this way, but rather the one who stimulates others to grapple with the questions of the day and thus to develop themselves and their society. The teacher is not necessarily the person with all the answers, but rather one who stimulates students by asking the right questions and pointing out possible avenues of approach. Too often in the past the teaching or prophetic role of the Church has been seen in giving answers or pronouncements to particular questions. This approach wedded to a claim of absolute certitude actually hindered the Church from properly fulfilling its teaching and prophetic function. The Church at times is in the best position to raise the embarrassing questions and also to show other institutions and society by its own actions what type of approaches might be taken to the problems of contemporary life.

The understanding of the teaching function of the Church described above has many important implications. From an ecumenical viewpoint, such an understanding of the teaching mission of the Church in these specific moral questions should not be an obstacle to the union of Christians, for it closely resembles many of the theoretical approaches adopted in Protestant circles today. The most important implications for the present involve the need for the Roman Catholic Church to realize not only in theory but also in practice such an understanding. The Roman Catholic Church badly needs the structures by which the magisterial character of the whole Church as well as the special hierarchical teaching office will exercise their proper roles in the teaching of the Church, which roles can never be viewed primarily in terms of pronouncements but which must always include this aspect of teaching.

NOTES

1. For a summary of some critical comments on situation ethics, see *The Situation Ethics Debate,* ed. Harvey Cox (Philadelphia: Westminster Press, 1968). On the question of the Church and social teaching, see Paul Ramsey, *Who Speaks for the Church?* (Nashville and New York: Abingdon Press, 1967).

2. For a fuller development of my stance, see Charles E. Curran, *New Perspectives in Moral Theology* (Notre Dame, Ind.: University of Notre Dame Press, 1976), pp. 47-86.

3. This particular criticism applies, for example, to W. H. van der Marck, O.P., *Toward a Christian Ethic* (Westminster, Md.: Newman Press, 1967).

4. For an example of a contemporary Protestant approach which departs from some of the theological bases proposed in orthodox Protestantism, see James Sellers, *Theological Ethics* (New York: Macmillan Co., 1966).

5. Paul Lehmann, *Ethics in a Christian Context* (New York: Harper and Row, 1963).

6. James M. Gustafson, *Christ and the Moral Life* (New York: Harper and Row, 1968), p. 28. The brief description of Barthian ethics in this paragraph is based primarily on Gustafson's summary, pp. 13-60.

7. Paul L. Lehmann, *Ethics in a Christian Context* (New York: Harper and Row, 1963), pp. 131 and 159-161.

8. Gustafson, *Christ and the Moral Life,* p. 59.

9. Ramsey, *Who Speaks for the Church,* pp. 58-118.

10. Ibid., pp. 118-147.

11. Ibid., p. 53. Ramsey earlier acknowledged that some would wrongly brand him as "one who believes the church to be a spiritual cult with no pertinent social outlook" (p. 20), but the distinction made above seems unfortunate precisely because creation, nature, and history do have a relationship to the reign of God in Christ.

12. Paul Ramsey, *Deeds and Rules in Christian Ethics* (New York: Charles Scribner's Sons, 1967), pp. 187 ff.

13. For apparent approval of the dropping of the atomic bomb, see Joseph Fletcher, *Situation Ethics* (Philadelphia: Westminster Press, 1966), pp. 167-168; W. van der Marck, O.P., *Love and Fertility* (London: Sheed and Ward, 1965), pp. 61-63.

14. H. Richard Niebuhr, *The Responsible Self* (New York: Harper and Row, 1963), pp. 55ff.

15. H. Richard Niebuhr, *Christ and Culture* (New York: Harper and Row, 1951; Torchbook, 1956), pp. 15-19.

16. James A. Pike, *You and the New Morality* (New York: Harper and Row, 1967), pp. 68-69.

17. James M. Gustafson, "Love Monism," in *Storm over Ethics* (no place given: United Church Press, 1967), p. 33.

18. Donald Evans, "Love, Situations, and Rules," in *Norm and Context in Christian Ethics*, ed. Gene H. Ontka and Paul Ramsey (New York: Charles Scribner's Sons, 1968), pp. 369 ff.

19. Joseph A. Komonchak, "Ordinary Papal Magisterium and Religious Assent," in *Contraception: Authority and Dissent*, ed. Charles E. Curran (New York: Herder and Herder, 1969), pp. 101-126.

20. Komonchak, "Papal Magisterium," p. 115.

21. Daniel C. Maguire, "Moral Absolutes and the Magisterium," in *Absolutes in Moral Theology?*, ed. Charles E. Curran (Washington: Corpus Books, 1968), pp. 57-70.

22. Yves M. J. Congar, O.P., *Lay People in the Church* (London: Geoffrey Chapman, 1959), basically develops the second part of this work, originally written before World War II, in accord with the threefold participation through baptism in the office and mission of Jesus.

23. Bernard Häring, "The Encyclical Crisis," *Commonweal* 88 (Sept. 6, 1968), pp. 588-594.

5: Utilitarianism, Consequentialism, and Moral Theology

The last few chapters have indicated that within the last decade in Roman Catholicism there has been a growing theological literature questioning the existence of absolute behavioral norms in moral theology. More specifically, many theologians have objected to exceptionless moral norms in which the moral action is described in terms of the physical aspect of the act. At the same time there has been a growing debate in philosophical ethics about the adequacy of a utilitarian approach. Often these debates have been taking place in isolation. The purpose of this chapter is to compare the different debates that have taken place within utilitarian thought, to examine the arguments proposed against a utilitarian position in order to clarify the terms of the discussion, to situate the debate which has taken place in Roman Catholic ethics in the light of the discussion about utilitarianism, and to suggest approaches for Roman Catholic ethics.

Debates within Utilitarianism

Utilitarianism is described as the ethical attitude which seeks to produce the greatest good for the greatest number. Since the morality of an action depends in some way on producing good and/or avoiding evil, utilitarianism is generally understood as a form of teleological ethics or consequentalism. Teleological theories are generally contrasted with deontological theories which maintain that it is possible to have a moral obligation to do an act which does not produce the most good or avoid the most evil in the manner suggested by teleologists. Utilitarianism is a form of consequentialism because moral obligation is determined by the good or bad consequences produced. J. J. C. Smart, a contemporary defender of utilitarianism, describes it as the view that the rightness or wrongness of an act depends only on the total goodness or badness of the consequences.[1]

Calculating Consequences

Utilitarians themselves as well as their opponents have frequently recognized some difficulty in calculating consequences. Bentham attempted a calculus of pleasure and pain by indicating seven different dimensions which had to be taken into account. John Stuart Mill, reacting to Bentham's calculus based on quantity, introduced a qualitative distinction between higher and lower pleasures.[2] But the problem of calculating the consequences is even more complex. Whatever utility means, the theory of utilitarianism calls for it to be maximized. Since our actions very often affect more than one person and many societal institutions, it must be possible to calculate the total net utility to all affected by the various alternative actions which are open to the subject. Different theories of calculation are still being proposed by various contemporary thinkers (e.g., Braybrooke, Rescher, and Brandt).[3] Most philosophers recognize the difficulty in constructing such a calculation of the consequences of acts.

Two points deserve mention in response to the problem of calculating consequences. Utilitarians do not believe that human beings should always attempt to make such exhaustive calculations before acting. They readily accept rules of thumb often called summary rules. Such summary rules are not absolute and should be violated if the violation brings about better consequences, but ordinarily one can follow such rules of thumb as the distillation of experience about what usually produces the most utility.

Secondly, one must admit there is no universal agreement even among utilitarians on how consequences of acts should be calculated. The difficulty or lack of agreement does not constitute a totally convincing argument against utilitarianism or any consequentialist theory. Calculating consequences is a problem for all other types of ethics as well. Roman Catholic manualistic moral theology has often appealed to consequences to justify the morality of particular actions. The principle of proportionality in war maintains that the good to be achieved by the war must outweigh the evils involved. Here one is asked to consider the consequences of alternative actions involving many different human values including the taking of human lives and the very existence of peoples and nations. Traditional Catholic moral theology thus has to face the same difficulty as utilitarians although not all the time.

Act-utilitarianism and Rule-utilitarianism

A very significant and important debate among utilitarians concerns the difference between act- and rule-utilitarianism. Until the last two or three decades utilitarianism was understood in terms of act-utilitarianism — the rightness or wrongness of the action is determined by the consequences of the act itself. Antiutilitarians brought up a number of objections to utilitarianism because by making the consequences of the individual act morally determinative one goes against many accepted moral teachings, e.g., punishment of the innocent, judicial murder, not voting in an election, not keeping secrets, not telling the truth, etc. Michael Bayles has collected an anthology of essays to show the development of rule-utilitarianism as a refinement of the basic utilitarian approach which was proposed in the intervening years to overcome some of the above objections.[4] According to rule-utilitarianism acts are to be regarded as right only if they conform to rules which can be supported on utilitarian grounds. Urmson maintains that John Stuart Mill himself was really a rule-utilitarian and not an act-utilitarian.[5]

In the 1960s David Lyons and others maintained that rule-utilitarianism and act-utilitarianism, if properly understood as including all the circumstances, especially threshold phenomena, are equivalent so that there is no real difference between them.[6] Lyons' thesis of equivalence has been attacked,[7] but it is safe to describe the present state of the debate by indicating that there is a growing consensus among utilitarians themselves that rule-utilitarianism very frequently if not always collapses into act-utilitarianism.[8]

The debate within utilitarianism about act- and rule-utilitarianism does not have any immediate parallels in the current debates in Roman Catholic moral theology. However, it seems that Roman Catholic moral theology might profit from this discussion with its emphasis on the principle of universalizability. Richard A. McCormick has recently proposed that some norms (e.g., direct taking of innocent life, direct killing of noncombatants, difference between commission and omission as seen in so-called passive and active euthanasia) are "teleologically established and yet are virtually exceptionless." In weighing all the consequences of actions one comes to the conclusion that the actions are wrong and that the dangers and risks that might result from any exceptions are so great that the norm is virtually exceptionless. The establishment of such a norm is based on an analogy with the establishment of a positive law on the basis of a presumption of a common and universal danger.[9]

McCormick's argument for exceptionless norms consists in a wedge argument that any possible exceptions would ultimately lead to greater evils than the good that might possibly be achieved in the one exception. The debate about act- and rule-utilitarianism has frequently made use of the principle of universalizability or generalizability which might be employed here to allow certain exceptions without necessarily involving all the evils that McCormick fears might come from any exceptions.

McCormick himself maintains that the existing laws or norms accepted in Catholic moral theology have ultimately come about by refining the principle that killing is wrong except where there is a proportionate reason. Exceptions have been made in this general norm for proportionate reasons (self-defense, killing in war, etc.) without endangering the value to be preserved by the norm itself.[10] Now one might attempt to push the question one step further — can exceptions be made in the now accepted norms of no direct killing of the innocent and no active euthanasia which could allow for some exceptions without entailing all the evil consequences that McCormick fears if one no longer accepts the existing distinctions?

In the case of directly killing noncombatants in war I am in basic agreement with McCormick's fears, but in the case of directly killing the innocent, it might be possible to make some very limited exceptions. Consider a case which was proposed by Williams. A foreigner comes across a scene where a tyrannical military captain is prepared to shoot a group of villagers taken at random to discourage other protesters in the village and bring about loyalty to the existing government. The captain offers the foreigner the privilege of killing one of the villagers with the promise that he himself will then let the others go free. The presuppositions are that the captain will do as he threatens and there is absolutely no other way to save the villagers or any number of them.[11] Is it not possible to acknowledge some exception clause for hard cases like this without necessarily involving the many long-range consequences feared by McCormick? Could one not accept the rule — directly killing the innocent is wrong except in those cases where one is forced into a situation in which there is certitude that this is the only way a far greater number of innocent persons can be saved? Such a restricted exception clause could allow such killing in a few cases and still maintain the general principle of not killing innocent people in almost all situations. Here it is necessary to insist on the sin-filled aspects of the situation and on the certitude that one has that this is the only way in which a far greater number of innocent persons can be saved. Such a condition is rarely present and impossible in the complex situation of warfare and the direct killing of noncombatants.

In the case of the difference between killing and letting die as acts of commission and omission, is it not possible to make some nuanced distinction which acknowledges there is not always an absolute difference between the two but still avoids some of the bad consequences that McCormick fears? I have proposed that once the dying process begins the distinction between omission and commission ceases to be of decisive importance. More practically, the dying process can be identified as the time that extraordinary means could be discontinued as now being useless, since there is no hope of success in thus treating the patient. Is there that great a difference between turning off the respirator with the intention of allowing the person to die and positively interferring at the same time to bring about the same effect? The presumption is that in both cases the death of the person will follow certainly, inevitably, and with about the same degree of immediacy from either the act of omission or commission. In the vast majority of cases the two acts of omission and commission would not be the same regarding certainty, inevitability, and immediacy of the effect of death, and thus one avoids most of the dangers mentioned by McCormick. However, there is the difference that in the case of shutting off the respirator I am not the cause of the death in exactly the same way as in an act of commission, but the difference does not seem to constitute the basis for a different moral judgment where the conditions mentioned above are the same.

Utilitarianism, Teleology, and Consequentialism

Clarifications and Rejection of Utilitarianism

In the recent literature there has been a general tendency to point out the insufficiency of utilitarianism as a moral theory and to advocate other approaches as at least modifications of the utilitarian approach. The terms involved have been defined in different ways, but in the context of the utilitarian debate, utilitarianism, teleology, and consequentialism are generally understood as ethical theories which determine the moral rightness or wrongness of the act (or rule) solely on the basis of the consequences of the act (or rule). J. J. C. Smart maintains that the rightness or wrongness of an action depends only on the total goodness or badness of the consequences; i.e., on the effect of the action on the welfare of all human beings.[12]

In a critique of utilitarianism especially with the theory of Smart in mind, Bernard Williams devotes a large section of his monograph to the structure of consequentialism and emphasizes that the alternative to consequentialism does not involve the acceptance of the position that there are certain actions which one should do or never do whatever the consequences. Williams himself admits some circumstances in which direct killing of the innocent would be morally good. The denial of consequentialism only involves the admission that there would be some situations in which acts would be good even though the state of affairs produced by doing these acts would be worse than some other state of affairs accessible to the actor. In other words to oppose consequentialism it is necessary to hold that consequences are not the only morally relevant considerations; one does not have to affirm that it is always wrong to do acts no matter what the consequences.[13]

In the more recent debate authors who modify or reject utilitarianism such as Rawls and Lyons employ the word teleological in this same sense. Lyons states in the very beginning of his book that teleologists claim that the rightness of acts depends solely on their utility; whereas deontologists claim that rightness is not simply a function of utility.[14] Rawls insists that in teleological theory the good is defined independently of the right. In accord with this description Rawls maintains that if the distribution of the good is also counted as a good and perhaps a higher order one, we no longer have a teleological view in the classical sense.[15] Such an understanding of teleological is in accord with the position of William Frankena who defines teleology as the system in which the moral quality or value depends on the comparative nonmoral value of what is produced or brought about. Deontological theories, as opposed to teleological theories, affirm that there are at least other considerations which make an action or rule right or obligatory besides the goodness or badness of consequences. Frankena recognizes that deontologists can be of two types: either those for whom the principle of maximizing the balance of good over evil is not a moral criterion or those for whom such a principle is not the only basis or ultimate one.[16]

Objections to the theory of utilitarianism or teleology or consequentialism as proposed by Rawls, Frankena, Williams, and others in the contemporary debate are not based on the fact that these authors necessarily maintain that some actions are always right or wrong whatever the consequences. Rather, their objections to utilitarianism, teleology, or consequentialism may be summarized as follows: (1) Aspects other than consequences must be taken into account; (2) the good cannot be determined independently of the morally right; (3) not only the consequences of the action but also the way in which the actor brings about the consequences has moral significance. To refute utilitarianism, teleology, or consequentialism, these authors do not have to maintain that certain actions are right or wrong whatever the consequences, but they must accept that acts can be the right thing to do even though the state of affairs produced by acts would be worse than other states of affairs accessible to the actor.

A consideration of promise keeping which is often mentioned in the literature about the adequacy of utilitarian ethics illustrates well the differences between utilitarians and their opponents. The case is often proposed about a promise to a dying person on a desert isle to give this person's money to a jockey club. When the survivor comes back to civilization should he say the dying man wanted his money given to the jockey club or to a hospital which could do much more good for people? The utilitarian or consequentialist would judge only upon what would have the best consequences — giving the money to the jockey club or to a needy hospital. The consequentialist recognizes the importance of promise keeping in society and must consider this aspect, but in this case the presupposition is that no one knows about the promise. Since no one else knows about the promise, there would be no harm done to society if the maker of the promise did not keep it. Working on the supposition that the promisor is a good utilitarian, such a person would never feel guilty about now giving the money to the hospital.

The antiutilitarian argues that in addition to consequences there is an obligation of fidelity on the part of the promisor which must be taken into account. The antiutilitarian, together with the traditional textbooks of Catholic moral theology, acknowledges that promises are not always to be kept, for a change in the matter or the person might make the promise no longer obliging. The antiutilitarian argues here that the good consequences cannot be considered apart from the criterion of the right and something other than consequences (namely, the obligation of fidelity) must be taken into account. Likewise, the integrity of the person who made the promise is involved.

In the light of this understanding of utilitarianism, consequentialism, and teleology, the antiutilitarians attempt to show the inadequacy of utilitarianism in the following areas: questions of fidelity, gratitude, and punishment; questions of distribution involving justice and fairness; intentionality and integrity of the person. The antiutilitarian appeals to questions of fidelity, gratitude, and punishment because here there are sources of moral obligation other than the future consequences. In fidelity, moral obligation arises from the promise made in the past. In gratitude, moral obligation arises from the past act of generosity or beneficence. In punishment, moral obligation arises from the wrong act which the person did in the past. It is not necessary to assert that an absolute moral norm can be derived from these other sources of obligation, but at least it must be asserted that these sources of moral obligation must be considered as well as the future consequences. However, very often the utilitarian and the antiutilitarian conclusions will coincide.

Questions of distribution, justice, and fairness have frequently been proposed as problems for a utilitarian ethic. The only controlling moral criterion cannot be the net aggregate of good over evil achieved by the act, for one must also consider the distribution of the good. Rawls first proposed a form of rule-utilitarianism in his famous essay, "Two Concepts of Rules," as a means of strengthening the utilitarian view especially in matters of justice and promises. On the basis of that article Rawls was often wrongly called a rule-utilitarian, but he himself expressly indicted he was not proposing the rule-utilitarian position as completely defensible.[17] Later, in his *Theory of Justice,* Rawls indicates that utilitarianism needs to be modified by considerations of justice and fairness which call for a proper distribution of benefits and burdens, rights and duties. Rawls develops these principles of justice relating to the basic equality of all and to the way in which all inequalities in societies are to be arranged.

In this connection of justice, one can consider the frequently debated example of the sheriff who, to avoid a race riot in which many blacks would be killed in a southern town in the United States, frames and executes one innocent black person. Philosophers have been arguing about this case and now Catholic moral theologians, e.g., Connery and Schüller, have taken different sides of the argument. However, both in the philosophical literature and now in the theological literature it seems as if the exact force of the particular case is often overlooked by both sides. Some argue that if all the consequences are properly taken into account, then one could never accept judicial execution. However, a staunch act-utilitarian such as Smart recognizes the bite of this particular case. If no one knows an innocent person was framed, and the presupposition is that no one can find out about it, then there would be no harmful effects on the role of justice and criminal law in society if the innocent person were executed. Smart admits that it is logically possible for such a situation to exist and that the utilitarian must logically opt for the judicial murder in this case, but existentially he hopes the case would never happen.[18] Again the importance of the illustration shows what are the differences between the two approaches.

Another series of objections proposed against utilitarianism emphasizes the intentionality of the agent. The bottom-line consideration of the net good over the net evil is not the only factor to be considered — one must also consider how the good and evil were accomplished. There is a difference between effects or consequences that are merely foreseen by the agent and those that are intended by the agent. The way in which the agent brings about the effects is also important. The case of judicial murder also illustrates this problem as exemplified in the already-mentioned case of a foreigner who in a South American country comes upon a military captain who is about to kill innocent villagers. The point is that the foreigner is not the cause of the death of the others in the same way he would be the cause of the death of the one. An individual's actions and decisions flow from one's projects, but in this case the foreigner's action is determined by the project of the captain. It is absurd to demand that the foreigner leave aside his own deepest projects and decisions and base his actions only on the utilitarian calculus of the number of lives ultimately lost when this has been greatly determined by the project of another. Williams who proposes such a case leans toward doing the deed, but considerations other than consequences enter into the moral decision.[19]

Another Antiutilitarian Position

Within the body of recent literature specifically discussing utilitarianism, the antiutilitarian approach generally agrees with the position just expounded and does not directly appeal to or accept the principle that certain actions are right or wrong no matter what the consequences.[20] However, within the philosophical literature in general, if not in the utilitarian literature specifically, there is another form of the antiutilitarian approach which is based primarily on accepting such a principle.

G. E. M. Anscombe includes all modern moral philosophy under indictment for leaving open to debate whether such a procedure as judicial murder might not be the right one to adopt. Although some of the present Oxford moral philosophers think it permissible to make a principle never to do such a thing as judicial murder, Anscombe condemns them for proposing a philosophy according to which the consequences of such an action could morally be taken into account to determine if one should do such an action. Anscombe opposes such a theory because it is willing even to consider the possibility of exceptions based on consequences. She thus places all modern moral philosophy under the indictment of what she calls consequentalism. (One can thus see the terminological problem which exists in the philosophical literature.) Anscombe and her followers accept the principle that there are actions which are right or wrong whatever the consequences.[21] In subsequent literature the position defended by Anscombe and others has been called absolutist,[22] conservative,[23] and Catholic.[24] This position can properly be called Catholic (even though authors like Bennett reject the term) because it describes the position generally taken in the manuals of moral theology that certain actions are intrinsically wrong, e.g., contraception, sterilization, direct killing of the innocent, and can never be justified no matter how much good might result. Likewise, Catholic philosophers such as Anscombe and John Finnis defend this position.[25]

Concluding Clarifications

In conclusion, an overview of the philosophical literature indicates that there are three different positions, but terminology differs in describing these different opinions. The following descriptions will not agree with the terminology employed by many of the authors themselves, but it seems to be necessary to bring about needed clarifications. The first position is properly described as utilitarianism, strict teleology, or strict consequentialism. The third position, Anscombe et al., may be described as nonconsequentialism or even deontology — some actions are wrong no matter what the consequences. I will call the middle position a mixed consequentialism or mixed teleology. This middle position differs from strict teleology or strict consequentialism because it maintains the following three points: (1) moral obligation arises from elements other than consequences, (2) the good is not separate from the right; (3) the way in which the good or evil is achieved by the agent is a moral consideration. Since such an opinion does not necessarily hold that certain actions are always wrong no matter what the consequences, it has been called consequentialist by Anscombe. The good consequences are able to be determinative of the right and wrong of actions. The terminological confusion increases when one realizes that some proponents of this middle position can also properly be identified as deontologists; e.g., W. D. Ross who speaks about *prima facie* obligations. Ross acknowledges morality consists in such *prima facie* obligations but also recognizes the existence of conflicts in which the consideration of good consequences can be equally determinative of which obligations one must follow.[26]

Situating Catholic Moral Theology

Where does Catholic moral theology fit into such a schema? The moral theology of the manuals definitely belongs under the third position — the nonconsequentialist position which maintains that some actions are intrinsically wrong no matter what the consequences. (I realize that some contemporary theologians are trying to reinterpret what this meant, but at least there is no doubt that as generally understood the teaching of the manuals belongs under this category.)

In the 1960s some Roman Catholic moral theologians reacted in general and especially in the context of the debate over artifical contraception against what I have called physicalism — the tendency to indentify the moral act with the physical structure of the act. The physical is only one aspect of the human and the totality of the human cannot be identical with just this one aspect. Many authors refer to physical or premoral or ontic evil as distinguished from moral evil. In this light these theologians (rightly in my judgment) rejected the traditional teaching that contraception, sterilization, masturbation for seminal analysis, artificial insemination even with the husband's seed and the killing of the fetus to save the mother were always wrong. Beginning with Knauer an appeal was made to commensurate reason or proportionate reason to justify some of the actions which the manuals described as intrinsically wrong.[27] Schüller and others spoke of a teleological justification and a consequentialist calculus to determine if such actions were right or wrong.[28] Reforming Catholic theologians thus appealed to commensurate reason, proportionate reason, or the calculation of consequences to indicate that premoral evil could on some occasions be justified. Knauer also argued that one should not speak of the evil as being an effect with the act as its cause but rather spoke of the effects as an aspect of the act so that one might see here some similarity with the position maintaining there is no difference between effects which are foreseen and effects which are intended. In the light of the terminology and of some of the reasoning, the question arises if these Catholic authors are utilitarians or consequentialists in the strict sense.

Notice that early in the discussion within Roman Catholicism the debate centered almost exclusively on problems present in the Catholic theological tradition such as contraception and sterilization. The questions that were being discussed in the debate about utilitarianism such as promise keeping, fidelity, gratitude, justice, punishment, and integrity were not even discussed by the Catholic moral theologians. Once some of these questions such as the prohibition of direct killing of noncombatants or questions of judicial murder began to be discussed by the reforming Catholic ethicists, their understanding of consequentialism and teleology became clear. McCormick rightly insists on a difference between an intending and a permitting will.[29] Schüller recognizes that the consequences alone are not the only considerations and that consequences are always considered in the light of what is right.[30] Thus as the debate progressed it became quite evident that the reforming Catholic theologians generally speaking do not embrace utilitarianism or what Rawls, Frankena, Williams, and others have called teleology or consequentialism. In the schema proposed above, they fit into the middle category which can be described as mixed consequentialism.

Even in the general statement of their theories, it is clear that the reforming Catholic theologians do not belong to the first position of strict consequentialism or utilitarianism. Knauer himself insists on commensurate reason, and thus attributes some value to the physical act in relationship to the end which is sought. Fuchs gives attention to all three aspects of the human act — object, end, and circumstances.[31] Janssens sees a reciprocal causality existing between the material and the formal element of the human act so that the consequences alone are not determinative.[32] Milhaven requires an objective evaluation of the consequences in light of moral criteria.[33] Yes, there is a problem in terminology, but as the debate continued it became more evident that these Catholic authors do not embrace utilitarianism or strict consequentialism or strict teleology. Thus I disagree with the contention of John Connery that many of these Catholic authors are tending to consequentialism, which he understands in the strict sense.[34] In light of the three different positions explained above, most of the reforming authors in the Catholic tradition fit into the second position called mixed consequentialism, but perhaps this position should be described differently.

Clarifications and Relationality

Problems exist both in the philosophical literature and in the literature of Catholic moral theology about the exact meaning of the terms teleology and consequentialism. Teleology is generally contrasted with deontology, yet the second position described above as mixed consequentialism also includes people like Ross who are often classified as deontologists.

In my judgment at least part of the confusion arises from the fact that the difference between teleology and deontology can refer to two different realities in ethical discussion — the general model of the moral life and the more particular question of the establishment of moral norms or the criterion for decision making in concrete cases. When referring to the model of the ethical life, teleology refers to an approach which sees the moral life primarily in terms of goals and ends. In this view Aristotle and the manualists of moral theology are teleologists, as well as all utilitarians. Deontology understands the moral life primarily in terms of duties, obligations, and laws. Kant serves as an example of deontology, but Ross with his emphasis on *prima facie* obligations also fits under this category. From the viewpoint of theological ethics, Rudolf

Bultmann's insistence on morality as radical obedience also makes him a deontologist.[35] However, in terms of the more limited aspect of determining moral norms or the criterion of concrete obligations one could characterize these ethicists differently. Certainly Aristotle and some manualists of theology would not be characterized as determining moral norms on the basis of consequences and strict teleology. Ross has been classified as a consequentialist (at least by Anscombe). Bultmann is often described as a situationist. There is a difference between the level of ethical model and the level of the formulation of the ethical norms.

One of the unfortunate aspects of the debate about situation ethics and norms in the last decade has been that moral theology is often reduced to the one question of whether or not there is a law. Questions of attitudes, dispositions, ideals, values, goals, perspectives, and intentionalities have not received the attention they deserve in a complete consideration of moral theology. The ultimate model of the ethical life therefore should be broad enough to consider all the more specific questions and topics that form part of ethics and moral theology. Therefore both in practice and in theory one can legitimately distinguish between the level of the ethical model and the level of establishing norms or the criterion for decision making in specific cases.

On the level of ethical model I prefer to accept an ethical model of relationality and responsibility as a third model distinguished from both teleology and deontology. Such a model seems to be more in keeping with both theological and ethical data. Theology views the life of grace and the reality of sin primarily in terms of relationships as is evident in the concepts of covenant and love. In the perspective of Christian eschatology the individual does not have that much power and control over one's end and destiny. The cross and the paschal mystery remind us that our end or goal is not completely in our hands. We as Christians live in the hope that the evils and problems of the present can be transformed somewhat even now by the power of God and ultimately transformed into the fullness of life.

A phenomonological reflection on all human existence also seems to indicate that our lives are more understandable in terms of responding to the many happenings of human existence rather than adhering to a prearranged plan in search of our goal. Teleological and consequential models emphasizing only the goal or consequences obviously laid the foundation for a technological model of human existence, but technological progress can never be identified with truly human progress. Likewise an emphasis on consequences, goals, and ends very readily places all value in terms of what one does, makes, or accomplishes. The Christian approach does not seem to react in the same way, for there will always be a Christian bias in favor of those who do not accomplish or are not successful — the poor, weak, and the outcast. One might retort that the teleological model does not necessarily involve the kind of problems that I have described here, but even at its most refined understanding, the teleological model seems less apt than the relationality responsibility model of the ethical life of the Christian.[36]

On the level of the formulation of moral norms and the criteria for concrete decision-making I would opt for the second position described above as mixed consequentialism. The problem of terminology has already been pointed out since strict teleology is different from this position, and both teleologists and deontologists rightly fall into this category. Here again I am trying to develop a relationality approach as a third type distinct from both teleology and deontology, but this needs much greater development in my thought at the present time. At the very least it solves the terminological problem which now exists. Such a relational type has the advantage of including all the elements that should be considered and not reducing reality only to consequences or to duties. One might also argue that the relationality approach is not merely a middle approach between the other two but in a sense also opts for a somewhat different understanding of the moral decision-making process. Certainly it is not as rationalistic as the consequentialist approach. Likewise, it avoids the inflexibility that might often be associated with various aspects of the nonconsequentialist approach. By seeing all reality in terms of relationships one is less willing to absolutize any one aspect or one individual, since the individual by definition exists in multiple relationship with others; but the theory can still insist on the fundamental importance of the individual person. However, this approach obviously needs much further development.

Conflict Situations

In general one might say that the entire discussion deals with conflict situations — a point which is even more true when it is limited to the discussion of philosophical literature but which can also be verified in the literature of Catholic moral theology. In my judgment it is important to recognize that there are different sources of conflict situations. Specifically I propose four sources of conflict situations which Christian ethics can and should distinguish: (1) conflicts arising from the difference between the subjective and the objective aspects of human acts; (2) conflicts arising from creaturely finitude and limitation; (3) conflicts arising from eschatological tension; (4) conflicts arising from the presence of sin. In concluding this essay it is not possible to develop these different sources of conflicts at length, but a brief description will suffice. However, since my theory about the source of conflicts resulting from sin has often been misunderstood, some further clarification is necessary.[37]

Catholic moral theology traditionally recognized the distinction between the objective and the subjective aspects of the human act. An act might be objectively wrong but the individual is not subjectively guilty or responsible for it because of various impediments to a voluntary act. The manuals traditionally referred to the question of invincible ignorance of the obligation, but many contemporary authors rightly insist that the notion of invincible ignorance today must be seen in the perspective which emphasizes the existential totality of the human person so that invincible ignorance is a matter of the inability of the person to realize a moral obligation because of the situation in which one finds oneself. Moral philosophers recognize the same reality in the distinction between reasons which justify an act and reasons which excuse an act. Here the objective evaluation of the act is not changed, whereas in the other three types of conflict situations the objective evaluation of the act is changed.

The second source of conflict situations is human finitude and limitation. Here one finds most of the problems in which the physical aspect of the act has become absolutized, for different premoral values will often exist in conflict with one another so that one cannot be absolutized. Here too the principle of double effect has been employed to solve some conflict situations such as the birth room dilemma of mother or child. The third source of conflict situation arises from the tension between the eschatological fullness and the present. Since Catholic moral theology in the past was so heavily based on natural law and did not appeal to grace and eschatological realities as being morally obligatory for all, this type of conflict seldom arose. However, it is quite present in the situation of divorce which in my judgment cannot be an absolute prohibition. The fourth source of conflict situation is the presence of sinfulness. In response to the presence of sin I have developed a theory of compromise which in the light of subsequent debate needs to be properly understood.

The theory of compromise was never meant to apply to all conflict situations but only to those conflict situations in which sinfulness predominates. The problem of physicalism or what others call physical evil as distinguished from moral evil constitutes a distinct question. The conflict here most often arises from finitude and limitation either of time or space. As chapter 2 clearly shows, I do not appeal to compromise to solve the questions of contraception, sterilization, artificial insemination, many cases solved by double effect, etc. However, it was a mistake to use the term the "theory" of compromise as if it were primarily an ethical term, for it refers primarily to a theological reality — the source and the cause of the ethical conflict. The ultimate ethical solution of the conflict requires an ethical approach such as those discussed earlier. I would apply in these situations the second or mixed approach which I prefer to call a relational approach which involves weighing all the values involved.

From a theological perspective it is more accurate to distinguish the various sources of conflict even though in particular cases it might be difficult to discern if the conflict is due primarily to one or the other sources; e.g., finitude, sin, or the eschaton. Even in the ethical order there are important ramifications in distinguishing the conflicts arising from sinfulness. Sinfulness as the origin of conflict situations might be understood in three different ways — the universal sinfulness existing in the world which was the basis for Thomas Aquinas' teaching on the ownership of private property; the sinfulness incarnate in the human situation which in my judgment affects the person who is an irreversible homosexual; and the sinful actions of another person affecting my action as illustrated in the case of the captain threatening to shoot a large number of innocent villagers unless I shoot one of them myself.

Some philosophers claim that many of the examples proposed in the debate about consequentialism are rather bizarre.[38] To a certain extent this is true, but the bizarre character of the examples often comes from the fact that personal human sinfulness is present as in the South American example. The exceptions will be less and severely limited when it is a case of the personal sinfulness of another. Likewise the sinfulness of the social situation affects a limited number of people. Finitude affects all in a more comprehensive way than sin when it is not the universal sin of the world. The Christian must try to limit all evil, but evil resulting from finitude and limitation will always exist together with the human. Evil resulting from sin is somewhat different. Its presence does not come from the human condition as such, and the Christian has an obligation to try to overcome the effects of sin. However, in the imperfect world in which we live it is never possible to overcome all the effects of sin this side of the eschaton — sometimes one must accept the limitations of the sinful situation. This explains the theological concept of compromise because of which an act which in ordinary circumstances would be wrong for this person in the sinful situation is not wrong. But the exact determination weighing all the values involved depends upon ethical criteria.

This chapter has not attempted a complete discussion of the philosophical debates about utilitarianism but has considered only those aspects most instructive for the current considerations of Roman Catholic moral theologians. In the process it has been possible to clarify and perhaps advance the discussions within Roman Catholic ethics.

NOTES

1. J. J. C. Smart in J. J. C. Smart and Bernard Williams, *Utilitarianism: For and Against* (Cambridge: Cambridge University Press, 1973), p. 4.

2. J. B. Schneewind, "Introduction," in *Mill's Ethical Writings*, ed. J. B. Schneewind (New York, Collier Books, 1965), pp. 19, 20.

3. For an analysis of the present debate on the measurement of utility and for a comprehensive view of recent debates in utilitarianism, see Dan W. Brock, "Recent Work in Utilitarianism," *American Philosophical Quarterly* 10 (1973), 245-249.

4. *Contemporary Utilitarianism*, ed. Michael D. Bayles (Garden City, N.Y.: Doubleday Anchor Books, 1968).

5. J. O. Urmson, "The Interpretation of the Moral Philosophy of J. S. Mill," *The Philosophical Quarterly* 3 (1953), 33-39.

6. David Lyons, *Forms and Limits of Utilitarianism* (Oxford: Clarendon Press, 1965).

7. J. H. Sobel, "Rule-Utilitarianism," *Australasian Journal of Philosophy* 46 (1968), 146-165.

8. Brock, *American Philosophical Quarterly* 10 (1973), 261.

9. Richard A. McCormick, *Ambiguity in Moral Choice*, the 1973 Père Marquette Theology Lecture, Marquette University, 91ff.; McCormick, "The New Medicine and Morality," *Theology Digest* 21 (1973), 319ff.

10. Richard A. McCormick, "Notes on Moral Theology," *Theological Studies* 36 (1975), 98.

11. Williams, *Utilitarianism: For and Against*, p. 98.

12. Smart, *Utilitarianism: For and Against*, p. 4.

13. Williams, *Utilitarianism: For and Against*, pp. 82-93.

14. Lyons, *Forms and Limits of Utilitarianism*, p. xii.

15. John Rawls, *A Theory of Justice* (Cambridge, Mass.: Harvard University Press, 1971), p. 25.

16. William K. Frankena, *Ethics* (Englewood Cliffs, N.J.: Prentice Hall, 1973), pp. 13, 14. In the light of these definitions, it seems that what is often called ideal utilitarianism would not fall under this description of utilitarianism.

17. John Rawls, "Two Concepts of Rules," *The Philosophical Review* 64 (1955), 4.

18. Smart, *Utilitarianism: For and Against*, p. 72.

19. Williams, *Utilitarianism: For and Against*, pp. 108-118.

20. Brock, *American Philosophical Quarterly* 10 (1973), 261-269.

21. G. E. M. Anscombe, "Modern Moral Philosophy," *Philosophy* 33 (1958), 1-19.

22. Thomas Nagel, "War and Massacre," *Philosophy and Public Affairs* 1 (1972), 123-144.

23. Jonathan Bennett, "Whatever the Consequences," *Analysis* 26 (1965-66), 83-102.

24. R. W. Beardsmore, "Consequences and Moral Worth," *Analysis* 29 (1968-69), 177-186; R. G. Frey, "Some Aspects to the Doctrine of Double Effect," *Canadian Journal of Philosophy* 5 (1975), 259-283.

25. John Finnis, "Natural Law and Unnatural Acts," *Heythrop Journal* 11 (1970), 365-387; Finnis, "The Rights and Wrongs of Abortion," *Philosophy and Public Affairs* 2 (1973), 117-145.

26. W. D. Ross, *The Right and the Good* (Oxford: Clarendon Press, 1930); Ross, *The Foundations of Ethics* (Oxford: Clarendon Press, 1939).

27. P. Knauer, "La Détermination du bien et du mal moral par le principe du double effet," *Nouvelle Revue Théologique* 87

(1965), 356-376; Knauer, "Das rechtverstandene Prinzip von der Doppelwirkung als Grundnorm jeder Gewissensentscheidung," *Theologie und Glaube* 57 (1967), 107-133.

28. Bruno Schüller, "Zur Problematik allegemein verbindlicher ethischer Grundsätze," *Theologie und Philosophie* 45 (1970), 1-23; Schüller, "Typen ethischer Argumentation in der katholischen moral Theologie," *Theologie und Philosophie* 45 (1970), 526-550.

29. McCormick, *Ambiguity in Moral Choice*, pp. 72ff.

30. Bruno Schüller, "Neuere Beiträge zum Thema 'Begründung sittlicher Normen,'" *Theologische Berichte* 4, (Einsiedeln: Benziger, 1974), pp. 109-181.

31. Joseph Fuchs, "The Absoluteness of Moral Terms," *Gregorianum* 52 (1971), 445ff.

32. Louis Janssens, "Ontic Evil and Moral Evil," *Louvain Studies* 4 (1972), 123ff.

33. John Giles Milhaven, "Objective Moral Evaluation of Consequences," *Theological Studies* 32 (1971), 407-430.

34. John R. Connery, "Morality of Consequences: A Critical Appraisal," *Theological Studies* 34 (1973), 396-414. I do have one difficulty with many of these authors — the use of premoral evil to cover diverse realities which at best are only analogously related. For example, killing a person and contraception are not premoral evils in exactly the same way. Many people in society rightly see little or no premoral evil in contraception. Catholic authors tend to call contraception premoral evil because they want to maintain some continuity with the official teaching that contraception is morally evil. Why is contraception a premoral evil? The same is true of sterilization so that there is no practical moral difference in my judgment between direct or indirect sterilization. Also these authors must consider more questions of social ethics. Even here one might properly say, for example, that discrimination because of race, creed, or color is only a premoral evil which in extreme situations of compensatory justice to others in society might be morally overriden. One could also argue that in social ethics we are often dealing with formal and not material norms as in Rawls' concept of justice. However, these questions deserve greater attention.

35. Thomas C. Oden, *Radical Obedience: The Ethics of Rudolf Bultmann* (Philadelphia: Westminster Press, 1964).

36. For a further development of this model, see my *Catholic Moral Theology in Dialogue* (1972; reprint ed., Notre Dame, Ind.: University of Notre Dame Press, 1976), pp. 150-183.

37. These different conflict situations have been discussed in my other writings especially *Ongoing Revision: Studies in Moral Theology*, (Notre Dame, Ind.: Fides Publishers, 1976).

38. E.g., Anscombe, "Modern Moral Philosophy," p. 13.

6: Sin

Does sin have any meaning for modern people? Is sin a vital reality for the twentieth century Christian? Maybe the sense of sin was just a morbid concept from the Middle Ages which people come of age have rightly put behind themselves.

There is a reluctance on the part of all of us to admit our sinfulness, but it seems that sin still retains an importance in contemporary human experience. Technology and science have given us an awesome power over creation; knowledge has been increasing at an ever growing rate; we are continually finding out more about ourselves and our world. But sinfulness also marks the lives of individual human beings and of society. In times of great scientific strides and progress we human beings tend to forget our own limitations and sinfulness, but a meditative reflection on reality cannot help but uncover even in our modern world the existence and importance of sin.

Sin can simply be described for the present as a lack of love and an alienation from God and others. If we are honest with ourselves, we have to admit our own sinfulness. Our own selfishness and unwillingness to go out of our way to help others are factors we cannot forget as much as we might like to. Are we willing to share what we have with the poor? Are we willing to embrace the outcast and the forgotten? Are we primarily motivated by the demands of our neighbor in need or rather by our own selfish needs? Are we really willing to change the established structures of our society in which we hold privileged positions at the expense of others? If sin is the opposite of love, then there is quite a bit of sin in our lives, despite the fact that we become uncomfortable when we think about it.

But sin is not just an individual phenomenon. Sin shows its effects in our society as a whole and perhaps is most present in the fact that many of us are unwilling to admit our own sinfulness. A few years ago the death of God theology and the secular city theology tended to downplay the reality of sin. Charles West of Princeton Theological Seminary has described the two opposing viewpoints at the 1966 Conference on Church and Society sponsored by the World Council of Churches as the "theological technocrats" versus the "theological guerrillas."[1] The theological technocrats were those who celebrated the joys of the secular city in which human beings are becoming progressively more whole and more free. However, their opponents pointed out that while these people were finding salvation and freedom in the secular city, this same secular city society was imprisoning two-thirds of the world in hunger, misery and poverty. Today we can be thankful for the protest movements that have reminded us of the sins that are existing in our society. We must acknowledge that our sins both individually and collectively have been hurting many others.

How easy it is to forget our own sinfulness while at the same time condemning the sinfulness of others. A few years ago there was a television documentary on the Hitler regime in Germany. The final portion of the film showed the last days of the Third Reich and portrayed Hitler as a megalomaniac whose distorted pride and fury made him keep fighting to the bitter end despite all the human death and suffering caused by him. However, never once did the film even suggest that part of the responsibility might have been ours. What right did we as Christians have to demand an unconditional surrender? Perhaps we were just as responsible as Hitler in prolonging the carnage of war. Some years ago the Sunday Magazine section of the *New York Times* had an article on the end of the hippie movement which was called "The Death of Love." The hippie community was an attempt to have people live together in the bonds of love, but the experiment was unsuccessful precisely because people forgot the existence of sin. Sin ultimately entered the hippie community in the form of drugs, taking advantage of others, self-promotion and feuds. How often today many overly romantic people fail to realize the existence of sin in the world! On the surface it might seem that we have outgrown the reality of sin, but a moment's reflection reminds us of the existence of sin in our own lives and in our own world. Unfortunately, sin is alive and well in the twentieth century.

The Christian message has always realized the importance of sin; in fact, the Christian mystery does not make sense apart from the reality of sin. "It was a fundamental assertion of the kerygma that Jesus came into the world to save sinners, and that he in fact did so by his death."[2] According to the Matthean account (1:21) he was called Jesus precisely because he would save his people from their sins. The redemptive work of Jesus has meaning only in terms of sin; the Paschal Mystery is ultimately the triumph over sin and death. Although his death showed forth the power of sin and the separation between sin and Jesus, the resurrection was the sign and promise of victory. The gospel message clearly sees the mission of Jesus in terms of redemption and victory over sin. The early Church was aware of its call to continue this mission and free people from sin and bring them into the newness of life in Christ. Christian anthropology recognizes the limited and sinful nature of human beings; in fact, anthropology which does not give sufficient attention to sinfulness cannot claim to be Christian.[3]

Despite the importance of sin in the Christian message, Catholic theology has been negligent in developing an adequate understanding of sin. Too often sin has been considered only in terms of the model of law and obedience which emphasizes sin as a specific external action. These actions were then thoroughly categorized and catalogued in lists. Sin as an external action viewed in the light of obedience to the law of God is a very inadequate model for understanding the reality of sin. A mechanical, individualistic, and actualistic concept of sin robbed sin of its real existential meaning for the Christian. Perhaps it is true that the world has lost the sense of sin, but even more unfortunate is the fact that Catholic Christians have lost a true understanding of sin.

A renewed understanding of sin should find its basic inspiration in the Scriptures but also make use of the insights of contemporary understandings of anthropology.[4] Both Scripture and contemporary understandings argue for a view of sin that follows the model of relationality. The individual person is a creature living in a multiplicity of relationships, sin is that which destroys these relationships. Perhaps the best illustration of the meaning of sin in the Scriptures is the account given in the first chapters of the book of Genesis. Modern scripture studies remind us that the Genesis account is not an historical account of two people but rather a reflective meditation many years later on the reality of sin. The authors of Genesis faced the basic problem that confronts all who believe in a good and gracious God. If the good God made all things, why is there so much evil in the world? Their answer? Sin. The Judaeo-Christian message makes no sense without an understanding of sin, and the authors here narrate in a very fanciful way their understanding of sin. Contemporary theologians can only marvel at the insight of the authors of Genesis.[5]

The convenant relationship characterizes the whole of the scriptural understanding of the relationship between God and his people. The story of salvation is the story of God's loving choice of a people as his own. Sin is the refusal of creatures to accept the gift of God's love. Although creatures spurned this gift, God is so faithful in his commitment that he sent his Son to restore the relationship of love and offer all human beings an opportunity to enter into his covenant relationship. The Christian believes that all people receive this same invitation in one way or another from God. Thus in Genesis sin is viewed not primarily as a particular external act or even as a particular act of disobedience seen in itself (these are aspects of the reality of sin but not the primary aspect), but rather as the refusal of human beings to accept their relationship of loving dependence on God. Creatures wanted to be like God — this was the temptation which was proposed by the evil one.

The fact that sin is to be seen in terms of a relationship is more evident in other details of this story. The author implies that God came down and walked with Adam and Eve in the evening in the cool of the garden — a very fanciful way of picturing the relationship of love between them. As a consequence of sin, however, Adam and Eve hid themselves when Yahweh came to walk with them in the garden. As a result of their sin Adam and Eve were expelled from the garden, a sign they had truly broken their relationship of loving dependence on God. Death, according to Genesis, is the penalty of sin; but such a penalty cannot be conceived as merely an arbitrary punishment for wrongdoing. Since sin itself is separation from the author of life, then death is the natural consequence of sin and not just an extrinsic penalty or punishment.

But sin also affects one's relationship with fellow creatures. Genesis is lyrical in its description of the love union of Adam and Eve. Eve is the helpmate and companion that Adam was not able to find in the rest of creation; she is flesh of his flesh and bone of his bone. The love union of the two is described by the fact that they left all other persons and things to become one body. But sin deeply affected that union of love, as is portrayed in Adam's reaction to Yahweh after his sin. Adam, instead of defending and protecting his wife with whom he formed one body, now placed the blame on her — "It was the woman you put with me; she gave me the fruit, and I ate it" (Genesis 3:12). The very next chapter describes how the children of Adam and Eve killed one another. The author graphically makes his point: sin affects the relationships existing among human beings.

The Genesis narrative develops its meditative reflection on sin by illustrating that sin also affects our relationship with the world. Before the "fall," Adam is portrayed as the king of all creation which exists in perfect subordination to him as is evidenced by the fact that Adam gave a name to all the animals. Sin brings discord into this marvelous harmony of the world. In that which is most characteristically masculine, man's relationship with the cosmos is changed through sin. From henceforth he will know suffering, sweat, and fatigue as he tries to work the fields to provide for his needs and those of his family. The remarkable harmony in which the world would have been as putty in his hands is shattered so that man will now know pain and suffering in work as he tries to eke out his existence against the forces of the world rather than in harmony with them. Sin's effect on our relationship to the world is also graphically illustrated in the case of Eve, for she is affected in that which (in the mentality of the author) is most characteristically womanly — the bearing of children. As a result of sin she would now know the pains of childbirth and bring forth her children in pain and suffering. Thus the membranes of her own body would resist the process of childbirth and cause her pain rather than exist in perfect harmony with the birth process. One can only admire the theological acumen and literary genius which thus presents the reality of sin as affecting our relationship to God, neighbor and the total cosmos.

The opening eleven chapters of Genesis and much of the Old Testament underline the dynamic aspect of sin especially in its cosmic dimension. In the last few years Catholic theology and catechetics have emphasized the concept of salvation history, but the opening chapters of Genesis are truly a history of sin. Human beings continue to fall into sin which then by incarnating itself in society and structures tends to grow and increase. The Old Testament frequently recalls the many saving interventions of God (e.g., Noah, Abraham, Moses, etc.); but despite all these saving interventions, the people fall back into the condition of sin. The Old Testament was very conscious of the cosmic aspect of sin which has been emphasized in the concept of the sin of the world developed by some contemporary theologians.[6] Sin affects the individual and incarnates itself in the structures, customs and institutions of our environment, and thus the reign of sin grows and increases. In such an environment other individuals easily become contaminated by sin. There are many ways in which one can view the reality of sin, e.g., disobedience to the divine commands; but the model of multiple relationships from the viewpoint of the Scriptures and the best insights of contemporary anthropology appears to be the most adequate.

In the Christian understanding, salvation or redemption is the gracious act of God freeing human beings from sin and restoring them to the relationship of love. Catholic theology has always required the free acceptance of this gift of God's love which involves a change of heart and entrance into a relationship of love with the Father through Christ Jesus, which affects all the relationships which constitute the person. This gift of salvation, which some theologians today call wholeness, is offered in one form or another to all persons; but for the Christian it is made explicit in the gospel message preached by the Church, which continues the mission of Jesus in time and space. Does the Christian ever overcome the sinful condition? The answer is yes and no. Traditional Catholic theology understands that when the individual accepts the gracious gift of salvation he or she has now overcome the radical separation from God and neighbor, but every human being in this world falls short of the fullness of love in relationships with God and neighbor. In this sense the Christian is at the same time justified and a sinner (*simul justus et peccator*). Thus conversion, justification, or salvation (whatever term is chosen to describe this reality) is never perfect but always striving for a greater wholeness. Also there is the possibility that one might entirely break off that relationship of love with God and neighbor and thus again separate oneself in sinful isolation. Human sinfulness and sin occupy an important place in the Christian understanding of reality, so that if one does not know or experience the reality of sin and sinfulness then the concept of conversion or penance is meaningless.

The above description corresponds to the traditional concept of mortal and venial sin, but the distinction is not viewed primarily in terms of a particular action. Mortal sin from the scriptural viewpoint is better interpreted in terms of a relationship which affects not only the individual's relationship with God but also the relationship with one's neighbors and the whole world, thus affecting the very core of the person. According to the Scriptures conversion is the process of passing from death to life, from darkness to light, from the old to the new, from flesh to the spirit, a change of heart animated by the gift of the life-giving Spirit.[7] Mortal sin is the opposite of this process and is described in the older categories as the passing from the state of grace to the state of sin.

Contemporary theologians with this scriptural basis and borrowing insights from various philosophical viewpoints have lately described sin in terms of a fundamental option.[8] From a Thomistic viewpoint mortal sin is seen as the orientation of the person away from God as one's last end with the substitution of another ultimate end, which in the last analysis is oneself. From an existentialist perspective, mortal sin is the project of existence which overturns the foundational orientation and tendency of the life of the person. From a personalist understanding, sin is the breaking of the relationship of love with God and neighbor. All these different viewpoints emphasize the fact that mortal sin is not just an external action viewed in itself but rather a fundamental orientation of the person, a notion which corresponds with the biblical concept of a change of heart.

In the past moral theology distorted the concept of mortal sin by understanding sin primarily in terms of an external act, thereby viewing sin more as a thing than as a relationship. Catechisms and textbooks frequently classi-fied the catalogues of actions which were mortal sins. Thus sin lost its intensely personal meaning, to say nothing of its social and cosmic dimension. If mortal sin is viewed as just an external act, then the existence of mortal sin appears to be much more frequent than in the concept of a relation-ship.

A more relational understanding of sin especially as specified in the theory of the fundamental option gives less importance to the external action itself. The external act in such a theory is essentially ambiguous, for it has meaning only insofar as it is revelatory of the human per-son and the person's relationships with others. Common sense and prudence have always accepted the reality that you cannot judge a person on the basis of just one short meeting or in the light of one particular action. One can-not judge the ability of an athlete by just seeing the results of one particular action. The sharp word that a person utters may have a variety of meanings. It could very well indicate an intense dislike for the person with whom one is talking, or it might only be indicative of impatience, a migraine headache or the failure to have had a second cup of coffee. Modern psychology also emphasizes the ambigu-ity of the external act. The full personal meaning of a particular act very often can never be truly known, for even the individual is not always that conscious of his per-sonal motives. A particular act would involve mortal sin only if the act were expressive of this breaking of a funda-mental relationship of love with God and neighbor.

Catholic theology has long recognized that the individ-ual goes from "sin" to "grace" not by one action but by a long series of actions which form one process. Mortal sin must now be viewed in the same way. One does not change so fundamental a relationship just in one particular action, but ordinarily there is a process taking place over a period of time in which this relationship gradually becomes weakened and then is finally broken. This process must ultimately culminate in an action which involves the very existential core of the person and such actions are not frequent in our lives. In such an understanding it is impossible for a person to be in and out of mortal sin two or three times a week. The poor approach of the past has cheapened the very notion and concept of mortal sin which as a consequence has lost real meaning for many Catholics today. Mortal sin is not a common occurrence, and is generally the culmination of a development lasting over a period of time. Again, personal experience reminds us how difficult and hard it is for us to change some of our basic human orientations. This experience in our relationships with others and with ourselves should reveal some understanding of the reality of our relationship with God.

The stress on the external act in the past definitely distorted the concept of mortal sin. In fairness even to the catechism requirements for mortal sin, it must be pointed out that they included other criteria in addition to the act itself. The threefold criteria for the existence of mortal sin included: grave matter, full knowledge, and full consent of the will. These three conditions if properly understood call for an almost total reaction from the depth of the person, a truly fundamental option or orientation. Unfortunately, theology and catechetics gave primary importance to the matter itself as the ultimate determining criterion of the existence of mortal sin. Such a concept even led to the conclusion that certain actions always involve grave matter.[9] The theory behind this insistence on the matter of the external action itself in its best possible interpretation was the presumption that grave or important matter will ordinarily involve the person in the very core of his or her existence, whereas light matter will ordinarily not evoke a total response on the part of the person. Today our knowledge of human beings and human relationships is such that it is difficult to place much importance on such presumptions especially because we now appreciate the difficulty involved in saying that any one action expresses the very depths of the person. Once sin is viewed in terms of the fundamental relationship between the person and God which consists primarily in a basic orientation and not in individual actions, then even the presumptive nature of the older approach no longer retains great value or usefulness.

What then are the criteria for establishing the existence of mortal sin? In actuality there are no certain criteria by which one can establish the existence of mortal sin. Perhaps the best approach remains that found in the Scriptures. Our relationship with God is known and manifested in our relationship with our neighbors. This is the gist of the so-called judgment scene in Matthew. "Lord, when did we see you hungry or thirsty, a stranger or naked, sick or in prison, and did not come to your help?" (Matt. 25:44). John reminds us that we cannot love the God we do not see if we do not love our neighbor whom we do see. The Christian commandment joins together love of God and love of neighbor into a unity so that the best criterion of our love for God is precisely our love for our neighbor, but even this criterion fails to be very specific and remains difficult to apply accurately, again because of the essential ambiguity of the external act. It always remains difficult to tell if one has broken this multiple relationship of love. Even the individual person in many cases cannot be aware of it in any reflexive way because of the very nature of this relationship and because of the difficulties of totally understanding one's own motives.

Some theologians conscious of the ambiguity of the external action viewed apart from the orientation of the person have tended to introduce other distinctions in the understanding of sin. For example, a threefold distinction is made: Mortal sin, serious sin, venial sin. Mortal sin is reserved for that which really separates us from love;

whereas serious sin is an action viewed in itself which is of serious nature but by itself cannot indicate whether the relationship of love is broken or not.[10] Another theologian introduces such distinctions as sin, mortal sin, serious sin, subjectively non-serious sin, venial sin, light sin, subjectively no imputation of sin.[11] I do not believe that such distinctions are necessary or ultimately even that helpful from a theological or catechetical viewpoint. At best they tend to be only presumptions, and the danger always exists of making them into rigid categories. While such elaborate distinctions serve as a salutary reminder of the complexity and ambiguity of the reality of sin, they remain only approximations which tend in a somewhat simplistic way to analyze the relationship between God and his creatures. It seems to be better to retain just the concepts of mortal sin and venial sin with the realization that mortal sin is the breaking of this multiple love relationship and thus involves a core decision of the whole person, whereas venial sin refers to the lessening of the relationship without involving a total break in that relationship. Naturally there are many degrees involved in the way in which this relationship can be affected without being severed.

However, there is a possible danger of dualism in the approach which sees sin primarily in terms of this fundamental relationship or option which involves one in the very core of one's being. In the past there was an overemphasis on the external act itself, but in the newer perspective there is the danger of not giving enough importance to the external act itself. Mortal sin should be viewed primarily in terms of intentionality, subjective involvement, and personalist categories; but there remains the danger of forgetting about the external act itself. Catholic theology in the last decade has embraced the more personalist categories of thought, but there is an inherent danger that such thought patterns will not pay enough attention to the social, political, and cosmic aspects of reality. The problems facing the world today are of such social complexity that a narrowly personalist approach will not be able to cope with them.[12] The human act remains a very complex entity. In theology most problems arise not from positive error but from a failure to give the proper weight to all the elements involved.

The notion of mortal sin described above views the individual act insofar as it is an expression of the whole person existing in his fundamental relationships with God and neighbor. However, the complex external act can be viewed from other aspects; for example, one can consider the external act insofar as it affects the persons and the world itself independently of the personal intentionality and involvement of the person placing the act. When a deranged person maims another, there is very little subjective involvement of the core of personhood in such an act, but such an action does have very drastic consequences on the unfortunate victim and on society itself. A highly scientific and technological society (which, however, is not to be canonized) appreciates the importance of the external act, as does a theology which sees the Christian as called to help create the new heaven and the new earth by one's own actions. If one is going to reserve the word sin for the fundamental option of love, then perhaps it would be helpful to speak of the external act viewed in relationship to self, others and the cosmos apart from the intentionality of the person in terms of right or wrong. Thus one could say that certain actions (cruelty, indiscriminate warfare, etc.) are wrong without necessarily involving grave sin on the part of the person.

An older Catholic theology did appreciate the problem by making the distinction between formal and material sin. Formal sin was precisely the external act insofar as it proceeded from the knowledge and will of the subject, whereas material sin was the act viewed in itself apart from the subjective involvement of the person in the act. One could even employ the term sin in a true but analogous way to describe the external act viewed in terms of its "objective" relationships, but perhaps the need to emphasize the reality of sin as the deeply personal orientation of one's life in terms of the primary relationships which constitute that existence would argue against using the term sin to describe this other aspect of the external act. No matter what terminology is chosen, an understanding of sin in terms of relationality and the fundamental option must avoid the danger of not paying sufficient attention to the external action viewed in its relationships to self, others, and the world apart from the intentionality of the agent. This problem in the understanding of sin points to the deeper philosophical problem involving a proper understanding of the relationship between subjective and objective. Theology today is striving to overcome a false dichotomy, but at times some distinctions such as those made above will be necessary.

Thus a better approach views mortal sin in terms of personal relationships, the involvement of the subject in one's own orientation, and a process which gradually develops over the course of time. Such an understanding of sin has important practical and pastoral consequences. In practice one cannot speak of the act viewed in itself as mortal sin. There is no possible answer to the question: Is killing or lying or adultery or blasphemy a mortal sin? (It would be a legitimate question to ask if such an action were right or wrong.) In fact one cannot even have mortal sins. The plural form indicates that sin would be a thing, but if mortal sin is properly understood in terms of a broken relationship of love then it does not admit the plural usage. There are no definite criteria for determining the existence of mortal sin precisely because of the essential ambiguity of the external act. Mortal sin seen as the culmination of a gradual process resulting in the breaking of these fundamental relationships is obviously a rare occurrence in comparison with an older understanding of mortal sin.

The reality behind the concept of venial sin must also be viewed in terms of a condition of the person and that person's fundamental relationships with God, neighbor, and the world. Catholic teaching has maintained that the ordinary Christian cannot avoid the reality of venial sin in one's life. This is another way of saying that the Christian always remains, *simul justus et peccator* (justified and a sinner at the same time), for the relationship of love with God, neighbor, and the world is never perfect. The individual act of venial sin refers to an action which does not come from a core personal involvement in an orientation away from God but rather is expressive of a coolness or lack of full dedication in this relationship of love. In the theory of the fundamental option venial sin remains a peripheral action which does not involve the core decision of the person. In the Thomistic perspective venial sin involves an illogical act because while the person in the core of his being is still united to God as ultimate end, this particular act is contrary to that orientation. However, the act remains on the periphery of the self and does not change the reality of one's orientation to God as ultimate end. Venial sin illustrates the condition of the Christian who constantly falls short of the total love union with God, neighbor and the world to which all are called. An emphasis in the past on particular acts has tended to see venial sin primarily in terms of particular acts of commission, whereas the realization of the sinful condition of the person opens up the wider horizons of the human condition itself and also acts of omission as well as commission.

New approaches in moral theology have been criticized by some for doing away with the concept of sin; in fact, people have applied to some contemporary theologians the scriptural words: "Behold the one who takes away the sins of the world." There is no doubt that an older theology and catechetics tended to develop a very warped notion of sin in the minds of many. The danger remains that in rejecting such inadequate notions the contemporary Catholic is at times tempted to forget the whole concept of sin. But the Christian message is robbed of its true meaning if one does not appreciate the reality of human sinfulness.

The loving gift of God in Christ to all of us presupposes the sinful condition of all in which we would be imprisoned without the gracious gift of God's redeeming love. No one can appreciate the great gift of God's love without an understanding of the reality of sin from which we have been freed by his gracious mercy and forgiveness. Mortal sin is a comparatively very rare occurrence in the Christian life, but this should only emphasize its importance and its true meaning as the breaking of our multiple relationships of love with God, neighbor and the world. The contemporary Christian also needs to be more conscious of our enduring, sinful condition — the fact that even though we are united in love with God and neighbor, nevertheless, we constantly fall short of the love that is asked of us. Superficial thinking at times does tend to forget the reality of sin. The history of theology furnishes many examples of theologies which have forgotten the existence of sin and its impact on our existence. The naive hopes of utopian dreams have been dashed against the reality of human sinfulness. Despite all the progress of science and technology we have not been able to overcome the basic human problems of selfishness, exploitation, self-interest, and the failure to accept responsibility for the neighbor in need. Many Catholics today have passed from a triumphalism of the Church to a triumphalism of the world. We are now very much aware of the sinfulness of the Church and the fact that a pilgrim Church is constantly in need of reform and renewal, but frequently we forget the reality of sin existing in the world itself with the suffering, hardship and frustration which that will entail. The perennial danger is to be lulled into forgetting the existence of sin. Then one's whole life and one's Christianity can become very comfortable. Is this not the problem with much of what passes for Christianity today?

The contemporary Christian needs to become more aware of the reality of sin — not in a morbid and scrupulous way, but in a manner that enables one to appreciate more the reality of God's loving gift, to understand the continuing failure to respond totally to that gift, and to encourage the individual Christian to join with the Risen

Lord in the struggle against sin. Catholic theology has explained the sacramental system in terms of the extension of the Incarnation in time and space. The love of God for us and our response become visible in the sacramental celebration. The reality of sin also becomes incarnated in time and space through the actions of human beings in the world, so that there are truly "sacraments of sin" — signs which make present the reality of sin in our human existence. Poverty, war, discrimination, alienation, sexism, institutional violence — these are all among the many sacraments of sin existing in our world.

How easy it remains for the contemporary Christian to forget the existence of sin, but a thoughtful reflection on human existence today in the light of the scriptural message of love of God and neighbor, especially the neighbor in need, reveals the continuing presence of sin in our life and world. Since Christianity so joins together the love of God and neighbor that the love for neighbor becomes the sign and criterion for our love for God, so too our sinful condition is manifested above all in our relationships with our neighbor and the world. The inequities of our world, the fact that the rich people and nations exploit poor people and nations, the will for power and the subjection of the weak and the failure of people to accept their responsibilities for the world and others are all signs of the reality of sin. The social, political, cultural, economic, and even religious aspects of our human existence all contain elements that show forth the failure of Christians to live the gospel message of love of God and neighbor. Through the eyes of faith the conscientious Christian sees the sacraments of sin in our world. Just as the sacraments celebrate the loving gift of God to us so too the sacraments of sin constantly remind us of the reality of our failures to love. How can the Christian be complacent and uninvolved in the presence of sin in our lives and our world?

In the neo-Orthodox phase of Protestantism, sin was emphasized as reminding the individual Christian of boundaries and limitations so that one became more conscious of the need for God's merciful love. In the last few years, as exemplified to an extreme in the "death of God" theology, Protestant theology has stressed not the imperfections and the limitations of human beings but especially human power and responsibility. People come of age now must take responsibility for the shaping of their earthy existence. Today there seems to be a tendency to realize that the thinking of the last few years might have been too naively optimistic. A balanced theological perspective should keep in view both the aspect of sin as it points up our continuing need for God's loving mercy and also our redeemed vocation to take responsibility and struggle against the forces of sin in our lives and in the world. (Remember that this gift of redemption is offered to all human beings.) A proper understanding of sin is necessary for the contemporary Christian to appreciate the gift of God in Christ by which we have been saved from sin and death, for redemption is meaningless unless we can appreciate the gratuitous, loving gift of our redemption. The Christian message sees the reality of sin as manifesting itself primarily in the very death of Jesus who died because of the power of sin and death. Sin is so important an aspect of human existence and so strong that it brought about the death of Jesus, but his death and resurrection also marked the triumph and victory over sin and death.

The Christian now allied through baptism with the Paschal Mystery of Jesus is called to overcome sin and death in daily life and in the world through the same life-giving love whose greatest sacrament remains the Paschal Mystery of Jesus. Sin still exists in our world and always will exist until the end of time, but the Christian cannot merely sit back and be content in the presence of sin. The Christian is called to cooperate in the redemptive work of Jesus in overcoming the forces of sin and death in one's life and in the world. This will be a continual struggle which will never completely be successful and which will end in death, but a death which is also a share in the victory of Jesus over sin and death itself. To forget the reality of sinfulness is to forget a very indispensable part of the Christian mystery. Only one who is conscious of sin and sinfulness can appreciate the greatness of the gift of redemption and the Christian vocation to struggle against and ultimately triumph over the reality of sin through a self-giving love which gives even unto death.

NOTES

1. Charles West employed this description in a paper read at the 1967 meeting of the American Society of Christian ethics.

2. Jerome Murphy-O'Connor, O.P., "Sin and Community in the New Testament," in *Sin and Repentance,* ed. Denis O'Callaghan (Staten Island: Alba House, 1967), p. 18.

3. Roger Lincoln Shinn, *Man: The New Humanism* (Philadelphia: Westminster Press, 1968), pp. 145-164.

4. Ph. Delhaye et al., *Théologie du péché* (Tournai: Desclée et Cie, 1960), which has been published in English by Desclée in a number of small volumes, the most important of which is Albert Gelin and Albert Descamps, *Sin in the Bible* (New York: Desclée, 1965). *Il Peccato,* ed. Pietro Palazzini (Rome: Edizioni Ares, 1959), a 928-page volume which has appeared in English in three smaller volumes published by Scepter.

5. Stanislaus Lyonnet, S.J., *De Peccato et Redemptione,* vol. 1 (Rome: Pontifical Biblical Institute, 1957).

6. Piet Schoonenberg, S.J., *Man and Sin* (Notre Dame, Ind.: University of Notre Dame Press, 1965), pp. 98-123.

7. Bernard Häring, C.SS.R., "Conversion," in *Pastoral Treatment of Sin* (New York: Desclée, 1968), pp. 87-176.

8. John W. Glazer, S.J., "Transition Between Grace and Sin: Fresh Perspectives," *Theological Studies* 29 (1968), 260-274, summarizes some of the recent literature on the fundamental option especially from a more existentialist viewpoint. Other articles on the subject with appropriate bibliographies include: M. Flick, S.J., and Z. Alszeghy, S.J., "L'opzione fondamentale della vita morale e la grazia," *Gregorianum* 41 (1960), 593-619; Pierre Fransen, S.J., "Toward a Psychology of Divine Grace," *Lumen Vitae* 12 (1957), 203-232. The approach adopted in this study tries to do justice

at one and the same time to the subjectivity of the individual person and one's relationships with God, neighbor, and the world. The core decision or option of the human person is seen primarily in terms of these multiple relationships. The denial or lack of emphasis on transcendence in some contemporary theological writing tends to over-emphasize the relationship to neighbor and the world at the expense of the person's relationship to God. It is true that an older theology pretended to know too much about this relationship, but a theological vision of the human must always consider this most important aspect of human existence and unceasingly try to give a better understanding and appreciation of it. For a somewhat "updated traditional Thomistic" approach to the question, see F. Bourassa, S.I., "Le Péché Offense de Dieu," *Gregorianum* 49 (1968), 563-574.

9. Anton Meinrad Meier, *Das Peccatum Mortale ex Toto Genere Suo: Entstehung und Interpretation des Begriffes* (Regensburg: Verlag Friedrich Pustet, 1966).

10. F. J. Heggen, *Confession and the Service of Penance* (Notre Dame, Ind.: University of Notre Dame Press, 1968), pp. 70-77.

11. Kevin F. O'Shea, "The Reality of Sin: A Theological and Pastoral Critique," *Theological Studies* 29 (1968), 241-259.

12. Johannes B. Metz, "The Church's Social Function in the Light of a Political Theology," *Concilium* 36 (June 1968), 2-18. Metz incorporates this article and others developing the same theme in his book *Theology of the World* (New York: Herder and Herder, 1969).

7: Sin and Sexuality

The Roman Catholic theology of sexuality has been frequently criticized in the past because it was too negative and gave an undue importance to sexuality. In the last few years the renewal in moral theology has stressed the primacy of love and service of the neighbor and not sexuality as the hallmark of Christian life. An appreciation of human sexuality based on the theology of creation, incarnation and bodily resurrection at the end of time has replaced the antimaterial and antisexual prejudices of an older theology. A total Christian view of sexuality also sees the limitations of human sexuality; the imperfections involved in time and space, the fact that sexuality is just one aspect of human life, and the reality of human sinfulness which affects sexuality and all human life.[1]

However, there remain many questions about sexual ethics. One very important obstacle in the attempt to arrive at a more balanced view of human sexuality and its role in the life of the Christian is the teaching that all sins against sexuality involve grave matter. Is that statement true? What was the reasoning process that led to such a conclusion? Will a changed understanding of the gravity of sins against chastity change any of our other teaching on sins against sexuality? This essay will attempt to explain the older approach in Catholic theology to sins against chastity and their gravity. The older approach will be criticized, and then the final section will survey some general and particular guidelines for an understanding of sins against sexuality in contemporary Catholic moral theology. There remain many other even more important aspects of human sexuality which Catholic theology must consider, but first of all it is necessary to show the inadequacies in the older way of understanding sins against sexuality and their gravity and to point out newer approaches.

I. The Older Teaching and its Development

In general, Catholic moral theology has approached the question of sexuality in the light of a natural law methodology. Such a methodology recognizes that there exists a source of ethical wisdom and knowledge apart from the explicit revelation of God in the Scriptures. Whereas individual texts from the Scriptures were used by the theologians in pointing out the malice of certain actions, Catholic theology realized the insufficiency of the revealed Scriptures for furnishing a complete and adequate understanding of the way in which the Christian should view human sexuality. Natural law methodology as such does not necessarily imply the existence of any absolute norms. Since natural law in its best understanding is right reason, such a methodology is deliberative rather than prescriptive.[2] Unfortunately, the natural law approach to sexuality in Catholic theology illustrates the problems developed at great length in chapter 2 including the ambiguity in the very concept of natural law.

In the natural law understanding of sins against chastity, nature does not mean right reason. In this context nature means the physical, biological, or natural processes which are common to humans and all the animals. Theology textbooks from Thomas Aquinas until a very few years ago divided the sins against sexuality into two classes — sins against nature (*peccata contra naturam*) and sins according to nature (*peccata iuxta naturam*).[3] Nature in this distinction refers to the physical, biological process common to humans and all the animals in which male semen is deposited in the vas of the female. Sins against nature are those in which this natural process does not take place and are generally listed as masturbation, sodomy, homosexuality, bestiality, and contraception. Sins according to nature are sexual actuations in which the biological or "natural" structure is observed, but they are opposed to the distinctively human aspects of sexuality. These sins include fornication, adultery, incest, rape, and sacrilege.[4] Chapter 2 has shown that this understanding is logically and historically influenced by the ideas of Ulpian.[5]

A second inadequacy in the textbook natural law approach to sexuality is the over-emphasis on procreation as the primary end of marriage and also of sexuality.[6] Such an understanding of the primary end of marriage theoretically follows from the natural law understanding of Ulpian. Ulpian himself gives the example of procreation and education of offspring as the classical example of natural law as that which is common to humans and all the animals.[7] Ulpian's theory would of necessity relegate the love union aspect of marriage and sexuality to a secondary end. The primary or fundamental in humans is what the human shares with the other animals. The specifically human aspect is something which is another layer merely placed on top of the primary layer of animality. Since relationality and love union do not enter into animal sexuality, these aspects are relegated to secondary ends of sexuality and marriage.

The emphasis on procreation and education shows through in the arguments proposed for the malice of certain sexual sins. Sins against nature are wrong because they violate the order of nature and thus impede the procreation of offspring.[8] However, even the sins according to nature are wrong primarily because they are against the primary end of procreation and education. Even though there may be no other circumstances present, such as the injustice to another marriage in adultery or the lack of consent in rape, all sins according to nature partake in the basic malice of fornication. Simple fornication is a grave sin because both parents are needed to provide for the proper education and upbringing of the child who might be born as a result of such an act.[9]

Imperfect medical and biological knowledge merely heightened the importance attached by the older theologians to the physical and procreational aspects of sexuality. Contemporary Catholic theologians too often forget the recent and rapid advances in scientific knowledge about human reproduction and sexuality. The very word "semen," taken from the agricultural metaphor of seed, indicates that the male semen merely had to be put in the fertile spot provided by the female. The classical authors in moral theology knew nothing of the exact contribution of the female to the human reproduction process. Very little progress in any type of anatomic knowledge was made until the sixteenth century because of the difficulty in obtaining corpses. In the sixteenth century, Gabriele Falloppio discovered the fallopian tubes in the woman, but he did not understand their true purpose.[10] In 1672 De Graaf described the female ovaries and the follicle which bears his name, but he made the mistake of identifying the ovum with the entire follicle. Only in the nineteenth century was the theory of De Graaf revived and corrected by the realization that the ovum is contained within the follicle.

In 1677, Van Leeuwenhoek, the great microscopist, discovered spermatozoa. Even after the discovery of spermatozoa a number of scientists thought that the male element was the only active element in reproduction. Some of Van Leeuwenhoek's overzealous followers even published pictures of the "homunculus" or little man which they found outlined in the spermatozoa![11] Obviously, such an understanding would attach great importance to human semen and spermatozoa.

In 1875, Oscar Hertwig showed that fertilization was effected by the union of the nuclei of ovum and sperm. Thus, only within the last hundred years or so has science realized that the woman is not fertile for the greater part of her menstrual cycle. Procreation is not possible after every act of sexual intercourse but only during a comparatively short time each month.[12] Thinkers like the classical moral theologians who lacked the knowledge of modern medicine necessarily would give too great a value to human semen and see too strong a connection between the individual sexual actuation and procreation.

Catholic theologians generally followed the teaching of St. Thomas that sins against sexuality are grave because they go against an important order of nature or because the absence of marriage between the parties fails to provide for the education of the child who might be born of such a union. Thomas also considered the question whether touches and kisses are grave sins. Thomas responded that an embrace, a kiss or a touch is not mortal *secundum speciem* because such actions can be done for some reasonable cause or necessity. However, something can be mortal because of its cause; and if these actions are done for a libidinous reason, they are mortal sins. Thomas had earlier argued that consent to the pleasure of a mortal sin is itself a mortal sin; therefore, if such actions are done from a libidinous intention, they are mortal sins.[13]

The commentators on St. Thomas approached the question of embraces, kisses, etc. in this Thomistic context. Martin Le Maistre (1432-1481) disagreed with Thomas.[14] Martin denied that such actions *secundum quod libidinosa sunt* are mortal sins. If such a kiss is done for the pleasure involved in the kiss and is not ordered to fornication, such a kiss is not a mortal sin. There remains the problem of what is meant by libidinous. However, for the purpose of our present study, the stage is thus set for the famous question of the existence of parvity of matter in sins against sexuality. Martin of Azpilcueta, the famous Doctor Navarrus (1493-1586), was apparently the first theologian to affirm that in matters of sexuality there can be parvity of matter; i.e., not all offenses against sexuality involve grave matter.[15] Navarrus proves his point by merely stating that the transgression of any precept is excused from grave sin because of parvity of matter and the precept governing chastity should be no different.[16] The opinion of Navarrus was accepted by Thomas Sanchez (1550-1610) who maintained there could be a slight venereal pleasure which would not involve lethal guilt provided there is no danger of pollution and no danger of consent to a carnal act.[17]

In 1612, the General of the Society of Jesus, Claudius Aquaviva forbade Jesuits to maintain the existence of parvity of matter in deliberately willed, imperfect sexual actuation or pleasure. This was later extended to imperfect sexual actuation which may have arisen indirectly but was later consented to. The opinion proposed by Sanchez was ordered to be changed in all the editions of his work.[18] (In 1659, the Revisores of the Society of Jesus did admit that the opinion affirming the existence of parvity of matter in questions of chastity was still extrinsically probable and penitents holding such a position could be validly absolved.)[19] The teaching denying the existence of parvity of matter in the sixth commandment gradually became so strong that some contemporary theologians claim it is temerarious to deny it.[20] The ruling by Father Aquaviva has obviously prevented any true discussion of the question by the Jesuit theologians who have been most influential in the area of moral theology. Since the issue was not allowed to be discussed, one can and should seriously question the validity of the apparent consensus of Catholic theologians on this point.

Jose M. Diaz Moreno recently published a protracted historical study of eighty theologians from Cajetan to St. Alfonsus to determine if the opinion admitting parvity of matter ever enjoyed probability. Only nine of these authors affirmed that parvity of matter excuses from grave sin in matters of sexuality.[21] However, the author concludes his lengthy investigation by saying that the arguments advanced by the proponents of parvity of matter are so generic or open to other interpretations that they do and did not constitute a solidly probable opinion. Nor do the nine theologians who maintained such a teaching constitute an extrinsically probable opinion either because many of them do not enjoy great esteem or because the reasons proposed by some (e.g. Navarrus and Sanchez) are not convincing.[22]

There have been no definitive interventions of the hierarchical magisterium concerning the question of parvity of matter.[23] Some statements definitely indicate and even presuppose the teaching denying the existence of parvity of matter in sexual sins.[24] A number of statements have condemned those who would assert that kisses, embraces, and touches that are done for carnal pleasure are only venial sins.[25] Also one response of the Holy Office presupposes there is no parvity of matter in the sixth commandment.[26] All of these are comparatively minor statements and must be judged today in the light of many different circumstances.

Since the seventeeth century theologians have generally taught that even imperfect sexual actuation or pleasure outside marriage does not admit of parvity of matter. There was some dispute, but only concerning the ultimate reason for such a teaching. Was the teaching based on intrinsic and theoretical reasons or merely practical and moral reasons?[27] Just a decade ago theologians maintained that the teaching denying parvity of matter was so certain that the contrary opinion was temerarious.[28] The reasons proposed by theologians for their opinion denying parvity of matter in the sixth commandment have taken different forms. Diaz Moreno summarizes the two arguments proposed by the authors he studied from Cajetan to St. Alphonsus. The first argument is based on the fact that all these imperfect sexual actuations are ordered to sexual intercourse, and thus all venereal pleasure, even the smallest, is the beginning of copula or pollution. The second argument consists in the danger of consent to a complete act which is intimately connected with these previous acts.[29] Fuchs proposes what he considers to be the best intrinsic argument in this way: in incomplete sexual actuation outside marriage there is a substantial breaking of an order of great importance, insofar as the individual desires for oneself that which was ordained by the creator for the good of the species.[30]

In fairness to the theologians one must carefully examine what is meant by the axiom that there is no parvity of matter in sexual matters. According to the best interpretations, the axiom means this: imperfect sexual actuation or pleasure outside marriage, which is directly willed, whether purposely procured or consented to, is by reason of matter always a grave sin.[31] Note well that the axiom denying parvity of matter in the sixth commandment does not mean that every sin against the sixth commandment constitutes a mortal sin. Sexual actuation or pleasure within marriage and indirect sexual actuation outside marriage are not grave matter. Although the matter is always grave in the other cases, the theologians constantly taught that sufficient reflection and full consent of the will are necessary for mortal sin. St. Thomas very wisely remarked that libido in the sensitive appetite diminishes sin because passion reduces culpability. Thomas admits that passion in sexual matters is very strong and difficult to overcome.[32]

What has been described as the older approach to sexuality in the Roman Catholic tradition still continues to exist. A good example of such an approach is found in "The Declaration on Sexual Ethics" issued by the Congregation for the Doctrine of the Faith on December 29, 1975. This document considers the three questions of masturbation, homosexuality, and premarital sexuality in the light of such an approach. The remaining two sections of this essay serve as a critique of both the methodology employed and the conclusions proposed in this declaration.

II. Evaluation of the Older Teaching

What about the teaching of the theologians that complete sexual actuation outside marriage is always grave matter and that direct, imperfect sexual actuation or pleasure outside marriage is always grave matter? I believe that such opinions and axioms are not true.

Contemporary moral theology views mortal sin in the light of the theory of the fundamental option which has been developed at great length in the last chapter. The difference between mortal and venial sin does not reside primarily in the difference between grave and light matter. Mortal sin involves the core of the person in a fundamental choice or option, a basic orientation of existence. Venial sin is an action which tends to be more peripheral and does not involve such a change in basic orientation. At best the distinction between grave matter and light matter is a presumption. The presumption is that grave matter will usually call for an involvement of the core of the person whereas light matter tends to call for only a peripheral response. If grave and light matter are at best presumptive guidelines, then such axioms as *ex toto genere suo gravis* or *non datur parvitas materiae* lose much of their rigidity.[33] However, my contention is that one cannot maintain the presumption that all complete sexual actuations outside marriage and all directly willed, imperfect sexual actuations outside marriage constitute grave matter. In the following arguments much of the attention will be directed to the case of complete sexual actuation outside marriage. However, if such complete sexual actuation outside marriage does not always involve grave matter, *a fortiori* directly willed, imperfect sexual actuation does not always involve grave matter.

The older view of the theologians rests upon a very inadequate notion of natural law which has exaggerated the importance attached to actions against sexuality. The Christian should be especially alert to a theological axiom which would seem to give primary importance to sexuality and chastity and not to the primary element of Christian love. Negative attitudes towards sexuality have definitely accented the over-emphasis on the importance of sexual sins. However, our discussion will center on the concept of natural law underlying the meaning and appreciation of sexuality and sexual sins in the teaching of the Catholic theologians before the last few years.

The manualistic concept of natural law applied to questions of sexuality distorts the meaning and importance of sexuality because it sees sexuality only in terms of the physical, biological process. No mention is made of the psychological which is just as objective an aspect of human sexuality as the physical. The older theologians can be excused because science has become aware of the psychological only within the last century. However, to deny the value and importance of the psychological distorts the meaning of human sexuality. For example, psychology reminds us that masturbation is not a very important matter in the life of some people such as the developing adolescent.[34]

The natural law concept underlying sexual morality in the manuals also fails to see the individual action in relation to the person. The Pastoral Constitution on the Church in the Modern World calls for theology to take into consideration the person and his or her acts.[35] The older approach viewed just the act in itself. There is a danger in some ethical thinking today which tends to give little or no importance to individual actions. However, it is equally fallacious to consider the act apart from the person placing the action. Masturbation may mean many different things depending on the person acting.

The exclusive emphasis on the physical aspect and the individual act apart from the person fails to do justice to the full meaning of human sexuality. One cannot brand all premarital sex under the same blanket condemnation of fornication. There is quite a bit of difference between sexual relations with a prostitute and with a spouse to be. Criteria which cannot come to grips with the differences involved in such cases do not seem to be adequate criteria. An emphasis on the physical and the natural, as opposed to the personal aspect of the action, also fails to see the need of growth and development as a person gradually strives to achieve a mature sexuality. Growth and development might even involve temporary problems along the way, but these are to be seen in view of the overall effort to reach the goal of an integrated human sexuality.

Perhaps the greatest error in the older approach is the close connection seen between every sexual actuation and procreation. Procreation is a very important human value. If every sexual actuation outside marriage involves a direct going against actual procreation, then there would be reason to assert the generic gravity of sins against sexuality. However, Catholic theology now realizes the over-importance attached to the relationship between sexuality and procreation in the past. The more recent statements of the hierarchical magisterium no longer mention procreation and education of offspring as the primary end of marriage.[36] Even the acceptance of the rhythm system of responsible parenthood argues that not every sexual actuation is closely connected with possible procreation. Ironically, an approach to sexuality exclusively in terms of procreation could logically lead to interesting consequences. Thomas Aquinas saw the generic grave malice of fornication in the harm done to the child who might be born of that union. The use of contraception would destroy the primary argument of St. Thomas asserting the generic malice of fornication!

Older biological notions also exaggerated the importance attached by Catholic theologians to the connection between sexual actuation and procreation. Even from a physical viewpoint the vast majority of sexual acts will not result in procreation because the woman is sterile for the greater part of her period. Modern science with its knowledge of the prodigality of nature in giving spermatozoa and the realization that semen is not the only active element in procreation indicates that human semen is not as important as older theologians seemed to think. Contemporary medical knowledge thus argues against the reasons assigned for the generic importance attached to sins of sexuality in the past.

From the pastoral viewpoint, it is most important to discard the view denying parvity of matter in sexual sins. Such a view gave an undue importance to sexuality in the overall view of the Christian life. In addition such a teaching tended to stifle a proper understanding of human sexuality and human sexual development. Sex was always connected with the fear of mortal sin. Such fear impeded the development of a proper attitude toward human sexuality on the part of many Catholics and even brought about grave repercussions in their adult attitude to sexuality.

III. Contemporary Approaches

It would be impossible to develop a coherent and systematic approach to the question of sexuality within the context of this study, even if there were such an approach. I will merely attempt to point out some of the problems involved, the generic approaches that are being taken, the important questions remaining, and the present state of the question on the morality of particular sexual acts as seen by some Roman Catholic theologians.

The question of sexual ethics raises again the problem of moral methodology which underlies most of the present discussions in Christian ethics and moral theology. The Christian ethicist certainly looks to the Scriptures for guidance. However, there is a realization today that the Scriptures cannot be used as proof texts to definitely indicate that one particular action is always wrong.[37] Scripture scholars remind us that the Scriptures are historically and culturally limited. Since the Scriptures reflect the historical conditions of their own times, they might not be applicable in changed circumstances. In some cases the words of Jesus may refer to an ideal of behavior rather than a norm required in all circumstances. The Scriptures tell us of the basic thrust of the Christian life and the attitudes that characterize such existence. The revelation of God in the Scriptures may also enunciate norms, and even particular norms for the Christian life. However, modern biblical scholarship does not permit the ethician to accept something as an absolute norm just because it is mentioned in the Scriptures.

The Christian theologian also pays great attention to tradition. Tradition records the experience of other men and women who have lived under the inspiration of the Spirit. One must give serious attention to such experience and reflection. However, historical changes, sociological developments, and increased knowledge brought to light through the recent knowledge explosion caution the ethician against a mere repetition of the traditional formulae and an unquestioning acceptance of the teaching of the past.

Chapter 2 has given a detailed critique of the natural law approach of the manuals of theology and pointed out some of the contemporary approaches. Contemporary theological notions stress the personal rather than the natural, the human rather than the physical, the relational rather than the substantial. Moral theology is also more conscious of the historical and cultural relativism that is a part of our evolving human existence. A more *a posteriori* approach gives more importance to what the other sciences tell us about human life and actions. Likewise, more importance is given to the experience of Christian people and all people of good will in determining the morality of particular actions.

Moral theology views sexuality in the light of the full Christian message. Sexuality reflects the goodness of God since it is part of creation and is destined to share in the resurrection of the body. Human sexuality shares not only the goodness of all creation but also the inherent limitations of human existence here and now — the limitations of time and space as well as human sinfulness. Revelation and personal reflection remind us of the tragic aspect which is present in the human story of sexuality and marriage. Sexuality forms an important aspect of human existence, but not the only or most important aspect of human existence.

All must admit the negative and even unhuman approach to sexuality which existed in the past both in Catholic theory and practice, but fortunately a much more positive approach is beginning to prevail. However, there lurks the danger of becoming so lyrical about sexuality that one forgets the imperfections, limitations and tragedy that mark sexuality, as well as everything human. An overly optimistic theology which has flourished in the last few years has tended in general to forget the aspect of the total Christian vision which reminds us of imperfection, sin and death. That is why one must insist today on the total vision. The imperfections of human sexuality stem from the creaturely limitations of space and time; the full sexual union lasts but a fleeting moment and cannot overcome the limitations of space and time. There is a rhythm of life and death in sexual actuation itself which is a constant reminder of limitation and incompleteness. Pierre Grelot devotes eight pages to the tragic aspects of the couple in the Old Testament literature and concludes: "All these facts show what is the real situation of sexuality and the human couple in a sinful world: a frail thing, constantly threatened and far removed from its original ideal."[38] But the Christian does not despair, for sexuality and marriage, again like all human reality, share in the redemption and the promise of the future. This study is considering the comparatively narrow aspect of what has been called the sins against sexuality, but it is helpful to present a brief overall view of sexuality that should be the starting point for any more particular consideration.

Christian ethics has traditionally seen the meaning of human sexuality in terms of love and procreation although too great an importance was attached to procreation at the expense of the unitive purpose of sexuality. Generally all Christian ethicists today, Protestant and Roman Catholic, view human sexuality in terms of a personal relationship between man and woman. Sexuality is not a mere object or even a faculty divorced from the person, but a very personal and intimate way of woman and man giving themselves to one another in a relationship of love. There are some theologians who argue that sexual intercourse as a personal act of loving does not always demand the binding and total commitment of man and woman. However, Catholic theologians generally and most Protestant theologians still hold to the principle that the union of two bodies *generally* calls for the total and complete union of two hearts which is the commitment of marriage.[39]

What about the relationship between sexuality and procreation? In the past, Catholic theology seems to have erred by seeing a connection between every act of sexual intercourse and procreation. Those who would argue for extramarital or premarital sex would naturally deny any necessary connection between sexuality and procreation. It is obvious that there is some connection between sexuality and procreation. The creation story in Genesis bears witness to this relationship. But even the approval of rhythm, to say nothing of the widespread rejection of the ethical conclusion of *Humanae Vitae*, indicates that not every act of sexual intercourse has to be open to procreation. Catholic theologians generally speak now of a connection between procreation and sexuality to the extent that sexual intercourse has meaning only within a realm of procreative acts or with a person with whom one is joined in a procreative union; in other words, in marriage. Sexuality as an expression of love also calls for some real connection with openness to procreation. Love itself is creative. The covenanted love of husband and wife tends to procreation just as the covenant of Yahweh with his people and Christ with his Church is a life-giving covenant of love. A problem arises in those cases in which even a married couple should not have children (e.g., because of a genetic problem or even societal reasons), for even their marital sexuality should not be procreative. Paul Ramsey answers this objection by saying that such married partners would still be saying that *if* either has a child it would come about only through their one flesh unity.[40] Moreover, some committed Christians today are purposely entering childless marriages with the very best of motives and intentions.

Another aspect that is too often left out of consideration by some extreme contextualists is the effect on society of such behavior. The societal aspect could call for the fact that certain practices are always observed even though in a particular case an individual might be greatly inconvenienced or even harmed to some degree. Catholic theology holds that the seal of the confessional is always binding because of this societal factor. Without such absolute assurances some Catholics might have difficulty in confessing their sins in the sacrament of penance. At least this societal aspect must be considered in the question of human sexuality, since marriage and sexuality affect many people and the entire society.

In the light of the inadequacies of the past approaches and the newer considerations a brief survey of the questions of masturbation, homosexuality, and premarital intercourse will follow. However, it will first be useful to call to mind an important distinction made in the preceding chapter: the distinction between sin and right or wrong. In the theory of the fundamental option mortal sin is seen as the change of the basic orientation of the person. Sin thus considers the action in relationship to the responsibility and personal involvement of the one placing such an action. But the human act is complex. The human act must also be considered in relationship with other acts and other persons. Right or wrong can be used to designate the human act under this aspect. Thus an action may be wrong, but not sinful; e.g., the act of becoming drunk is wrong, but for this particular person because of his personal make-up this might not be gravely sinful. Too often even professional ethicians seem to confuse the two different aspects which I have designated in terms of sin or right and wrong.

Masturbation. The blanket and sinful gravity of masturbation in the older teaching was derived from the one-sidedly physical approach, the emphasis on the connection of each sexual act with procreation, and the erroneous importance attached to male semen. A more personal approach and better psychological as well as physical knowledge point out that masturbation is ordinarily not that important a matter. There is no blanket gravity that can be assigned to every act of masturbation. Masturbatory activity is generally symptomatic; it can be symptomatic of many different things. Masturbation might be expressive of a deep-seated inversion or just an adolescent growing-up process.[41] Generally speaking, I believe masturbation falls short of the ideal since it fails to integrate sexuality into the service of love. Masturbation indicates a failure at a total integration of sexuality in the person. This wrongness is usually not grave; in fact, most times it is not. In the developing adolescent individual acts of masturbation are definitely not that important at all provided the individual is trying to develop his personality and enter into healthy relationships with others.

Catholic educators should openly teach that masturbation usually does not involve grave matter and most times, especially for adolescents, is not that important. Thus, masturbatory activity should not be a reason preventing an adolescent from full participation in the Eucharist. Also such a teaching would remove the fear so often induced by the inadequate teaching that masturbation always involves grave matter. However, the teacher should not leave the adolescent with the impression that there is absolutely nothing wrong with masturbation. Mature sexuality has meaning only in terms of a relationship of life-giving love to another. Sexuality should develop in this direction. Individual masturbatory actions are not that important provided there is a general growth toward the ideal of communion with others and interpersonal relationships.

Homosexuality. It would be impossible even to summarize the recent literature on the subject of homosexuality.[42] I believe that homosexual actions are wrong. Sexuality seems to have its meaning in terms of a life-giving love union of male and female. The priest as counselor must not speak primarily in terms of grave sinfulness. The theology of sin in terms of the fundamental option and modern psychological knowledge indicates that most often homosexual actions do not involve the person in grave or mortal sin. Help should be available to the homosexual so that he can come to a better development of sexuality. What about the cases in which modern medical science cannot help the homosexual? In these cases it seems to me that for such a person homosexual acts might not even be wrong. I am not saying that such acts are ever a goal or an ideal that should be held up to others to imitate. Homosexual acts for such a person, provided there is no harm to other persons, might be the only way in which some degree of humanity and stability can be achieved. This would be a practical application of the theology of compromise. Compromise maintains that because of the existence of sin in the world (not personal sin) a person might be forced to accept some behavior which under ordinary circumstances would not be chosen.[43] Since many experts trace homosexuality to psychological roots springing from the lack of love in early development, the application of compromise because of the existence of sin seems most appropriate in these cases.

Premarital sexuality. The older approach with its naturalistic criterion grouped all premarital or extramarital sexuality under the same generic gravity and wrongness. A more personalist approach realizes that there is quite a difference between sexual relations with a prostitute and sexual relations between an engaged couple. The gravity is inversely proportionate to the degree of personal commitment involved. The gambit of personal relationship can run all the way from prostitutional to playboy, to casual, to friendly, to committed. The same generic degree of wrongness cannot apply to all these different sexual relationships short of the commitment of marriage. However, the degree of personal commitment cannot be the sole criterion of the moral judgment in these cases, for other aspects must also be considered.

Catholic theologians generally uphold the teaching that sexuality outside marriage is wrong. Even the extreme situationists admit that sexuality calls for some degree of personal relationship and commitment. The position affirming that sexual relations outside marriage is wrong employs different arguments. Sexual relationships are a personal giving of one to another as persons. They are more than just chance encounters. In a sexual encounter one accepts responsibility for another; to accept full responsibility means that the persons are totally committed to one another. The biblical understanding sees two in one flesh as the sign of the total giving of one to another in marriage. Such a union of two in one flesh becomes the analogue of the covenant that God has made with his people. Just as fidelity marks the covenant of God with his people, so personal fidelity must characterize the union of two in one flesh. This is the fidelity of the marriage commitment. A similar argument views the sexual union as the language of total commitment. The union of two bodies in one flesh is the sign and the symbol of the union of two hearts. The union of bodies is a lie and a false sign unless it bespeaks a total union of two hearts. Likewise the defenders of the traditional Christian teaching against premarital sexuality point to the connection between sexuality and procreation. (Even the small failure rate in contraception is a reminder that sexuality has a relationship with procreation.)[44]

There also seem to be lacunae in some of the arguments proposed in defense of the theory that premarital sexuality is sometimes right. The societal dimension is often forgotten. In fact, frequently the situation is reduced to the very immediate and does not extend beyond the present moment. The fact that under the emotional impact of the present moment other important values might be forgotten does not enter into the argument. James Gustafson, himself a moderate contextualist, complains that the ethics of Fletcher often restricts the situation much too narrowly.[45]

Premarital and extramarital sexuality could have grave repercussions on the very important social realities of marriage and the family. Also, it is extremely difficult to know one's true motives and feelings. Can one be sure one is not taking advantage of another? Does the boy particularly realize the different psychological attitude of the girl and her different reactions? As in many emotional situations, for example, war and sex, there is always the danger of escalation!

Underlying many of the arguments in favor of premarital sexuality seems to be a false dualism. How often does one hear the argument: as long as both parties agree, there is nothing wrong with it. However, in the phrase of Paul Ramsey, the human person is the soul of his body just as much as he is the body of his soul.[46] To say that one can sin only against the soul (freedom) and not against the body appears to presuppose an inadequate anthropology.

However, some contemporary Catholic theologians are aware of the difficulty of stating that sexual relationships outside marriage are always and everywhere wrong. The more historical and relational approach that characterizes contemporary moral theology is more willing to see exceptions in absolute norms. I personally do see occasions where sexual intercourse outside marriage would not be wrong, but the exceptions are quite limited. Others have argued that sometimes sexual relations for the engaged couple would not be wrong, but it seems to me that such people may already have made the total commitment to one another even though they have not publicly expressed this commitment in the marriage ceremony.[47] In the theory of compromise one could imagine certain situations in which sexual relationships outside marriage would not be wrong. Also in view of proper medical experimentation and knowledge, sexual intercourse outside marriage would not seem always wrong (although by no means do I intend to justify all that is presently being done along these lines).

The theologian is also aware that many young people have a difficult time in seeing the generally accepted teaching on premarital sexuality. Perhaps they are blinded by the immediacy of their own situation. Or could it be that they are saying something to the professional theologian? Theologians will have to continue grappling with these questions.

This essay has attempted to show the inadequacies of the older approaches to sexual sins and their gravity and also to indicate some of the current approaches to sexuality in general and to particular sexual problems. Although these inadequacies do not necessarily call for a total rejection of the older teaching, many aspects of the older approach must be rejected. The very fact that theologians are more certain about the insufficiencies of the past than the approaches of the present is most revealing. Although uncertainty and greater hesitation will characterize the theological approach of the future, the moral theologians must continue their consideration of ethical methodology and its bearing in the area of sexuality.

NOTES

1. For a nontechnical but well-balanced approach to sexuality from within a Catholic context, see Sidney Cornelia Callahan, *Beyond Birth Control* (New York: Sheed and Ward, 1968).

2. Thomas Aquinas, *Summa Theologiae, Ia IIae*, q. 91, q. 94. Josef Fuchs, *Natural Law*, trans. Helmut Reckter and John A. Dowling (New York: Sheed and Ward, 1965), distinguishes both an ontological and a noetic element in the Thomistic concept of natural law. For a description of natural law ethics and Thomistic ethics as deliberative rather than prescriptive, see Edward LeRoy Long, Jr., *A Survey of Christian Ethics* (New York: Oxford University Press, 1967), pp. 45-52.

3. *IIa IIae*, q. 154, introduction and a. 11. E.g., H. Noldin et al., *Summa Theologiae Moralis: De Castitate*, 36th ed. (Innsbruck: Rauch, 1958), pp. 21-40.

4. Thomas Aquinas has practically the same enumeration as found in the more recent manuals of moral theology.

5. Ulpian's definition and theory is briefly cited in Justinian's *Digest*, 1. I, tit. I, I.

6. For a survey of the teaching on procreation as the primary end of marriage and sexuality, see John C. Ford, S.J., and Gerald Kelly, S.J., *Contemporary Moral Theology*, vol. 2: *Marriage Questions* (Westminster, Maryland: Newman Press, 1963), 1-127.

7. Ulpian in Justinian's *Digest*, 1. I, tit. I, I.

8. *IIa IIae*, q. 154, a. 1, *in corp.*; a. 11, *in corp.* Note that Thomas does speak about such actions as also being against right reason, but Ulpian's notion of natural law appears to have been the determining factor of what Thomas considered against right reason in this area. Lottin admits that Thomas in his attitude toward earlier definitions of natural law definitely "shows a sympathy for the formulae of Roman Law." Odon Lottin, *Le Droit Naturel chez Saint Thomas d'Aquin et ses prédécesseurs*, 2nd ed. (Bruges: Charles Beyaert, 1931), p. 67.

9. *IIa IIae*, q. 154, a. 2, *in corp.* Noldin, p. 23, like Thomas, mentions that fornication is wrong because it is against the good of offspring and the propagation of the human race. No mention is made of the unitive or love union aspect of sexuality.

10. The historical information on the development of knowledge of human reproduction is taken from the following sources: George Washington Corner, "Discovery of the Mammalian Ovum," *Publications from the Department of Anatomy, School of Medicine and Dentistry, University of Rochester*, (1930-33), 2, no. 38, 401-423; Richard A. Leonardo, *A History of Gynecology* (New York: Forben Press, 1944); Harvey Graham, *Eternal Eve: The History of Obstetrics and Gynecology* (Garden City, N.Y.: Doubleday, 1955); Harold Speert, *Obstetric and Gynecologic Milestones* (New York: Macmillan 1958).

11. Leonardo, *History of Gynecology*, p. 202.

12. The rhythm method of family planning, which is based on this comparatively recent information, only became scientifically acceptable through the independent work of Ogino and Knaus in the late 1920s.

13. *IIa IIae*, q. 154, a. 4, *in corp.*

14. Martinus DeMagistris, *Quaestiones Morales*, vol. 2 (Paris, 1511), *De temperantia, Quaest. de luxuria*, fol. 54.

15. In the historical development of the question of parvity of matter in the sixth commandment, I am following quite closely the work of Jose M. Diaz Moreno, S.I., "La doctrina moral sobre la parvedad de materia 'in re venerea' desde Cayetano hasta S. Alfonso," *Archivo Teologico Granadino* 23 (1960), 5-138.

16. *Operum Martini ab Azpilcueta (Doct. Navarri)*, vol. 2 (Rome: 1590), *Commentaria in Septem Distinctiones de Poenitentia*, d. 1, cap. *si cui*, n. 17. Navarrus here admits that he has found no other theologians who admit "a small venereal pleasure."

17. Thomas Sanchez, *Disputationum de Sancto Matrimonii Sacramento*, vol. 3 (Venice, 1606), lib. 9, dis. 46. n. 9. Compare this with the change made in the later editions of his work in accord with the order of Father Aquaviva — e.g., the Antwerp edition of 1626.

18. Josephus Fuchs, S.I., *De Castitate et Ordine Sexuali*, 3rd ed. (Rome: Gregorian University Press, 1963), p. 139; Diaz Moreno, 42-47.

19. Arthurus Vermeersch, S.I., *De Castitate et De Vitiis Contrariis* (Bruges: Charles Beyaert, 1919), n. 352, p. 357.

20. Marcellino Zalba, S.I., *Theologiae Moralis Summa*, vol. 2: *De Mandatis Dei et Ecclesiae* (Madrid: Biblioteca de Autores Cristianos, 1953), pp. 340, 341.

21. Diaz Moreno lists the following as arguing in favor of parvity of matter in the sixth commandment: Navarrus, Thomas Sanchez, Cunhafreytas, John Sanchez, Marchant, Caramuel, Bassaeus, Hurtado and Verde. However, four of these authors treated the question only indirectly in the context of the question of solicitation in confession.

22. Diaz Moreno, "La doctrina moral," 135.

23. This statement is made by the contemporary manualist M. Zalba, p. 340. Waffelaert maintains that the opinion admitting parvity of matter was not condemned by the Pope or rejected as improbable. G. J. Waffelaert, *De Virtutibus Cardinalibus: De Prudentia, Fortitudine et Temperantia* (Bruges, 1889), n. 188, p. 303. Obviously this statement is limited to the time before Waffelaert wrote his manual.

24. Response of the Holy Office of February 11, 1661, concerning the denunciation of solicitation in confession: "Cum in rebus venereis non detur parvitas materiae, et, si daretur, in re praesenti non dari (detur?), censuerunt esse denuntiandum, et opinionem contrariam non esse probabilem." *DS*, 2013.

25. One of 45 propositions condemned by decree of the Holy Office, March 18, 1666, as at least scandalous. *DS* 2060. For the order issued under Clement VIII and Paul V to denounce to the inquisitors those who assert that a kiss, an embrace, or a touch done for carnal pleasure is not a mortal sin, see Zalba, p. 340.

26. A decree of the Holy Office of May 1, 1929, withdrew from commerce the book of P.A. Laarakkers, *Quaedam moralia quae ex doctrina Divi Thomae Aquinatis selegit P. A. Laarakkers* (Cuyk aan de Maas, 1928) in which the author argued in favor of parvity of matter in the sixth commandment. For details, see Benedictus Merkelbach, *Questiones de Castitate et Luxuria* (Liege, 1936), pp. 28-31.

27. Fuchs, *De Castitate*, p. 139.

28. Ibid.; Zalba, *Theologiae Moralis Summa*, p. 341. Bernard

Häring, C.S.S.R., *The Law of Christ*, vol. 3 (Westminster, Md.: Newman Press, 1966), p. 291, says that it would be presumptuous to place the traditional thesis in doubt.

29. Diaz Moreno, "La doctrina moral," pp. 135-137.

30. Fuchs, p. 141. Note the emphasis here on procreation and the good of the species. The same explanation with the same emphasis is found in Noldin, pp. 16, 17 and Zalba, pp. 342, 343.

31. The authors mentioned in note 30 all agree with this interpretation.

32. *IIa IIae*, q. 154, a. 3, ad. 1.

33. Anton Meinrad Meier, *Des Peccatum Mortale Ex Toto Genere Suo* (Regensburg: Verlag Friedrich Pustet, 1966).

34. As an example of such assertions made by Catholic psychologists, see Frederick von Gagern, *The Problem of Onanism* (Cork: Mercier Press, 1955), p. 95; George Hagmaier, C.S.P., and Robert Gleason, S.J., *Counseling the Catholic* (New York: Sheed and Ward, 1959), p. 81.

35. Pastoral Constitution of the Church in the Modern World, para. 51.

36. The Pastoral Constitution on the Church in the Modern World does not mention the question of the ends of marriage and their mutual relationship in its consideration of marriage, sexuality and responsible parenthood. The addresses of Paul VI on the precise question of responsible parenthood (June 23, 1964; March 27, 1965; October 29, 1966) seem to studiously avoid the question of the relationship between the ends of marriage. Even the encyclical *Humanae Vitae* does not speak of procreation as the primary end of marriage.

37. For one approach to the methodological question of the role of the Scriptures in moral theology from a Catholic viewpoint, see E. Hamel, S.J., "L'Usage de l'Écrite Sainte en théologie morale," *Gregorianum* 47 (1966), 53-85. For a fine summary of the use of Scripture in recent Protestant ethics, see James M. Gustafson, "Christian Ethics," in *Religion*, ed. Paul Ramsey (Englewood Cliffs, N.J.: Prentice-Hall, 1965), pp. 309-320. For a recent study of the question, see Bruce C. Birch and Larry L. Rasmussen, *Bible and Ethics in the Christian Life* (Minneapolis: Augsburg Publishing House, 1976).

38. Pierre Grelot, *Man and Wife in Scripture* (New York: Herder and Herder, 1964), pp. 54-55.

39. For a review of some of the moral literature on the question, consult the "Notes on Moral Theology," which generally appear every June and December in *Theological Studies*. Joseph L. Walsh, C.S.P., "Sex on Campus," *Commonweal*, Feb. 24, 1967, 590 ff., raises questions and doubts about the traditional teaching against premarital intercourse. A good summary of three different methodological approaches now current in Christian ethics to the question

of premarital sexuality is found in *Sex and Morality: A Report of the British Council of Churches* October 1966 (Philadelphia: Fortress Press, 1966), pp. 25-31. A more contextualist approach to morality would tend to be against absolute norms although not all contextualists would permit sexual intercourse outside marriage.

40. Paul Ramsey, "A Christian Approach to the Question of Sexual Relations outside Marriage," *The Journal of Religion* 45 (1965), 100-113.

41. A. Plé, O.P., "La Masturbation: Réflexions théologiques et pastorales," *Supplément de la Vie Spirituelle* 77 (1966), 258-292

42. As examples of the abundant literature on homosexuality, see from a Catholic perspective: John Harvey, O.S.F.S., "Morality and Pastoral Treatment of Homosexuality," *Continuum* 5 (1967), 279-297; Henri J. M. Nouwen, "Homosexuality: Prejudice or Mental Illness?" *National Catholic Reporter*, Nov. 29, 1967; John G. Milhaven, S.J., "Homosexuality and the Christian," *Homiletic and Pastoral Review* 68 (May, 1968), 663-669. From other Christian perspectives: Canon D. A. Rhymes, "The Church's Responsibility towards the Homosexual," *Dublin Review* 241 (1967), 83-95; Morton T. Kelsey, "The Church and the Homosexual," *Journal of Religion and Health* 7 (1968), 61-78. My own position is explained at greater depth in my *Catholic Moral Theology in Dialogue* (Notre Dame, Ind.; University of Notre Dame Press, 1972), pp. 184-219.

43. See my article, "Dialogue with Joseph Fletcher," *Homiletic and Pastoral Review* 67 (1967), 828, 829.

44. The crucial theological problem is if these reasons plus the question of societal needs and practices mentioned above warrant the conclusion that premarital intercourse is always wrong. Richard F. Hettlinger accepts the arguments based on personal commitment and a connection of sexuality with procreation, but he does not conclude that premarital intercourse is always and under all circumstances wrong. However, he does not give enough attention to the question if there is a need for rules and practices because of the good of society. In general, Hettlinger exemplifies a "summary rule approach" which sees a great and important value in such rules but does not categorically state that such rules are always to be followed. Hettlinger, *Living with Sex: The Student's Dilemma* (New York: Seabury Press, 1966). See also note 39.

45. James M. Gustafson, "Love Monism," in *Storm Over Ethics* (No place given: United Church Press, 1967), pp. 31, 32. For a summary of different opinions expressed about situation ethics which is frequently illustrated by questions of sexuality, read *The Situation Ethics Debate*, ed. Harvey Cox (Philadelphia: Westminster Press, 1968).

46. Paul Ramsey in one of the papers in *The Vatican Council and the World of Today*, a collection of papers read at Brown University,

March 15, 1966, and prepared for publication by the Secretary of the University.

47. Dennis Doherty, "Sexual Morality: Absolute or Situational?" *Continuum* 5 (1967), 235-253. The author tries to show in continuity with the manualist theology that voluntary insemination apart from marital intercourse is not always evil. In the question of pre-marital sexuality, the author limits himself to the problem of sexual relations between engaged couples.

8: Conscience

Since conscience constitutes a very important theme in Christian morality, it is appropriate to conclude with a study of conscience. In addition a consideration of conscience will help synthesize, concretize, and develop many of the points made earlier. The first section will develop the meaning of conscience in the tradition of Roman Catholic theology which culminated in the treatises on conscience in the manuals of moral theology which were the usual textbooks both for theologians and for future priests. In the second section the approach of the manuals will be critiqued, and in a positive manner a different theory of conscience will be developed. The third section will bring together some practical conclusions for the formation of conscience.

Historical Development

Since conscience plays so important a role in human existence and is often discussed in Christian circles, one would expect to find a lengthy and extensive discussion about conscience in scripture. Such is not the case. The word *conscience* (the Greek συνειδησις) was introduced into the scriptures by Paul, and for all practical purposes does not exist outside the Pauline corpus. Where did Paul find the term *conscience*? Again there is general agreement among scholars that Paul borrowed the word from the Greek world, but there is some discussion as to whether his source was the stoic philosophers or just the ordinary usage of the time. Scholars generally agree that the Greek usage portrayed conscience almost always as a guilty conscience — conscience as a negative judge of our actions completed or at least already initiated.[1]

There is a great disagreement about the meaning of conscience in Paul. C. H. Pierce, in a monograph entitled *Conscience in the New Testament,* indicates that the biblical notion is quite different from the notion of conscience as found among contemporary theologians. Conscience today is understood as justifying, in advance or in general principle, actions and attitudes of others as well as of oneself. But in the New Testament conscience cannot justify; it refers only to the past and the particular — and to acts of the self, not of others.[2] Conscience comes into play only after at least the initiation of a wrong act. At most conscience, according to Paul, can only indicate the act was not wrong — not that it was right, or the only act, or the best possible act in the circumstances. Above all conscience can say nothing directly about future acts.[3] According to Pierce's analysis, *conscience* appears thirty-three times in the New Testament. It never refers to an action to be placed, and only once unambiguously and in two other places ambiguously refers to a good conscience. The overwhelming number of references are to various types of a negative or morally bad conscience. Thus conscience is generally a negative judge of past behavior.[4]

There is another school of thought. Eric D'Arcy claims that Paul introduced an entirely new phase in the history of conscience by giving conscience a directive role before an action takes place. For the pagan writers conscience appeared only after the action (what we call today *consequent conscience* as distinguished from *antecedent conscience*) and in a judicial role; but for Paul conscience has a legislative function and indicates an obligation as such.[5] Ceslaus Spicq also understands conscience in the New Testament as a norm of conduct.[6] Philippe Delhaye maintains that for Paul conscience exercises both a judicial and a legislative function in reference not only to personal acts but to acts of others. Delhaye even develops the criteria of the norm of conscience as antecedent legislator.[7] Exegesis is not the only factor involved in this discussion. The authors holding the second opinion are all Roman Catholics who tend to understand Paul in the New Testament in the light of the generally accepted Catholic understanding which includes the notion of conscience as a judgment about the rightness or wrongness of actions to be placed. Pierce adopts a position more in keeping with the classical Protestant tradition which emphasized the importance of faith and downplayed works. Conscience in this perspective often plays a theological role rather than an ethical role. In conscience one recognizes that all our works, struggles, and efforts do not bring us closer to God, but rather conscience accuses us of our sinfulness and brings us to realize that salvation comes only through faith as the acceptance of God's gracious gift.[8] Many Protestant scholars, however, do not agree with Pierce's interpretation of Paul.[9]

There is no doubt that Paul places heavy emphasis on the negative and consequent aspects of conscience, stressing the pain and remorse for past actions. To what extent Paul speaks of the antecedent conscience and the function of conscience as a guide or directive for action is a matter of dispute.[10] However, there seems to be general agreement that Christians must address the question of conscience as the guide for action. There are also other concepts in the scriptures such as wisdom, heart, or choice which do include the understanding of direction and guidance for our actions.[11]

In the medieval period there is no doubt that the concept of conscience as an antecedent guide to actions is present together with the notion of the consequent conscience which judges past actions and is often synonymous with pain and remorse. Twelfth- and thirteenth-century Roman Catholic Scholastic theologians developed the notion of conscience — especially antecedent conscience as a guide to moral actions.[12]

There is one fascinating development which sets the parameters for the discussion in the twelfth and thirteenth centuries. These medieval theologians generally distinguished between *synderesis* and conscience. Where did this distinction come from? St. Jerome in his commentary on Ezechiel describes the four powers in the soul — reason, spirit, desire, and a fourth element above and beyond the other three which the Greeks called *synderesis*. This passage and its interpretation became pivotal because Peter Lombard, whose *Sentences* was the primary theological textbook of the times, referred to the text of Jerome which thus became a point of departure for any future discussion.[13] Why did St. Jerome use such a new term as *synderesis*? Why did he not use the word *syneidesis*? A widely accepted theory claims that St. Jerome himself did not use the word *synderesis*. There are different manuscripts of Jerome's commentary, some of which use the word *synderesis* and some *syneidesis*. Apparently a monk transcribing the text mistakenly employed the term *synderesis* rather than *syneidesis*. There is no other use beside Jerome's use of *synderesis*. The medievalists knew the text of Jerome primarily through the *Glossa Ordinaria* which contained the reading *synderesis*. Thus the discussion proposed by the influential Peter Lombard on the basis of the mistaken transcription of Jerome distinguished between *syneidesis* (conscience) and *synderesis*.[14]

Lombard's text became the starting point for the ensuing discussions. Jerome's text understands *synderesis* as a fourth element of the soul above and beyond reason, spirit, and desire. It makes us feel our sinfulness, and it corrects the other elements when they err. This spark of conscience was not quenched even in the heart of Cain according to Jerome, but he adds in the same paragraph that in some people it has been overcome and displaced. Such a text naturally raised questions for the Scholastics. Being like reason, spirit, and desire, is *synderesis* a faculty? Does it belong to the cognitive order or the affective order — i.e., the intellect or the will? Can it be lost? Jerome seems to be contradicting himself on this point. What is the relationship of *synderesis* to conscience? What is conscience itself? The stage is set for the future discussions.

Stephen Langton (1205) in his commentary on Lombard's *Sentences* made what became a lasting contribution in Scholastic thought. *Synderesis* is a part of the power of reason concerned with very general moral judgments (Aquinas will later call it the habit of first principles). Disagreements existed as to whether or not *synderesis* refers to the appetitive (will) or cognitive (intellect) aspect of the person. St. Bonaventure, developing the thought of Philip the Chancellor, sees *synderesis* as a habit-like faculty of the will — a natural appetite for the morally good. Bonaventure, like the theologians before him, on the basis of the authority of Jerome refers to *synderesis* as a habit-like faculty — a concept which is not very clear — rather than just a habit. Conscience for Bonaventure is a habit belonging to practical reason which is partly innate and partly acquired, referring to all moral judgments, both general principles and particular conclusions.[15]

Albert the Great, a representative of the Dominican School influenced by Jerome, understands *synderesis* as a habit-like faculty but connected not with the will but with practical reason. *Synderesis* is the knowledge of the universal principles of morality just as speculative reason has a knowledge of the self-evident truths of the speculative order. Albert logically proposes a different understanding of conscience than Bonaventure. *Synderesis* gives the first universal principles which form the major premise of a syllogism. Conscience is a judgment about a particular case that is the conclusion of a syllogism whose major premise is given by *synderesis* whose minor premise is given by reason or experience.[16]

The stage is set for the teaching of Thomas Aquinas who discusses the question first in his *Commentary on the Sentences* of Lombard, then in his *De veritate,* and finally in his *Summa Theologiae* which will be briefly summarized here.[17] In the *Pars Prima,* question 79, articles 12 and 13, Aquinas deals with the meaning and nature of conscience. Here Aquinas finally throws off the influence of Jerome and claims *synderesis* is not a faculty but a habit belonging to practical reason by which one knows the first, self-evident principles of practical moral reasoning. By this Thomas means the principle of doing good and avoiding evil and acting according to right reason. This habit, which corresponds to the knowledge of the first principles in the speculative order (e.g., principle of noncontradiction), then impels us to the good and cannot be lost as long as one enjoys the use of reason.

Conscience according to Aquinas is neither a faculty nor a habit, but an act — the act of applying knowledge to conduct. Here both the antecedent conscience as directing and guiding actions and the consequent conscience of judging are mentioned. Thomas also mentions that since the habit is the principle of the act, sometimes the name *conscience* is given to this habit which he has called *synderesis.*

Our discussion has traced the very fascinating historical development of the meaning, function, and working of conscience. Aquinas, who stands as the most influential person in the development of Catholic teaching, treats another aspect of conscience — its obliging force, especially in terms of following an erroneous conscience. Albert the Great had broken with earlier authors and asserted that conscience is binding whether it be correct or erroneous. Before his discussion in the *Summa,* Aquinas treated the question in an earlier and different way in his *Commentary on the Sentences* and in the *De veritate.*[18]

In question 5 of article 19 of the *prima secundae* of the *Summa Theologiae,* Thomas asks if a will going against an erring reason is bad and immediately adds in his response that this is the same as asking if an erroneous conscience obliges. Thomas refutes some other positions and argues that, since the object of the will is what is presented by reason, the will in pursuing what is proposed as evil incurs guilt. For example, it would be a sin to embrace the Christian faith if a person judges it to be evil. Thomas finishes his response by saying that every act of the will which is at variance with reason, whether the reason is correct or erroneous, is evil. An erroneous conscience always obliges. In question 6 he responds to the question whether an act is good if the will follows an erroneous conscience. The response hinges on the difference between vincible and invincible ignorance — is the error blameworthy or not? The question is, as Thomas himself notes in beginning his answer, whether an erroneous conscience excuses. One is obliged to follow an erroneous conscience; but it is sinful to do so if the ignorance is voluntary or vincible. An invincibly erroneous conscience excuses from guilt. In these two very short discussions Thomas considers the nature, function, and obliging force of conscience. One of the great differences between Thomas and the manuals of Catholic moral theology concerns the length of the discussion on conscience. The manuals devote a long, separate tract to conscience — much of which comes from a controversy that absorbed Catholic moral theology in the sixteenth, seventeenth, and eighteenth centuries. The problem centered on the question of a doubtful conscience. How is one to act if one's conscience cannot certainly decide what to do? The so-called moral systems, while recognizing that one cannot act with a doubtful conscience, proposed ways of moving from theoretical doubt to practical certitude about acting. How can theorectical doubt be turned into practical certitude?

This debate took place within a number of very significant contexts.[19] Moral theology had become a very practical discipline concerned with training confessors for the Sacrament of Penance especially in their role as judges about the existence and gravity of sin. Moral theology was cut off from its speculative roots as well as from dogmatic and spiritual theology. The tone was often legalistic, extrinsicist, and minimalistic. Casuistry for many takes on pejorative overtones because of the way it was used in the moral theology of this period. Within this general context there were different approaches to the problem of resolving doubts of conscience depending upon the rigidity of the authors. On the one extreme were the Jansenists many of whom embraced an absolute or rigid tutiorism. When there existed a doubt in theory, one always had to follow the safer course in practice — that is, the course asserting there was an obligation. On the other side of the debate were the laxists who in theory held that one could follow an opinion in favor of freedom from the obligation of law even if arguments in favor of such a theory were only tenuously probable or even much less probable than those in favor of the obligation.

During this debate the papal magisterium through the Holy Office entered the discussion to condemn the extreme opinions. (Incidently this was the most significant intervention up to that time by the papal office in the area of moral theology and began a trend that has continued until contemporary times.) In 1679 under Pope Innocent XI the Holy Office condemned sixty-five propositions associated with moral laxism at the instigation of the University of Louvain, which had previously condemned many of these propositions and sent their condemnation to Rome. These opinions were taken from a number of authors some of whom were Jesuits such as Thomas Tamburini.[20] The Holy Office condemned the use of the less probable opinion and of even a tenuously probable opinion (*DS* 2102, 2103). Likewise in conferring the sacraments it was forbidden to follow a probable opinion leaving aside a more safe opinion (*DS* 2101). Some of the condemned propositions show the state of moral theology at the time and the minimalistic and juridical approach to morality. The following laxist opinions were condemned as at least scandalous and dangerous in practice: We do not dare to condemn the opinion that some-one sins mortally who only once in a lifetime elicits an act of the love of God (*DS* 2105). It is sufficient to elicit an act of faith only once in a lifetime (*DS* 2117). We are able to satisfy the precept of loving our neighbor by only external acts (*DS* 2111).

Sometime after these condemnations, the opponents of the Jansenists gathered together various opinions espoused by theologians in Belgium. They were sent to Rome in 1682; a study by the Holy Office was finished in 1686, but the decree containing the condemned errors was only promulgated in 1690, under Pope Alexander VIII (*DS* 2301-2332). The principle of absolute tutiorism, that one always had to follow the safest opinion even though the opinion for freedom from the law was most probable, was condemned (*DS* 2303). Other condemned opinions included the following: Although there exists invincible ignorance of the natural law, this does not excuse from formal sin one who in the state of fallen existence operates on the basis of such ignorance (*DS* 2307). The intention by which one detests evil and pursues the good merely to obtain heavenly glory is neither right nor pleasing to God (*DS* 2310). They are to be excluded from Holy Communion who do not have in them the most pure love of God which is in no way contaminated (*DS* 2323).

Although the extremes were condemned, bitter discussions still continued. Generally, at least after 1656, the Dominicans were associated with the theory of probabiliorism according to which one could follow the opinion for freedom only if it were more probable than the opinion in favor of the obligation. The Jesuits were generally associated with the theory of probabilism according to which one could follow the opinion for freedom from the obligation provided it was probable or, as sometimes phrased, solidly and truly probable.[21] Although some Jesuit theologians maintained opinions which were condemned as laxist, it would be entirely false to claim, as some have, that the Jesuits as a whole were laxists. They generally followed the opinion of probabilism.

The intensity and intrigue in the entire debate is well illustrated by the case of Thyrsus Gonzalez de Santalla, S.J., who was a professor at Salamanca. Gonzalez wrote a book dedicated to the General of the Jesuits, Father Oliva, in which he advocated probabiliorism; but he was denied permission to publish the book. Gonzalez's opinions were brought to the attention of Pope Innocent XI who issued a decree through the Holy Office in 1680. In this decree the Holy See told Gonzalez to preach, teach, and defend intrepidly with his pen the teaching about the more probable opinion. In addition the decree ordered the General of the Society of Jesus that he not only permit Jesuits to write in favor of the more probable opinion but he inform all Jesuit Universities that scholars are free to write in favor of the more probable opinion. It seems that this decree was never communicated to the members of the Society of Jesus. There exists another version of the same decree (judged by many to be not authentic) in which the Jesuits are forbidden to write in favor of probabilism. The story does not end here. Gonzalez, with some help from the Pope, was elected General of the Jesuits in 1687. But his book on the correct use of probabiliorism which he had secretly published in Bavaria around 1691 was still surpressed. In 1694, Gonzalez did succeed in publishing a version of the book he had originally written in 1671.[22]

The controversy finally came to an end with the moderate probabilism of St. Alphonsus Liguori, who worked out his moderate probabilism in the 1750s and 1760s. The opinion for freedom could be followed if it were equally probable as the opinion for the obligation. Alphonsus called his opinion equiprobabilism or moderate probabilism. In his later writings, he even changed his terminology but not his teaching in an effort to avoid being attacked by anti-Jesuits. With the demise of the Jesuits, Alphonsus became the champion of moderate probabilism.[23] St. Alphonsus was later named a doctor of the church and patron saint of confessors and of moral theologians.[24]

This long dispute had a great impact on the treatment of conscience in the manuals of moral theology. The characteristics of legalism and minimalism mentioned earlier became even more prevalent in the manuals of moral theology in the light of the long discussion. Until contemporary times the primary and most often asked question about a particular moral opinion in Roman Catholicism was whether or not such an opinion was probable and could be followed in practice. According to the theory an opinion could be probable either intrinsically, on the basis of the reasons proposed, or extrinsically, on the basis of the authority of the authors who maintained such an opinion. It was generally accepted that five or six authors of grave weight could constitute an opinion as probable.[25] Thus Catholic moral theology often "solved" moral problems by counting up the various authors who supported a particular opinion.

Unfortunately, the definitive history of the teaching on conscience still needs to be written, but this study has mentioned what appear to be the most important influences in the development of the Roman Catholic manuals of moral theology.[26] In the light of this one can both better appreciate and criticize the teaching of these manuals of moral theology on conscience.

The manuals of moral theology almost invariably divide their consideration of fundamental moral theology into the following treatises — the ultimate end (which is usually very short), human acts, law, conscience, sin, and virtue. The manual written and first published in 1952 by Marcellino Zalba, S.J., will be used for purposes of illustration. After his brief discussion of the ultimate end and a longer discussion of human acts, Zalba discusses rules, norms, or criteria which should direct our acts. These rules are basically two — the remote, objective, and extrinsic norm is law; the proximate, subjective, and intrinsic norm, which applies the law in particular cases and judges the morality of acts, is called conscience.

The first chapter under conscience treats the nature

and meaning of conscience. Moral conscience is defined as a dictate of practical reason or the ultimate practical judgment of reason about the morality of an act, here and now to be placed or omitted or already placed or omitted, according to moral principles. It is called the dictate of reason because conscience is formally an act of the intellect obtained by means of an at least virtual conclusion from general moral principles either by way of a strict reasoning process or by a certain sense and intuition of the right. Conscience is distinguished from other realities such as *synderesis* which is the innate habit of the universal principles of the moral order. Then the various distinctions of the types and kinds of conscience are given.[27]

The second chapter considers the necessity, truth, and certitude of conscience, dealing with the question of the erroneous conscience in the same general way as proposed by the theory of Thomas Aquinas — i.e., invoking the concept of vincible and invincible ignorance. Chapter 3 discusses the formation of conscience when one is doubtful. After a lengthy discussion of all the moral systems, Zalba chooses the system of probabilism according to which in cases of a law which is purely or principally preceptive, that is, about the mere liceity of an act, it is permitted to follow a less-probable opinion favoring liberty provided it is truly and solidly probable. However, probabilism cannot be used in a number of cases: a question of something probably necessary for salvation, actions concerning the validity of sacraments, acts involving the certain rights of another or, generally, a matter of the common good. The next section then discusses the various types of habitual conscience — tender, lax, perplexed, and scrupulous.[28]

In my judgment there are significant deficiencies in this understanding of conscience, which will be briefly mentioned. In the first place the basic approach is too legalistic with the resulting problems of minimalism and an extrinsic understanding of morality and the moral life. Second, conscience viewed as a faculty tends to give too little importance to the person as a whole — the subject of the action. Third, the understanding of conscience is too one-sidedly rationalistic — there is little or no mention of affectivity. Fourth, the emphasis is on a deductive reasoning process which bespeaks a classicist approach.

Toward a More Adequate Theory

Now it is time to propose a more adequate understanding of conscience which will avoid the criticisms briefly mentioned above. These criticisms of the manuals do not imply that there is nothing of value in the past Catholic tradition. It will be pointed out that the manuals, perhaps because of some aspects of the historical development mentioned earlier, do not necessarily represent the best of the Catholic tradition. On the other hand, there are changes called for in the light of contemporary understandings some of which have been mentioned in chapter 2.

As a preliminary consideration it is important to establish the different theological context within which the question of conscience is to be situated. The manuals operate almost exclusively within the realm of the natural as differentiated from and distinct from the supernatural. In the first chapter the importance of the Gospel ethic was stressed. The second chapter argued that the natural, rather than being considered as existing apart from the supernatural, must be incorporated into the total Christian vision or stance. Such a theological context is a very necessary prerequisite for a proper understanding of conscience.

The first and primary consideration involves the ethical model within which one situates the reality of conscience. There is no doubt that the manuals understand morality primarily in terms of deontology. The objective norm is God's law as this is mediated in and through other laws — divine positive, natural, and positive law. The impression is readily given that the law spells out all one's moral obligations and conscience passively conforms to the existing law.

As mentioned earlier, there are three possible models that can be employed for understanding the moral life — deontology, teleology, and relationality — responsibility. The legalistic theology of the manuals, which sees the moral life primarily in terms of law, seems totally inadequate and accentuates the negative characteristics of minimalism and juridicism which so often characterized this morality. Interestingly, the manuals of Catholic moral theology do not follow the approach of Thomas Aquinas. They continually quote Aquinas in their discussion of law and appear to be following him but in reality they do not.

Thomas Aquinas properly belongs under the category of teleology — morality is based on the ultimate end and acts are good or bad depending on whether or not they bring us to the ultimate end or impede this progress.[29] Thomas's first consideration is the ultimate end of human beings, followed by his discussion of the human acts by which we achieve the ultimate end. His next major treatise concerns the principles of human actions. The intrinsic principles are the various powers or potencies from which our acts comes — e.g., the intellect, the appetites; but these powers can be modified by habits which are stable ways of acting inclining us either to the good or to evil. Among the good habits affecting our powers or faculties, Aquinas considers at great length the virtues and also mentions the gifts of the Holy Spirit, the beatitudes, and the fruits of the Holy Spirit. Only then does Thomas consider the external principles of actions which are both law and grace.[30] The manuals unfortunately do not follow either the whole of the Thomistic teaching or the tone of that moral teaching.

However, as mentioned in the preceding chapters, I choose a relationality-responsibility model as the basic ethical model. The use of this model was illustrated in the consideration of sin in chapter 6. For a deontological model, sin is an offense against the law of God. For a teleological model, sin, especially mortal sin which is the primary reality, involves going against one's ultimate end. For the relationality-responsibility model, sin is the breaking of our multiple relationships with God, neighbor, self, and the world. As illustrated in chapter 6, the relationality-responsibility model better corresponds with the biblical data and with a more adequate understanding of the moral life in general and of sin in particular.

There are a number of important theological and ethical considerations arguing for the acceptance of a relationality-responsibility model for moral theology. The first important impetus has come from biblical ethics. In Roman Catholic theology the renewal associated with the Second Vatican Council first appeared in the area of scripture and then grew as scriptural insights were incorporated more and more into the whole of theology so that scripture truly became the soul of theology.[31] In biblical ethics it became clear that relationality-responsibility was a very significant ethical theme. The primary ethical category even in the Old Testament is not law but covenant which is the loving relationship that God has made with his people.[32] The Gospel ethic with its call to perfection fits much better in relational categories than in deontological terms as is evident in chapter 1.

The understanding of the scriptures also played a significant role in leading Protestant scholars to a relationality model. Protestant ethics had always been firmly based on the Scriptures. The more critical approach to the Scriptures made theologians realize that the Scriptures could no longer be used as a source of laws or norms universally binding in the Christian life. In the Scriptures God revealed himself in his loving acts so that the concept of propositional revelation was no longer accepted. Especially in Barthian ethics the God of the Scriptures is the God who acts with his mighty deeds. In relationship to the God who acts and saves the Christian is a responder.[33] I have already negatively criticized a theological actualism which can easily develop in the light of this approach, but such an abuse does not destroy the valid understanding of the moral life in terms of relationality and responsibility.

Theological emphasis on eschatology also influences the selection of the relationality model. Contemporary eschatology no longer sees its subject as the last things but rather the Kingdom of God is already somewhat present and trying to become more present in history. The Christian then has a responsibility to make the kingdom more present and to overcome the evils of social, economic, political, and sexual oppression which too often continue to imprison many human beings. Such a theme is particularly central in the theology of liberation which in the Roman Catholic context has been developing especially in South America.[34]

Theological anthropology today understands the individual person as called to creatively make the kingdom more present in the struggle against the reality of sin in the world. Such an anthropology, highlighting the powers and capabilities of human beings, does not view the individual primarily in terms of conformity to a minutely spelled-out law or plan. Here again there is a danger of abuse as mentioned in chapter 4. The true realization that the individual creates one's own meaning and value can be distorted to deny the limitations that continually exist for human beings.

From a more philosophical-anthropological perspective the relationality-responsibility model fits in better with the emphasis on historicity. The tone of the manuals of moral theology with their insistence on all embracing laws characterized by universality and immutability is the product of a classicist worldview. This is not to deny that there is a place for law or for considerations of universality in ethics and the moral life of the Christian, but primary emphasis does not belong here. Historicity favors the stress on growth and development which is also much better incorporated in a relationality-responsibility model. A proper understanding of our multiple relationship with God, neighbor, self, and the world does justice to all the aspects of human existence including the political and social dimensions.

The emphasis on the person and personalism rather than the natural has also influenced the shift toward a model of relationality-responsibility. The individual as person is seen as a subject interacting with other persons. As was mentioned in chapter 2 this approach rejects an understanding of natural law as based on physical and biological processes or the innate teleologies of particular faculties seen apart from the person.

The adoption of a relationality-responsibility model rests on convincing theological and ethical arguments. Naturally it is necessary to develop at great detail what precisely is meant by relationality-responsibility. I have already pointed out in chapter 2 what I see as some erroneous approaches. In many ways I accept the basic approach of H. Richard Niebuhr to the model of relationality-responsibility. Niebuhr understands responsibility as embracing four elements — response, interpretation, accountability, and social solidarity.[35] My approach differs from Niebuhr in two important aspects. First, my understanding of relationality has a more metaphysical basis to it. Second, I want to give a greater emphasis to the subject as agent and incorporate here some of the findings of transcendental philosophical approaches. This emphasis will now be developed at much greater length in the subsequent steps of this section within the context of a relationality-responsibility model.

The second step in developing a more adequate concept of conscience in the Catholic theological tradition concerns giving greater importance to the subject or the person as agent. The legalistic and extrinsicist view of the manuals saw the moral life primarily as actions in obedience to the law. The law was recognized as an objective norm of morality to which the individual conformed one's acts. In this perspective conscience formation consisted primarily in instructing people about what is in the law. To this in practice was often added a motivational aspect emphasizing the fear of sin and hell.

In general an emphasis on the person as subject or agent

accepts the fact that the acts of the individual must be seen not in relation to an extrinsic norm but in relation to the person acting. An older axiom in Catholic thought understood this reality very well — *agere sequitur esse* — action follows from being — in other words, what we do follows from what we are. Actions are expressive and revelatory of the person. The person expresses oneself and extends oneself in and through one's actions. The biblical metaphor expresses the reality very well — the good tree brings forth good fruit while the bad tree brings forth bad fruit. Loving and compassionate actions come from a loving and compassionate person.

But there is also another important aspect to the emphasis on the person as agent. Not only are actions expressive and revelatory of the person, but by one's actions the individual shapes and constitutes the self as subject and as moral agent. By our actions we make ourselves the moral agents we are. Truly the individual human person has the opportunity and the destiny to create one's own moral self.

In more technical ethical terminology emphasis is placed on an ethics of character or of the virtues. How often we talk about the character of the person coming through in one's action. Character, as distinguished from particular character traits, emphasizes that the person is more than what happens to the self. One can determine oneself and one's character, recognizing that there are some factors over which we have no control. James Gustafson has emphasized the role of the self, virtues, and character in Christian ethics.[36] Stanley Hauerwas, influenced by Gustafson, has recently developed an ethics of character, understanding character as the qualification of self-agency which is an orientation of the self.[37] Obviously there would be many ways in which one could develop an ethics of character.

An ethics of the virtues also rests on the recognition of the importance of the subject as agent. This emphasis was present to a degree in Aquinas who saw the virtues as good habits or stable ways of acting modifying the faculties or

powers and inclining them to the good.[38] Contemporary
Christian ethicists are speaking again about an ethic of the
virtues and some even want to develop an independent
ethic of virtues with no place for an ethic of obligation.[39]
An ethic of the virtues could be developed in many different ways, but all such approaches stress the importance
of the person as subject and agent.

Unfortunately this emphasis is missing in the approach
of the manuals and much of contemporary moral thought
which often reduces ethical considerations to the moment
of decision, forgetting about the self who continues from
decision through decision and who actually affirms and
creates one's moral self in and through those decisions.
Again the Catholic tradition with the understanding of
the virtues tried in some way to do justice to the importance of the subject and the person, but the manuals tended
to neglect this aspect in their development. Even when
treating of the virtues the manuals primarily discuss only the
acts of the virtues and the obligations to place such actions.

From a theological perspective Catholic ethics possessed
a strong basis for developing an ethic of the person as
subject. The Catholic theory of grace maintains that grace
produces an ontological change in the person. By freely
responding to the gracious gift of God's love in Jesus
Christ, one truly now becomes intrinsically changed, a
different person mystically and really united with Jesus in
the family of God. The Christian should then live in accord
with the new life which has been received in Christ Jesus
and grow in that life. The teaching of Aquinas can readily
be understood in the light of the agent transformed by
grace.[40] Some Protestant theology with its teaching on
justification and the lesser emphasis on sanctification
would have a greater difficulty in developing an ethic
stressing the fact that the moral subject constitutes oneself
as subject in and through one's actions and that the subject
grows and progresses in the moral life.[41] However, Hauerwas develops an ethic of character judged to be in accord
with some Protestant theories of justification.[42]

In the light of the importance of the person as agent and subject, the centrality of continual conversion in the moral life of the Christian emerges. Continual conversion has strong roots in the scriptural notion of *metanoia* and well illustrates the dynamism and call to perfection which characterizes a gospel inspired ethic. Bernard Häring has made conversion a central concept in moral theology.[43]

The Christian through responding to and accepting the gift of God's love in Jesus Christ becomes a new person, a new creature sharing in the life of Jesus. But one must continue to grow and deepen this new life. There is a true sense in which the individual remains *simul justus et peccator* — at the same time justified and a sinner. As mentioned in chapter 6 the reality of venial sin understood as the continuing sinfulness of the redeemed takes on added importance in this view, for the Christian constantly strives to overcome the sinfulness which is still present in the individual as well as in the world. The Christian continues both to express in actions the new life received in Baptism and to constitute self as a person ever more united with Jesus through the Spirit. Spiritual theology in the Catholic tradition, which unfortunately became separated from moral theology, has often insisted on the injunction to put on the Lord Jesus, to imitate Jesus and to live in union with the risen Lord. All of these notions, when made more dynamic in the light of continual conversion, underscore the personal growth of the subject who not only expresses this reality in one's actions but also constitutes one's moral self through these choices.

The biblical concept of conversion seen as the change of heart in response to the gracious gift of God in Jesus also avoids some of the dangers of Pelagianism which lurked in older approaches to morality in the Catholic tradition. With the insistence on works there was always the danger of thinking that one is saved by one's own efforts. Conversion as the opposite of sin has personal, social and cosmic dimensions and thereby views the Christian subject in the context of an ethical model of relationality-responsibility.

The virtues can be readily integrated into a theology of conversion and continual conversion. Virtues refer to the attributes and dispositions which characterize the Christian life. In the Thomistic presentation of the virtues some problems arose because of the faculty psychology on which they were based — virtues are habits modifying the individual faculties or powers of the soul. Likewise there exist some dangers of Pelagianism in the Scholastic understanding of the virtues. However, the basic concept of the virtues as the attitudes, dispositions, and inclinations characterizing the Christian person as subject must be seen as very important in the moral life of the Christian. One could develop the important virtues of the Christian on the basis of the beautitudes or the list of virtues in Paul or those characteristics such as hope, humility, mercy, and forgiveness, which so often appear in the New Testament.

The understanding of conscience must give central importance to the self — the person who acts and the characteristics of the person. Formation of conscience in this context can never settle merely for instruction in the law but rather must spur the individual to grow in wisdom, age, and grace as a follower of Jesus. What has been developed in this second step is a general emphasis on the subject and the person. The level of generality at which it was presented needs to be specified. The third and especially the fourth steps involve this process of specifying exactly how to understand the person as subject in deciding and acting.

The third step in a more adequate understanding of conscience is to overcome the one-sidedly cognitive aspect in the manuals of moral theology. Conscience should also have an affective dimension as well as a cognitive aspect. The affective dimension has taken on increased importance in light of work done in depth psychology and psychiatry. As the historical section points out there were different traditions within Roman Catholicism which saw conscience as either connected with the intellect as in the Thomistic approach or connected with the will as in the Franciscan approach.

In my judgment one of the sources for the problem in the Catholic tradition stems from an anthropology accepting a faculty-psychology approach. If conscience is viewed in terms of a particular faculty or power, then there lurks the danger of not giving enough importance to all the aspects of conscience.[44] It seems better to identify conscience with the moral consciousness of the subject as such. Bernard Lonergan shows how his intentionality analysis of the subject differs from the older faculty approach.

> The study of the subject is quite different, for it is the study of oneself inasmuch as one is conscious. It prescinds from the soul, its essence, its potencies, its habits, for none of these are given in consciousness. It attends to operations and to their center and source which is the self. It discerns the different levels of consciousness, the consciousness of the dream, of the waking subject, of the intelligently inquiring subject, of the rationally reflecting subject. It examines the different operations on the several levels and their relations to one another.[45]

A transcendental methodology which begins with the subject as conscious provides one way of overcoming the problems connected with the one-sided view of conscience as related to only one faculty or power and not to the whole subject. However, one must avoid any simplistic reduction and carefully distinguish the different levels of consciousness and operations in the subject — the levels of experiencing, understanding, judging, and deciding.

The recognition of the importance of the affective aspects and feelings in the formation of conscience have important practical ramifications. Much can be learned from all branches of psychology. Appeal must be made not only to the intellect but to the imagination and the affectivity of the person. In this connection one can mention an element which unfortunately has been lost in recent Catholic life — emphasis on the lives of the saints.[46] The saints furnished inspiration and supplied heroes for many younger Catholics in the past. These stories in their own way fired the imagination, triggered the feelings, and inflamed the hearts of those who strove to follow in the footsteps of the saints. With the passing of this emphasis on the lives of the saints, Catholic life has lost an important element in conscience formation.

A fourth step in arriving at a better understanding of conscience calls for a deeper understanding of the subject and how the subject arrives at its judgments and decisions. What do we mean by the self knowing, feeling, deciding, and how does the self do these things? Our inquiry starts with the traditionally accepted notion that a good conscience indicates that a good decision has been made. The precise question concerns what is a good conscience. When has the subject judged rightly and decided well? This question raises very fundamental issues about our understanding of human knowing, judging, and deciding. The approach developed here will differ from the considerations of the manuals which propose a heavily deductive reasoning process going from the universal to the particular and which see a correct judgment in terms of the correspondence of the mind to the objective reality existing "out there" or outside the subject.

As a preliminary note it can be pointed out that the neo-Thomist Jacques Maritain rejected the deductive reasoning process often proposed in the definitions of conscience. According to Maritain's interpretation the manner or mode in which human reason knows natural law is not rational knowledge but knowledge through inclination. Such knowledge is not clear knowledge through concepts and conceptual judgments. It is obscure, unsystematic, vital knowledged by connaturality or congeniality in which the individual in making judgments consults and listens to the inner melody that the vibrating strings of abiding tendencies make present in the subject.[47]

More radical solutions have been proposed in the context of transcendental method which sees objectivity not in conformity to the object out there but rather in terms of the human knowing, deciding, loving subject itself. Both Karl Rahner and Bernard Lonergan have made significant contributions to the understanding of conscience in this area.

Rahner has developed his approach in the context of discussions of the discernment of spirits and of a formal existential ethic.[48] The discernment of spirits has been a traditional part of Catholic spirituality.[49] There are three types of phenomena which the individual can experience — revelations and visions; internal enlightenment or impulses concerning some determinate object; general states of consolation or desolation. The discernment of spirits tries to determine the causes of these as either God and the good angels or the bad angels or human nature.[50]

Rahner develops his thought in commenting on the spiritual exercises of St. Ignatius. The whole purpose of the exercises is to bring the individual to make a vital decision — the election. According to Ignatius there are three times or occasions for making such an election. The first time arises when God moves the soul without any hesitation, as in private revelation. The second time occurs when light and understanding are derived through the experience of desolation and consolation in the discernment of spirits. The third time arises in tranquility when the soul is not agitated by different spirits and has the free and natural use of its powers. Rahner maintains that most commentators mistakenly interpret Ignatius as choosing the third time as the time for making the election. But Rahner argues, convincingly in the eyes of many, [51] that the second time is the usual time for making an election.[52]

Rahner attempts to explain the reality of discernment in the second time in light of his transcendental metaphysics. Knowledge does not mean only the conceptual knowledge of an object. In all human knowing there is also the concomitant awareness of the knowing self as the subject. This is not the knowledge of an object or even of the self as an object but is the subject's awareness as subject. Rahner interprets the Ignatian expression of consolation without previous cause as consolation without an object of that consolation. In all conscious acts the human being has an indistinct awareness of God as transcendent horizon but this awareness does not ordinarily emerge into explicit consciousness. Just as the individual is conscious to oneself as subject, so God as transcendent horizon but not as an object is present in consciousness. How, however, in this second time the soul explicitly feels oneself totally drawn to the love of God and thus experiences this consolation, peace, and joy which is coming from God's presence. This consolation is the nonconceptual experience of God as the individual is drawn totally into his love. If this consolation perdures when the person places oneself in accord with the projection of the election to be made, the individual rightly concludes that the prospective choice harmonizes with one's own human, Godward subjectivity. Obviously this requires that the person as subject to be truly open to the call of God. This experience by which the soul is wholly drawn to the love of God as God, unlike discursive or conceptual knowledge, possesses intrinsically an irreducibly self-evident, self-sufficient character.[53]

In an earlier essay Rahner proposes a formal existential ethic in addition to and in no way opposed to an essential ethic resulting in the general principles of natural law. Rahner agrees that in addition to one's essence each individual also has a positive individual reality. This positive individuality cannot be the object of reflective, objective knowledge which can be articulated in propositions. How does conscience perceive this individual moral obligation? Rahner again appeals to nonreflective, nonpropositional self-presence of the person to self in one's positive uniqueness.[54]

Rahner in this way tries to develop a theory of conscience which corresponds with the traditionally accepted idea of the peace and joy of a good conscience when a good decision has been made or is to be made.[55] Obviously there are questions that can and should be put to Rahner. One problem is that his transcendental method, while handling quite well questions primarily of a personal and individual nature such as vocation, does not even try to say anything to questions of social ethics. Perhaps this is just the appearance in the realm of moral theology of the reality that Metz criticized in Rahner's systematics for not giving enough importance to the social and political aspects of reality.[56] Likewise, in my judgment Rahner's approach does not seem to give enough importance to empirical reality.

Bernard Lonergan in his work on theological method and elsewhere has outlined a transcendental approach to ethics which seems to overcome the problems mentioned above with the theory of Karl Rahner.[57] Lonergan is opposed to deductive reasoning. He always begins with the concrete. Lonergan understands consciousness as the presence of the subject to oneself — not the presence of an object. In the following paragraphs Lonergan's approach to conscience or moral consciousness will be sketched although it is impossible to give a full and complete understanding of his complex thought.[58]

Conscience for Lonergan is seen in the context of the thrust of the personal subject for the authenticity of self-transcendence. The person shares sensitivity with the other animals, but the human individual can go beyond (transcend) this level of consciousness. In addition to the empirical level of consciousness and intentionalities, in which one perceives, senses, etc., human beings go beyond this to the intellectual level of understanding and to the rational level of judgment which not only goes beyond the subject but also affirms that which is so. On the next level self-transcendence becomes moral — in the order of deciding and doing not just knowing. By responding to questions about value we can effect in our being a moral transcendence. This moral transcendence is the possibility of becoming a person in human society. Our capacity for self-transcendence becomes fully actual when we fall in love. Being in love is of different kinds but being in love with God is the basic fulfillment of our conscious intentionality. This brings a joy and a peace that can remain despite failure, pain, betrayal, etc. The transcendental subjectivity of the person stretches forth toward the intelligible, the unconditioned, and the good of value. The reach of this intending is unrestricted.[59]

Within the context of self-transcendence Lonergan develops the three conversions which modify the horizon of the subject. Intellectual conversion denies the myth of the object out there as the criterion of objectivity and reality. This is a naive, comic-book realism. Lonergan strives for a critical realism. The real world for Lonergan is mediated by meaning and is not the world of immediate experience. The real world mediated by meaning is known by the cognitional process of experiencing, understanding, and judging, which is based on the thrust of cognitional self-transcendence. Moral conversion consists in opting for the truly good, for values against satisfactions when they conflict. Here we are no longer cajoled as children, but we freely opt for value. Thus we affect not only the object of choice but we decide for ourselves what to make of ourselves.

Religious conversion, the third conversion, is being grasped by ultimate concern. It is the total and permanent self-surrender of other-worldly falling in love.[60] Lonergan himself succinctly summarizes his understanding of the three conversions.

> As intellectual and moral conversion, so also religious conversion is a modality of self-transcendence. Intellectual conversion is to truth attained by cognitional self-transcendence. Moral conversion is to values apprehended, affirmed and realized by a real self-transcendence. Religious conversion is to a total being-in-love as the efficacious ground of all self-transcendence, whether in the pursuit of truth, or in the realization of human values, or in the orientation man adopts to the universe, its ground and its goals.[61]

How do we know our judgments have attained the true and our decisions have achieved the value? In other words, what are the criteria by which we know our judging and deciding have been good and proper? In the manuals of moral theology the criterion of judgment is conformity to the objective truth out there. Lonergan firmly rejects that criterion. In a judgment one arrives at truth when there are no more pertinent questions to ask. The self-transcending thrust toward truth is satisfied. The judgment for Lonergan is thus described as virtually unconditioned because the subject seeking the truth can now rest content. Thus we have established the radical identity between genuine objectivity and authentic subjectivity.[62]

Likewise, the criterion of value judgments is not the value or reality out there; rather, it is the satisfaction of the moral subject as a self-transcending thrust toward value. A rounded moral judgment is ever the work of a fully developed self-transcending subject or, as Aristotle would put it, of a virtuous person.[63] The drive to value rewards success in self-transcendence with a happy conscience and saddens failure with an unhappy conscience.[64] Thus once again the peaceful and joyful conscience of the authentic subject understood in terms of self-transcendence becomes the criterion of objective value. One might truly say that for Lonergan the norms for the proper formation of conscience are the transcendental precepts which correspond to the basic levels of consciousness of the subject and the basic operations — be attentive, be intelligent, be reasonable, be responsible.[65]

Lonergan is well aware of the dangers and difficulties in achieving authenticity and self-transcendence. Development is not inevitable; there are many failures. In moral conversion one must overcome enticing but misleading satisfactions and fears of discomfort, pain and privation. Lonergan speaks of bias as affecting authentic transcendence on all levels and going against the transcendental precepts.[66] He applies to all levels of self-transcendence what was said about intellectual conversion in *Insight*.

Bias as a block or a distortion appears in four principal matters: the bias of unconscious motivation brought to light in depth psychology; the bias of individual egoism; the bias of group egoism; and the bias of common sense.[67] The recognition of such obstacles in the way of authentic self-transcendence continually reminds the individual to be self-critical. Human authenticity has no room for complacency and self-satisfaction. One must continually question, inquire, and be open to learn.

Again, one should critique and discuss the theory proposed by Lonergan. One set of problems arises from the nature of conversion, the order of conversion (according to Lonergan there is usually, first, religious, followed by moral, and then, and only rarely, intellectual conversion),[68] and the frequency of conversion (Lonergan admits intellectual conversion is rare and describes the other conversions, especially religious, in such a way that they would seem to be very rare in practice).

I would make two suggestions. First, I do not think there is that great a difference or distinction between moral and religious conversion. The strictly theological data (love of God and neighbor) and existential experience seem to see the two conversions as basically one.[69] Second, Lonergan could introduce a variant of the notion of continual conversion to indicate that both conversions involve a continual growth and that these conversions might take place on a fundamental and beginning level even though the radical description of conversion has not yet been fully achieved.[70]

I have tried to develop through various steps a basic understanding of the reality of conscience and how it functions in the Christian life. First, conscience must be understood in the context of a relationality-responsibility model of the Christian life — never forgetting the multiple relationships within which one lives. The second step affirmed the importance of the self as agent and subject who expresses oneself in actions and also by those very

actions constitutes oneself as subject. The third step insisted on seeing conscience as more than merely cognitive
and strove to bring together the cognitive, the affective,
and the moral aspects of conscience. Finally, the fourth
step proposed specific metaphysical theories explaining
the reality of conscience and how one arrives at good
judgments and decisions. Lonergan's basic theory has
advantages over Rahner's for three reasons: (1) it deals
more adequately with the empirical; (2) it can handle
better the social aspect as well as the personal aspect of
moral existence; (3) it is a unified theory explaining all
knowing and deciding and does not distinguish between
the essential and the existential aspects of conscience
formation. This theory attempts to explain in a more
systematic and reflective way the traditionally accepted
notion that joy and peace mark the good conscience
which is the adequate criterion of good moral judgment
and decision.

One further point deserves mention. This understanding
of conscience recognizes the importance of the development of conscience. The approach proposed here calls for
and readily incorporates within its philosophical context
the work of developmental psychologists in describing the
way in which conscience itself develops and grows.[71] What
has to be remembered is that development occurs not only
in childhood, although it is obviously more dramatic in
childhood, but continues to occur throughout adult life.
Theologians must take the biblical concept of continual
conversion and see how this can be psychologically understood in terms of the development of conscience.

Practical Conclusions

The first practical conclusion of the discussion on conscience reaffirms the traditionally accepted teaching that
conscience is the norm of personal action. Yes, the conscience judgment and decision might be wrong, but the
individual must be true to one's own self. Authentic sub-

jectivity excludes the possibility of error, but authentic subjectivity is not always present. Many abuses have existed in the past in the name of conscience, and there will continue to be many abuses in the future. But this does not take away the basic realization that the individual must decide and act in accord with conscience. Christians and the Church should learn from the divine wisdom both to accept the freedom and responsibility of the individual to decide in conscience despite all the abuses of that freedom and to challenge the individual to achieve authenticity. God's loving gift of self to human beings respects human freedom and the choices made by human beings, even though God's gift is often spurned.

Second, however, one must be well aware of the dangers involved in judgments and decisions of conscience. Yes, the ultimate decision and judgment rest with the individual, but the individual must recognize the limitations and dangers involved in trying to achieve subjective authenticity which is synonymous with objectivity. In a practical way human experience reminds us of the many horrendous realities that have been done in the name of conscience — slavery, torture, atrocities, and deprival of basic human rights. The realization of the dangers involved becomes even more acute when recognizing how seemingly even good people can disagree over such basic issues as the use of force in the service of justice, abortion, or the just ordering of the economic system for the good of all. The authentic development of self-transcendence is threatened on every level.

The Christian can and should recognize the two basic sources of this danger as human finitude and sinfulness. Finitude is different from sinfulness. As a result of our finitude we are limited; we see only a partial aspect of reality; we cannot achieve all possible goods or values. Human sinfulness, on the other hand, stems not from creation itself but from the actions of ourselves or others and can be seen in the sinfulness both of the individual and of the society in which we live.

Although the basic sources of the dangers in a theological perspective are easy to identify, the actual dangers can take many different forms. Again, these dangers exist in the cognitive, affective, and moral levels and operations. Bias and prejudice can easily affect our judgments and decisions. Why is it that those who espouse the just-war theory generally judge wars of their own country to be just while rejecting the justice of the wars of their opponents? An examination of conscience reveals the lack of courage which prevents us from acting upon what we believe to be right or the lack of ardor which weakens our pursuit of value.

One example will well illustrate the complexity of the problem of how limitation and sinfulness can affect our judgments and decisions of conscience. Will better conscience decisions result if a person is involved in the problem or if a person is an "objective" observer? Frankly, there are pluses and minuses to both approaches. The one who is intimately involved in the struggle knows and appreciates the problem. One must honestly admit that white, male, middle-class theologians have not been as aware as we should be of the problems of racism, poverty, and sexism in our society. On the other hand, personal involvement in an issue might prejudice one's judgments and decisions. Do the heads of powerful governments or people desperately fighting for the rights of the poor and oppressed tend to resort too quickly to violence? Do people involved in equal rights and opportunities for women tend to overlook the fetus? Yes, it is not too difficult to become aware of the difficulties and dangers in making judgments and decisions of conscience.

Third, one must not only be aware of the dangers but strive to overcome them. This is what it means to live out a theory of critical self-transcendence. From the Christian perspective the basic disposition that we all need to cultivate is openness to the gift of God and the needs of our neighbor. The Christian should try to put aside all prejudice, bias, and egoism. There is much talk today about openness, but to be truly open is not easy. The fundamental importance of openness stems from the theory of conscience proposed on the basis of critical self-transcendence which sees the individual person in terms of an unrestricted thrust toward truth, value, love, and the unconditioned. The proof of a good conscience is had when one affirms the true and embraces the value. A false conscience arises from a lack of authenticity on the cognitive, affective, and moral levels of our existence. Openness therefore keeps one truly open to the truth, value, and love which alone can satisfy the unrestricted thrust toward the unconditioned. Openness also seems to be a very good understanding of the biblical attitude of humility of spirit. The humble in spirit are truly those who are open to the gift of God and the needs of neighbor. Openness aptly describes the primary disposition in conscience formation.

The individual should be critically alert to the many different ways of trying to guarantee that openness characterizes our existence in the quest for truth, value, and love. Many ways have been proposed but one must remember that they are usually only prudential specifications of the basic disposition of openness. The Gospel gives us a very significant way of trying to overcome our finitude and sinfulness — love your neighbor as yourself. To put ourselves in the position of the other person remains an excellent way to overcome our own finitude and sinfulness. This same wisdom is found in the golden rule — do unto others as you would have them do unto you. Some contemporary philosophers speak of the veil of ignorance. In choosing what social system should be in existence all individuals must choose from behind the veil of ignorance — that is, not knowing which of the various positions in society might be theirs.[72] Other philosophers speak of the ideal observer as the way of overcoming the prejudice and bias of any one individual.[73] The philosophical principle of universalization based on the understanding that one must always be willing to see all others act in a similar way in similar circumstances also serves as a strong antidote to individual bias, prejudice, and sinfulness.

Above all openness for the Christian calls for one to be an authentic self with all those attitudes and dispositions which should characterize a human and Christian person. In this way the person develops the feeling for the true and the good as well as the yearning and inclination to affirm and embrace them. The good conscience remains the work of a virtuous person.[74]

Fourth, community and especially the Christian community of the Church are very important in the formation of conscience. The discussion thus far has concerned only the individual, but the insistence on multiple relations and on the social aspects of morality recalls that the individual judges and decides in dialogue with other individuals and as members of various communities in which one lives. The various communities to which we belong play a very important role in personal conscience formation. These considerations will be limited to what for the Christian must be the most important community — that of the Church.

The Church as the people of God, called together to live in the risen Lord and to bear witness to that life, has a very significant role to play in the formation of the conscience of the individual Christian. The Church as the mediator and sign of the Gospel strives to have its own people become signs of that Gospel to others. From an ethical perspective, the Church is a great help in the formation of conscience precisely because it can overcome the two basic dangers of finitude and sinfulness which always threaten the individual. Because of our finitude we are limited historically, spatially, and temporally. The Church as a universal community existing in different cultures, in different times, and in different places is thus able to help overcome the limitations of finitude. The Church as the community of Gospel and grace also tries to overcome human sinfulness and egoism. Although the Church remains a sinful Church still in need of continual redemption, the believer sees in the Church the presence of redeeming grace and a power to overcome sin and its ramifications.

Take a particular example of how the Church is able to help conscience. In my judgment some Protestant clergy deserve great credit for the leadershp role they played through early opposition to the recent American involvement in the war in Viet Nam. Many of these people suffered greatly because their stand was far from popular when they first took it. Some of these clergy admitted that at the very beginning they favored American participation in the war, but their early opposition was greatly influenced by the questions posed to them by Christians from other countries. These other Christians in the light of a broader perspective could overcome the narrowness, limitations, and group egoism of Americans.

The Church by every means possible — challenging, accusing, approving, questioning, supporting, teaching — helps in the formation of the conscience of the individual Christian. There are myriad ways in which this formation can and should take place in the Christian community. The Roman Catholic believer also recognizes the God given function of the hierarchical magisterium as one mode in which the Church teaches and forms consciences. One way in which the whole Church and the hierarchical magisterium can inform conscience is by giving specific directions for specific actions. Chapter 4 has already alluded to the fact that the hierarchical magisterium must go through a proper discernment process to understand just what these specific directives are. Likewise, it was also pointed out that the Roman Catholic Church has recognized that this teaching of the hierarchical magisterium on specific moral matters cannot claim the certitude that excludes the possibility of error. At times the individual Christian, conscious of all the dangers, can rightly dissent from such teaching in theory and practice. Here again in making that decision one must carefully follow all the available approaches to conscience formation mentioned above. Here again, too, the ultimate criterion is the peace and joy of a good conscience.

This rather lengthy, but still unfortunately sketchy, consideration of conscience brings to a close our discussion of the most significant themes in fundamental moral theology. The concept of conscience proposed here overcomes the criticisms proposed against the theory of conscience found in the manuals of moral theology. Above all this theory of conscience incorporates an understanding of the Christian life which highlights its Gospel, personal, dynamic, historical, and social characteristics.

NOTES

1. C. A. Pierce, *Conscience in the New Testament* (London: SCM Press, 1955), pp. 13-53.

2. Ibid., p. 117.

3. Ibid., p. 109

4. Ibid., p. 62.

5. Eric D'Arcy, *Conscience and Its Right to Freedom* (New York: Sheed and Ward, 1962), pp. 11-12.

6. Ceslaus Spicq, *Théologie morale du Nouveau Testament,* vol. 2 (Paris: J. Gabalda, 1965), p. 603. See also C. Spicq, "La Conscience dans le Nouveau Testament," *Revue Biblique* 47 (1938), 50-80.

7. Philippe Delhaye, *The Christian Conscience* (New York: Desclée, 1968), pp. 37-50.

8. Emil Brunner, *The Divine Imperative* (Philadelphia: Westminster Press, 1947), pp. 156ff.

9. Ronald Preston, "Conscience," in *Dictionary of Christian Ethics,* ed. John Macquarrie (Philadelphia: Westminster Press, 1967), pp. 66-68. For a view of conscience in the Protestant tradition which recognizes a positive and antecedent function, see David Little, "A View of Conscience within the Protestant Tradition," in *Conscience: Its Freedom and Limitations,* ed. William C. Bier (New York: Fordham University Press, 1971), pp. 20-28.

10. For a Catholic scholar who sees the legislative and positive role of conscience in the New Testament as exceptional and differing from the usual usage, see James C. Turro, "Conscience in the Bible," in Bier, *Conscience,* p. 7.

11. Eric Mount, Jr., *Conscience and Responsibility* (Richmond: John Knox Press, 1969), p. 26.

12. For the development of the teaching in the scholastic period, see Odon Lottin, *Psychologie et morale aux XIIe et XIIIe siècles*, vol. 2 (Louvain: Abbaye du Mont César, 1948) pp. 103-350. For a shorter treatment in English which acknowledges a great debt to Lottin, see D'Arcy, pp. 20-48. My summary discussion is dependent on both of them.

13. *Liber IV Sententiarum*, lib. 2, dist. 39.

14. J. de Blic, "Syndérèse ou conscience? " *Revue d'Ascétique et de Mystique* 25 (1949), 146-157.

15. The question is whether *synderesis* is a faculty or power like reason or the will or whether it is a habit or disposition which modifies the reason or will. Philip the Chancellor, obviously influenced by Jerome, cannot say it is merely a habit. The Latin term he employs is *potentia habitualis*, which Lottin (pp. 140-142) translates as "faculté doublé d'habitus" and D'Arcy (p. 27) as "habit-like faculty." For Bonaventure's position see his *In II Sent.*, dist. 39, art. 1 and 2.

16. *Summa de Creaturis, secunda pars* q. 71, a 1; q. 72 a. 1.

17. *In II Sent.*, dist. 24, qu. 2 art. 3.; *Quaestiones Disputatae De Veritate*, q. 16.

18. For a brief historical summary of this discussion, see D'Arcy, pp. 76-105.

19. The source generally cited for this debate is Th. Deman, O.P., "Probabilisme," in *Dictionnaire de théologie catholique* (Paris, 1936), vol. 13, col. 417-619. (Hereafter referred to as *D.T.C.*). However, in my judgment this account is somewhat biased in favor of the probabiliorist approach against the probabilist approach. In this connection note Deman's dependence on a strong proponent of probabiliorism, Daniel Concina, *Della storia del probabilismo e del rigorismo*, 2 vols. (Lucca, 1743).

20. *Enchiridion Symbolorum Definitionum et Declarationum de Rebus Fidei et Morum*, ed. H. Denzinger, A. Schönmetzer, 32nd ed. (Barcelona: Herder, 1963), nn. 2101-2167. Hereafter referred to as *DS*.

21. Deman, *D.T.C.*, vol. 13, col. 502-510, 523-530.

22. *DS* nn. 2175-2177; Deman *D.T.C.*, vol. 13, col. 534-547; P. Bernard, "Gonzalez de Santalla, Thyrse," *D.T.C.*, vol. 6, col. 1493-1496.

23. For a recent and very accurate study of the development of St. Alphonsus's thought on probabilism, see the three part study of Domenico Capone, "Dissertazioni e note di S. Alfonso sulla probabilita e la conscienza." *Studia Moralia* 1 (1963), 265-343; 2 (1964), 89-155; 3 (1965), 82-149. The documentary evidence of how he changes his terminology in the light of political and religious pressures is found in *Studia Moralia* 2 (1964), 123ff.

24. I. Aertnys-C. Damen, *Theologia Moralis*, ed. J. Visser, 17th ed. (Rome: Marietti, 1956), 1: n. 95, pp. 103-105.

25. Marcellino Zalba, *Theologiae Moralis, Summa I: Theologia Moralis Fundamentalis* (Madrid: Biblioteca de Autores Cristianos, 1952), p. 306.

26. Recently there have appeared a number of anthologies bringing together different articles on conscience. In addition to the work edited by Bier which has already been mentioned, see *Conscience: Theological and Psychological Perspectives*, ed. C. Ellis Nelson (New York: Newman Press, 1973); *Conscience*, ed. John Donnelly and Leonard Lyons (Staten Island: Alba House, 1973); *Conscience*, ed. Curatorium of the C. G. Jung Institute, Zurich (Evanston, Ill.: Northwestern University Press, 1970).

27. Zalba, pp. 241-253.

28. Ibid., pp. 253-328.

29. For a categorization of Aquinas as belonging to a deliberative rather than a prescriptive motif, see Edward LeRoy Long, Jr., *A Survey of Christian Ethics* (New York: Oxford University Press, 1967), pp. 45-49.

30. This paragraph merely summarizes the outline of the *prima pars* of the *Summa Theologiae.*

31. Dogmatic Constitution on Divine Revelation, n. 24; Decree on Priestly Formation, n. 16.

32. Robert Koch,. "Vers une morale de l'alliance," *Studia Moralia* 6 (1968), 7-58.

33. James M. Gustafson, "Christian Ethics," in *Religion*, ed. Paul Ramsey (Englewood Cliffs, N.J.: Prentice Hall, 1965), pp. 309-320.

34. For the best theological explanation of liberation theology stressing especially the changed understanding of eschatology, see Gustavo Gutierrez, *A Theology of Liberation: History, Politics and Liberation* (Maryknoll, N.Y.: Orbis Books, 1973).

35. H. Richard Niebuhr, *The Responsible Self* (New York: Harper and Row, 1963), pp. 55-68.

36. James M. Gustafson, *Christ and the Moral Life* (New York: Harper and Row, 1968), pp. 1-5 and throughout the book; James M. Gustafson, *Christian Ethics and the Community* (Philadelphia: Pilgrim Press, 1971), pp. 151-216.

37. Stanley Hauerwas, *Character and the Christian Life: A Study in Theological Ethics* (San Antonio, Texas: Trinity University Press, 1975).

38. For a development of the Thomistic concept of the virtues, see George P. Klubertanz, *Habits and Virtues* (New York: Appleton-Century-Crofts, 1965). In the next step I will express my disagreement with the faculty psychology on which the Thomistic approach is based.

39. For example, see the following articles in the first issue (1973) of *The Journal of Religious Ethics:* Frederick Carney, "The Virtue-Obligation Controversy," pp. 5-19; William K. Frankena, "The Ethics of Love Conceived as an Ethics of Virtue," pp. 21-36; Arthur J. Dyck, "A Unified Theory of Virtue and Obligation," pp. 37-52.

40. Yves Congar, "Le saint Ésprit dans la théologie thomiste de l'agir morale," in *Tommaso D'Aquino nel suo VII Centenario, Congresso Internazionale, Roma-Napoli, 17-24 aprile, 1974,* pp. 175-187.

41. As an illustration of an unwillingness to accept such an approach, see Victor Paul Furnish, *Theology and Ethics in Paul* (Nashville: Abingdon Press, 1968), pp. 176, 239, 240.

42. Hauerwas, *Character and the Christian Life,* pp. 183-195.

43. Bernard Häring, *The Law of Christ* (Westminster, Md.: Newman Press, 1961) 1: 287-481; Bernard Häring, *Pastoral Treatment of Sin,* ed. P. Delhaye et al. (New York: Desclée, 1968), pp. 87-176.

44. For an illustration of the faculty-psychology approach to conscience, see Ralph McInerny, "Prudence and Conscience," *The Thomist* 38 (1974), 291-305. McInerny restricts conscience to the cognitive, but he recognizes other important affective aspects in the moral life.

45. Bernard Lonergan, *The Subject* (Milwaukee: Marquette University Press, 1968), pp. 7, 8.

46. Berard L. Marthaler, "A Traditional and Necessary Ingredient in Religious Education: Hagiography," *The Living Light* 11 (1974), 580-591.

47. Jacques Maritain, *Man and the State* (Chicago: University of Chicago Press, 1951), pp. 91, 92.

48. Karl Rahner, "The Logic of Concrete Individual Knowledge," in *The Dynamic Element in the Church* (New York: Herder and Herder, 1964), pp. 84-170; Karl Rahner, "On the Question of a Formal Existential Ethic," *Theological Investigations,* vol. 2 (Baltimore: Helicon Press, 1963), pp. 217-234.

49. For an overall view of this question, see Jacques Guillet, et al., *Discernment of Spirits* (Collegeville, Minnesota: Liturgical Press, 1970). This book is the authorized English edition of the article in the *Dictionnaire de spiritualité.* For a contemporary theological discussion, see Philip S. Keane, "Discernment of Spirits: A Theological Reflection," *American Ecclesiastical Review* 168 (1974), 43-61.

50. Joseph de Guibert, *The Theology of the Spiritual Life* (London: Sheed and Ward, 1956), pp. 130ff.

51. See, for example, the special issue of *The Way Supplement* 24 (1975), which is devoted to the spiritual exercises of Ignatius.

52. Rahner, *Dynamic Element in the Church,* pp. 89-106.

53. Ibid., pp. 129-170.

54. Rahner, *Theological Investigations,* vol. 2, pp. 217-234.

55. For an interpretation of Rahner's entire ethical theory, see James F. Bresnahan, "Rahner's Ethic: Critical Natural Law in Relation to Contemporary Ethical Methodology," *The Journal of Religion* 56 (1976):36-60. For a fuller development, see James F. Bresnahan, "The Methodology of Natural Law: Ethical Reasoning in the Theology of Karl Rahner and its Supplementary Development Using the Legal Philosophy of Lon L. Fuller" (Ph.D. Diss., Yale University [Ann Arbor, Mich.: University Microfilms, 1972, no. 72-29520]).

56. Johannes B. Metz, "Foreword: An Essay on Karl Rahner," in Karl Rahner, *Spirit in the World* (New York: Herder and Herder, 1968), pp. xvi-xviii.

57. The two major works of Bernard Lonergan are: *Insight: A Study of Human Understanding* (New York: Philosophical Library, 1957); *Method in Theology* (New York: Herder and Herder, 1972).

58. Of great value are two, unfortunately unpublished, dissertations: Walter Eugene Conn, "Conscience and Self-Transcendence" (Ph.D. diss., Columbia University [Ann Arbor, Mich.: University Microfilms, 1973, no. 73-26600]); John P. Boyle, "Faith and Community in the Ethical Theory of Karl Rahner and Bernard Lonergan" (Ph.D. diss., Fordham University [Ann Arbor, Mich.: University Microfilms, 1972, no. 72-20554]).

59. Lonergan, *Method in Theology,* pp. 103-105.

60. Ibid., pp. 239-241.

61. Ibid., p. 241.

62. Lonergan, *Insight,* pp. 279-316.

63. Lonergan, *Method in Theology,* p. 41.

64. Ibid., p. 35.

65. Ibid., pp. 53, 231.

66. Ibid., pp. 51-55.

67. Ibid., p. 231.

68. Ibid., pp. 243, 267.

69. Charles E. Curran, "Christian Conversion in the Writings of Bernard Lonergan," in *Foundations of Theology: Papers from the International Lonergan Congress 1970,* ed. Philip McShane (Notre Dame, Ind.: University of Notre Dame Press, 1972), pp. 41-59.

70. For different criticisms of the questions involving conversion in Lonergan's approach, see Conn, pp. 526ff.

71. Conn develops at great length the theories of Piaget, Erikson, and Kohlberg incorporating their findings in a critical way into his understanding of conscience.

72. E.g., John Rawls, *A Theory of Justice* (Cambridge, Mass.: Harvard University Press, 1971), pp. 136-142.

73. E.g., F. C. Sharp, *Good and Ill Will* (Chicago: University of Chicago Press, 1950), pp. 156-162.

74. For a discussion of discernment from the viewpoint of a Protestant ethician who approaches the question in a nonmetaphysical way, see James M. Gustafson, "Moral Discernment in the Christian Life," in *Norm and Context in Christian Ethics*, ed. Gene Outka and Paul Ramsey (New York: Charles Scribner's Sons, 1968), pp. 17-36.

Index

Abortion, 70–72
Accommodation, 19f.
Action
    ambiguity of external act, 155
    complexity of, 180
    emphasis on in moral theol-
        ogy, 87f., 201f.
    extrinsicist view, 202
    physical structure of, 34, 35,
        64f., 106f., 110, 134
    as self-constituting, 219–20
    subjective/objective aspects,
        139f., 158f., 203
    See also Physical-material
        reality
Actualism
    philosophical, 108f., 117
    theological, 102f., 117, 205
Aertnys, I., 228n.
Agape, 8, 96, 109f.
    and eros, 8, 109f.
Albert the Great, 36, 195, 196
Alexander VIII, Pope, 199
Alphonsus Liguori, Saint, 170,
    171, 200, 227n
Alszeghy, Z., 163n
Anscombe, G. E. M., 132f., 137,
    143n, 144n
Anthropology
    Aristotle's, 61

Christian, 147, 148
    contemporary theological,
        184, 206
    Ulpian's, 38–39
Aquaviva, Claudius, 170
Araud, Régis, 77n
Aristotle, 60f., 136, 218
Aubert, J. M., 76n
Augustine, Saint, 77n

Barth, Karl, 102f.
Bayles, Michael, 123, 142n
Beardsmore, R. W., 143n
Bennett, John C., 28
Bennett, Jonathan, 132, 143n
Bentham, Jeremy, 122
Bias, 218, 219, 222, 224
    veil of ignorance, 223
Birch, Bruce C., 24n, 188n
Blic, I. de, 227n.
Bonaventure, Saint, 195, 227n
Bonhoeffer, Dietrich, 28, 102
Bourassa, F., 164n
Boyle, John P., 230n
Bresnahan, James F., 230n
Brock, Daniel W., 142n, 143n
Brunner, Emil, 28, 226n
Buber, Martin, 21
Bultmann, Rudolf, 136–37

233